MW00749340

LISP
A FIRST LANGUAGE FOR COMPUTING

LISP
A FIRST LANGUAGE FOR COMPUTING

John A. Moyne

VNR VAN NOSTRAND REINHOLD
New York

Copyright © 1991 by Van Nostrand Reinhold

Library of Congress Catalog Card Number 90-22181
ISBN 0-442-00426-5

All rights reserved. No part of this work covered by the
copyright hereon may be reproduced or used in any form
or by any means—graphic, electronic, or mechanical,
including photocopying, recording, taping, or information
storage and retrieval systems—without written
permission of the publisher.

Manufactured in the United States of America

Published by Van Nostrand Reinhold
115 Fifth Avenue
New York, New York 10003

Chapman and Hall
2-6 Boundary Row
London, SE1 8HN

Thomas Nelson Australia
102 Dodds Street
South Melbourne 3205
Victoria, Australia

Nelson Canada
1120 Birchmount Road
Scarborough, Ontario M1K 5G4, Canada

16 15 14 13 12 11 10 9 8 7 6 5 4 3 2 1

Library of Congress Cataloging-in-Publication Data

Moyne, John A.
    LISP: a first language for computing / John A. Moyne.
      p. cm.
    Includes index.
    ISBN 0-442-00426-5
    1. LISP (Computer program language)   I. Title.
  QA76.73.L23M69   1991
  005.13′3--dc20
                                    90-22181
                                      CIP

For Nicholas and Parvin

Contents

Preface

This book attempts to teach Lisp as the initial language to be learned by a prospective computer programmer. Therefore, I do not assume any background in computing, and there will be elementary approaches to programming before we get on to more advanced topics and procedures. There will also be many intentional repetitions. While the book is not a self-study manual for a completely novice reader, for someone with a basic knowledge of computing and a familiarity with another programming language, it can be used for self-study.

When advanced students of computer or cognitive sciences start studying Lisp, they may know why it is called the "native language" of artificial intelligence (AI), and they will appreciate its symbol manipulation capabilities and its logical elegance. However, why should Lisp be used as the first language for a beginner? Thanks to the profusion of popular articles and media pronouncements, AI has become a household word, and any aspiring computer programmer would do well to learn its native language.

There is more, however, to learning Lisp than following fads. I believe that the expressive power of the language, and the logical beauty of its structure, will inspire students to appreciate computing and will make it easier for them to learn other languages and systems. Moreover, learning Lisp is an exercise in logical thinking and reasoning, which are the cornerstones of becoming competent scientists.

Much of this study is based on inductive learning, or learning by examples. Readers are presented with simple examples (and sometimes not so simple!) in Lisp and they are asked to find out what they do. Later on in the text, the examples are discussed and described in detail. I believe that if students are able to discover something by themselves, they will remember it more readily. A beginner is not, however, expected to find out or understand everything before the explanations are given. The trick is to get the reader involved—to think!

Since the invention of Lisp over three decades ago, it has developed many dialects. Students who have worked through this text should be able to use any of the dialects with minimal help from the technical manual of a particular dialect. The authors of textbooks on Lisp have traditionally selected a particular dialect as the medium for teaching Lisp. These dialects have ranged from the original, Lisp 1.5, to MacLisp, Franz Lisp, InterLisp, NIL, ZetaLisp, and many others. Perhaps the major reason for the development of the various dialects was the necessity for changes in the implementation of the language for different computers. More recently, a dialect known as Common Lisp (CL) has gained much popularity. Common Lisp has adopted the common features of some of the above dialects, so that it is a "common dialect" of other dialects. Its implementation on various machines will then include extensions to the basic language (there are already some subdialects of Common Lisp). The current versions of Common Lisp are powerful and extensive systems, with many capabilities and capacities far beyond the original design of the Lisp developers. Common Lisp is fast becoming the standard language for the AI and cognitive sciences, the development of PROLOG and other 'logic base' languages notwithstanding.

The dialects of Lisp mentioned so far have been developed as software packages (interpreters, compilers, etc.) for various computers. There are also the so-called Lisp Machines; computers exclusively constructed for Lisp, in which the language is built into the device (microcoded into the machine).

In this book, I will not deal exclusively with one dialect. However, whenever there are differences between major dialects, I will point them out to the reader. For expositional purposes, the reader is mostly exposed to Common Lisp and Lispvm; Common Lisp because of its universality and elegance, and because it is becoming more widely available for a variety of mainframes and personal computers; Lispvm because of its vastness and its representation of "uncommon" dialects.

During the late 1970s and early 1980s, several groups were working on the development of successors to some of the already highly developed Lisp systems: MacLisp (MIT), ZetaLisp (MIT), InterLisp (Xerox), and others. Individual implementations even in each language (e.g., MacLisp) kept diverging, as they were developed for different computing systems. The idea developed then to focus on a common core dialect, Common Lisp, to which any implementation can make extensions for compatability with hardware and for other purposes. Thus the goals of Common Lisp were to be portable from one computer environment to another, compatible with the three major Lisp systems mentioned above, and efficient—among others. There are also dialects called Standard Lisp and Portable Standard Lisp, which have similar goals, but have not gained the popularity of Common Lisp.

Lispvm (formerly Yorktown Lisp) was developed at the IBM Research Center in Yorktown Heights, New York. It is a representative of the "uncommon" dialects developed for individual computing systems. (I should point out that the commonality discussed here is a relative concept. All programming languages with the same name trivially have many identical features. For example, the FOR-TRAN or PASCAL languages developed for IBM and Digital VAX machines have many identical procedures.)

Lispvm is a very large and comprehensive system. It is not inhibited by the portability constraint of Common Lisp and it, therefore, attempts (sometimes excessively) to include features that can be difficult or awkward for implementation on other machines. I have included exposition of Lispvm in this study because of (a) its comprehensiveness, (b) its wide use in academic and industrial institutions with mainframe IBM computers as their main computing facility, and (c) the fact that, as far as I know, no other textbook has, so far, been written on this dialect.

However, as we progress through the text, the emphasis shifts more and more toward Common Lisp, until the last chapter, which is almost exclusively concerned with Common Lisp. I should point out further that, throughout the text, an attempt has been made, as far as possible, to write the examples in a way to make them compatible with all dialects. Whenever there are discrepancies, they are usually pointed out.

In addition to the major dialects, we will also see references to some dialects specifically designed for personal computers with more limited memories and facilities than are required by Common Lisp versions for personal computers. Such 'small' Lisp dialects include IqLisp, Mu-Lisp, XLisp, and others.

There is another departure in this book from the general practice. When a particular feature of a language is discussed, authors often give full details of the scope, variants, complexities, and extensions of the feature. While this approach has the advantage of keeping together in one place all of the details of each feature (and is suitable for a reference manual), it often taxes the beginner, who encounters a lot of technical terminology and details, without an appreciation of their significance or utility. In many cases in this text (especially in the first chapters), I will give the simplest form of a feature and illustrate its use. Later on, as the need arises, additional details are introduced.

Let me give an admittedly extreme example. In Common Lisp there is a procedure ("function") called **remove**. Given a list of elements, you can use the function to remove occurrences of a particular element in the list. For example, the following expression,

$$(\text{remove 'a '(a b c a a d e))}$$

removes all of the occurrences of 'a' in the list, and gives the list (b c d e). Now, there are several variants of this function, **remove-if, remove-if-not, remove-duplicates,** and more than half-a-dozen keywords that can augment, restrict, and enrich the **remove** function. In this text, we see the **remove** function in its simple form, when a situation calls for it, but the additions and augmentations come afterwards, only when we have a need for them and the reader has accumulated enough background to appreciate them. In this particular case, I called the example "extreme" because **remove** is introduced early in the text, but the full description and examples of its variations and extensions come at the very end of the book! At that point, however, the reader is familiar with such extensions, and can appreciate and use the function in its full capacity.

This book is designed so that students may experiment with the language while sitting at a personal computer that has a version of Lisp in its memory (or on a diskette), or is connected with a mainframe computer that has a dialect of Lisp available. In other words, it is designed for a hands-on approach to learning.

Some of the material presented in this book, particularly the editing and input/output procedures in Chapter 3, are system-dependent; that is, they depend on a particular computer implementation and set-up in a computer installation. Such data are often not included in general textbooks, because it is assumed that users know this, or get instructions from their respective computing facilities. I have included these procedures in this text because they are similar across different systems, and experience has shown that familiarity with one system greatly facilitates learning others. This familiarity is provided through a lot of examples and exercises for readers with no previous experience. Readers who are already familiar with the use of a particular system and its editing facilities need not read the sections in Chapter 3 that are specific for our set up. Appendix A contains a partial glossary of terms and examples for starting with Lisp in particular environments. Readers should benefit from reading this Appendix first.

Acknowledgments

I have used the material in this text for teaching graduate students in computer science, as well as in linguistics and other disciplines in the humanities and social sciences. I am grateful to these students for much insight and feedback. In particular, I am indebted to Lynette Ganim, who collected and tested much of data for Lispvm. I am also grateful to Chris Bosman-Clark and Norman Haas of IBM, for discussions and corrections of some of the material on Lispvm. Example (5.62) in Section 5.9.2 is reprinted with permission from *Common Lisp* by Dr. Guy Steele, copyright (©) 1984 Digital Press/Digital Equipment Corporation, 12 Crosby Drive, Bedford, MA 01730. The formula in Exercise 4, Section 3.9 is taken with permission from page 71 of *The Emperor's New Mind* by Roger Penrose, Oxford University Press, 1989.

The manuscript has been improved through a thoughtful review and imaginative recommendations by Constantine Kaniklidis. I am indebted to Dianne Littwin of Van Nostrand Reinhold for her enthusiastic undertaking of this project and to Ray Kanarr for the professional copyediting of the manuscript.

1

Beginning Lisp

1.0 WHAT IS LISP?

Lisp (an acronym of *List processing*) is a computer programming language. It was originally developed at M.I.T. in late 1950s to early 1960s by a group under the direction of John McCarthy. It was designed for the IBM 704 computer, and much of its original design structure and layout was influenced by the structure of that machine. Two of its famous function names are derived from instructions in that machine: **car** (**c**ontents of the **a**ddress **r**egister) and **cdr** (**c**ontents of the **d**ecrement **r**egister.) The first implementation that became generally available with a manual was called Lisp 1.5, and was used by groups of reaserchers and students in some of the early work in artificial intelligence, machine translation, and other activity that predominantly dealt with what came to be known as *symbol manipulation,* versus the *numeric data manipulations* that were then the stuff of programming languages. Early versions of Lisp had poor and inefficient mathematical capabilities. However, other institutions started implementing Lisp, and improvements and enhancements were made in each new implementaion. Before the end of the decade, Lisp 1.6, Lisp 1.75, Lisp 1.9, and (late in the 1960s) Lisp 2, which was a complete revision of the Lisp system, had been developed.

Since the early years in the history of Lisp, many new dialects and implementations have been developed for different computing systems and environments. Current Lisp dialects are powerful systems, having full and efficient mathematical and logical, as well as symbol and list processing, capabilities. In recent years, attempts have been made to 'standardize' Lisp, or to produce a core version for computer programs, which would be universal and independent of the various

1

machines. These attempts have resulted in a family of dialects, known under the generic name of Common Lisp. There have already been several important implementations of Common Lisp. Each implementation must have the common core, but it can have any number of extensions. As long as a programmer stays with the common core, the program should be exportable. (There are always some nagging problems of exporting programs from one computer system, to another, but this is not the appropriate forum to discuss these problems.)

There are also a large number of individual "uncommon" Lisp systems that are currently in use in a wide variety of applications in academic institutions, research organizations, and industries throughout the developed world. In this book, one "uncommon" Lisp has been selected as a representative of the group, for discussion. But the emphasis here shifts heavily toward Common Lisp.

Since, in this text, Lisp is advocated as a *first* language to learn for computing, nothing need be said about other languages. It should, however, be pointed out that, among the innovations that set Lisp apart from other languages, are its elegant underlying logical foundations and its facility for dealing with simple and complex list and symbolic structures. A major innovation is that the syntax or structure of data, and the instructions for manipulating data, are identical, so that with the stroke of a key, so to speak, data can be turned into instructions and instructions into data. Another important characteristic is the versatility of the langauge. The "keywords" or vocabulary of the language can be redefined to suit various needs and purposes. There are almost no keywords or reserve words in modern Lisp systems.

Programs in most classical programming languages must go through two separate processes. The program is written in, say, language L and must be submitted to a *compiler* for L. A compiler is a resident program (usually large and complex) in the computer, which will convert the program to codes that the machine can understand and manipulate. This code is returned as a *compiled program*. The compiled program must then be run on the computer to get results. Lisp was designed as an *interpretive* system. In an interpretive system, lines of program are translated and executed on the spot, so that the process becomes *interactive*. In modern Lisp systems, every element that is entered into the computer through the keyboard goes through a cycle known as read-eval-print, that is, the element is read, evaluated, and the result is displayed on the screen of the terminal. However, many of the modern Lisp systems give the option, as well, of "compiling" the program, and the system procedures are often precompiled for efficiency.

1.1 SOME EXAMPLES

Here are some examples of Lisp expressions. It is not expected that you will understand all of these at the very beginning, but it might be interesting for you to figure out as many of them as possible. As a general practice throughout this text, it will be assumed that the user will type inputs to Lisp in lower case letters, and that the computer will display responses or results on the monitor screen in capital letters (the examples in the text reflect this). However, we will see later that the output can be altered to be expressed in lower, upper, or mixed cases. In the early examples, the output from LISPVM is often used, because outputs in this dialect are clearly marked with the expression

$$VALUE = \ldots$$

Most other dialects of Lisp simply produce the output without marking it in this way. In general, when an expression is entered by pressing the *ENTER* key on the keyboard, the output or response will appear below the input. Later in this text, the output will either be printed directly under the input, or a double-shafted arrow, $\Rightarrow$, will be used to mark the output. Both of these methods are common in the literature.

```
(+ 3 4)                             VALUE = 7
(plus 3 4)                          VALUE = 7
(+ 3 4 6 10)                        VALUE = 23
(times 6 5)                         VALUE = 30
(* 6 5)                             VALUE = 30
(+ 3 (* 6 5))                       VALUE = 33
(+ (* 3 6) 5)                       VALUE = 23
(- 7 3)                             VALUE = 4
(difference 7 3)                    VALUE = 4
(/ 45 3)                            VALUE = 15
(quotient 45 3)                     VALUE = 15
(remainder 45 3)                    VALUE = 0
(remainder 45 4)                    VALUE = 1
(divide 45 3)                       VALUE = (15 0)
(divide 45 4)                       VALUE = (11 1)                    (1.1)
(append '(a b c) '(d e f))          VALUE = (A B C D E F)
(add1 4)                            VALUE = 5
(sub1 5)                            VALUE = 4
(add1 (sub1 4))                     VALUE = 4
(last '(john mary bill jerry))      VALUE = JERRY
(car '(john mary bill jerry))       VALUE = JOHN
(cdr '(john mary bill jerry))
                             VALUE = (MARY BILL JERRY)
(setq names '(john mary bill jerry))
                             VALUE = (JOHN MARY BILL JERRY)
(last names)                        VALUE = JERRY
(car names)                         VALUE = JOHN
(cdr names)                  VALUE = (MARY BILL JERRY)
(length names)                      VALUE = 4
(atom 'a)                           VALUE = TRUE
(atom  '(a b c))                    VALUE = NIL
(atom names)                        VALUE = NIL
(atom (length names))               VALUE = TRUE
```

```
(intersection '(1 2 3) '(a b c)) VALUE = NIL
(intersection '(1 mary 2 max) names)
                              VALUE = (MARY)
(setq digits '(2 4 6))        VALUE = (2 4 6)
(union digits names)
                  VALUE = (2 4 6 JOHN MARY BILL JERRY)
(sort names)          VALUE = (BILL JERRY JOHN MARY)
```

It should be pointed out that all of the above examples are not available exactly in the above format for all dialects of Lisp. Variations will be discussed in the course of the text. The reader can, however, find many of these variations by trial and error, and it is strongly recommended that the reader should try to find the variations for the particular dialect available on his/her own. Here is one example. In the arithmetic expressions given above, we see the forms

$$(+ 3 4)$$
$$(plus 3 4)$$

Both of these forms cause the computer to add 3 and 4, and to give the result 7, but in many dialects of Lisp written for personal computers or medium-size computers, the form with the addition operator "+" spelled out as **plus** is not available. In such dialects, (plus 3 4) will give an error message. From this, the user will know that this particular form is not available. We will see later, however, that the user can 'define' this word and make it a part of the vocabulary of the language. The vocabulary of Lisp is readily expandable by the user. (Parentheses in the above examples are part of the language in all dialects of Lisp and must be included as given. The format of the expressions will be discussed further in the text.)

The following section will give a preliminary description of how to get in and out of Lisp, so that the reader can experiment with the earlier examples. This would be a good way to find out what the examples do.

1.2 GETTING IN AND OUT OF LISP

Unfortunately, there is no standard procedure for working with a system. To work with a Lisp stored in a personal computer, the *installation* directions for the particular system must be followed, as well as the simple instructions for entering and leaving Lisp. Procedures for getting in and out of mainframes are normally set by computing facilities to suit their resources and needs. There are, however, certain general practices, and if the procedure is known for one system, it is easy to adjust to others. In Appendix A, the procedures for the systems that the author is using for the compilation of this text are given.

Once in a Lisp language, the user can start writing expressions or forms in that language. In Chapters 3 and 5 the use of an *editor* to correct programs, save, load, erase, and so forth will be discussed. At present, however, since you don't know how to use the editor, if serious errors are made, just get out of the program (see Appendix A) and rewrite the example from the beginning. Now begin by trying the material that was given in Example (1.1). As noted in the previous section, any symbol or expression that is input into the computer will go through the following cycle, which is common to all Lisp systems: *Read-eval-print* (REP). Thus, if you input the integer *56,* it will be read and evaluated to itself and the result 56 will be displayed. On the other hand, if the word *names* has previously been assigned the value (john mary bill jerry), as was done in Example (1.1), then if the word *names* was input, it would be evaluated to its value and the list (JOHN MARY BILL JERRY) will be displayed. Now try to do some more examples. The reader can make up his/her own examples, based on the examples that he/she has been able to figure out. When through with the exercises, exit Lisp and log off (Appendix A).

1.3 ARITHMETIC

Lisp is most suitable for doing symbol manipulation and list processing, which are particularly useful for developing intelligent and expert systems, for natural language processing and understanding, for communication with databases, and many other activities in modern computing that go beyond 'number crunching.' Nevertheless, modern Lisp dialects contain full and efficient arithmetic facilities. However, this text will not be much concerned with arithmetic, so some of the basic arithmetic facilities will be shown first, and then set aside for the present. This section will, therefore, describe the functions which operate on numbers.

Look at the first example in Example (1.1): (+ 3 4). It shows the structure that all forms and functions have in Lisp. An open parenthesis is followed by the name of a function (in this case the arithmetic symbol " + "), followed by the objects that the function is supposed to operate on. These objects are called *arguments* (in this case the numbers 3 and 4). This structure, in which the name of the function precedes the arguments, is called *prefix,* or Polish, notation. All functions in Lisp are in this format. The arguments of an arithmetic function are expected to be either numbers or *variables* that have been given numerical values. A variable is a name that can be assigned different values; for example, if "a" is a variable, the value 5 can be assigned to it (a = 5) or we can assign the value, say, *moon* to it. In that case, "a" would represent (or be the name for) 5 or moon, respectively. Note also that spacing is crucial in Lisp. The expression (+ 3 4) is a function, and instructs the computer to add 3 to 4 and give the result; the expression (+3 4), which has no space between the + and 3, is a list of two elements, +3 (positive 3) and 4, and does not give any instructions. Analogously, the expression (a b c d) is a list of four elements; the expression (abcd), which has no spaces between the letters, is a list of one element. The expression (+ 5 −3) means to add 5 to negative 3, and gives the value 2; the expression (+ 5 − 3), where there is a space between − and 3, has no meaning other than being a list of four elements.

In expressions with embedded parentheses, such as ($+$ 3 (* 6 5)), the parentheses are evaluated from inside out, in the normal arithmetic fashion. The * means to multiply. Thus:

```
(* 6 5) = 30
and (+ 3 (* 6 5))
means (+ 3 30)
so VALUE = 33.
```

This example and others in Example (1.1) show that simple expressions can be combined to make complex expressions, with any combination of arithmetic operators, such as $+$, *, /, etc.; or, in the case of Lispvm, any combination of operators and their names, such as *plus*, *times*, etc. Here is another set of examples of complex expressions:

$$(+ (* 6 (- 7 3)) (/ (* 2 4)(+ 2 2)))$$
$$(* (+ a b) c) \qquad (1.2)$$

In the first expression in Example (1.2), the following sequence of operations takes place, giving the final value of 26:

```
7 - 3 = 4
4 * 6 = 24
2 * 4 = 8
2 + 2 = 4
8 / 4 = 2
24 + 2 = 26
```

In the second expression, it is assumed that variables "a", "b", and "c" have been assigned some numeric values, and then "a" is added to "b", and the result is multiplied by "c". An example of a mixed expression for Lispvm and other dialects that accept operators in their spelled forms is this:

$$(plus (* 5 6)(times 3 2)) \qquad (1.3)$$

In the following table, a list of most of the arithmetic or numeric functions in Lispvm and other Lisp dialects with similar facilities, together with examples of their use, will be given. Some of them will be discussed further as a use is found for them. This table (and the one given later for Common Lisp) may be used as a ready reference. Don't worry if all of the functions are not understood at this point. In the following table, a *variable* is a symbol that can take on various values. For example, ($+$ a b c) will be erroneous unless some numeric values have been assigned to "a", "b", and "c". Thus, if "a", "b", and "c" were previously defined as a = 3, b = 5, and c = 10 (this is not how it is done in Lisp!), then ($+$ a b c) would make sense and would have the value: a + b + c, or 18. In Table 1.2, you will find similar data for Common Lisp. At the end of this section, in Table 1.4, a side-by-side comparison of some of the functions in Lispvm and Common Lisp that differ in their formats will be given. Although you will be using some particular dialect of Lisp, the Table will give an inkling of the kind of differences that may be expected in various dialects.

In Table 1.1, the first column contains the names of functions in Lispvm, the second column contains the description of the operation of each function, and the third column contains examples of the use of each function. In these examples, the expression VALUE = has been omitted from Lispvm outputs.

There are a number of other numerical and geometric functions in Lispvm, including abbreviations used in other programming languages, such as **lt** (less than), **gt** (greater than), **le** (less than or equal to), **ge** (greater than or equal to), and so forth. These will be presented in later chapters, as some use is found for them. The above functions, except **equal** and **nump**, expect numerical arguments, or variables with numerical values to be already assigned to them, otherwise, the output may be an error message or NIL.

Now, let us look at the **quotient** function in Lispvm once more:

$$
\begin{array}{lll}
\texttt{(quotient 15 3)} & \texttt{VALUE = 5} & \\
\texttt{(quotient 16 3)} & \texttt{VALUE = 5} & (1.4) \\
\texttt{(/ 17 3)} & \texttt{VALUE = 5} &
\end{array}
$$

Though the results in Example (1.4) may seem strange, there is a simple explanation. In Lisp, as in other programming languages, there are two kinds of numbers: integer and floating point (also called real or decimal-point). Integers are whole numbers without a decimal point, while floating point numbers, or real numbers, have decimal points. Thus, 3 is an integer, but 3., 3.0, and 3.15 are all real numbers. Inside the computer, real numbers are represented in floating point or the so-called scientific notation, and large numbers are often printed that way, but there is no need to be concerned with these details at present.

There are several functions in Lisp that treat these two kinds of numbers differently. In Lispvm, **quotient** is one of them. (The discussion of integer and floating point numbers in Common Lisp will be given in the following paragraphs.) In general, if all of the arguments of an arithmetic function are integers, then the result will be also an integer. That is, the result will simply ignore, or *truncate,* the decimal fraction, no matter how large it is. Thus, 4.99 will be represented as 4. On the other hand, if one or more of the arguments were given in decimal notation, then the result will be expressed in floating point. Now compare the following examples with those given in Example (1.4):

$$
\begin{array}{lll}
\texttt{(quotient 15 3.0)} & \texttt{VALUE = 5.0} & \\
\texttt{(quotient 16 3.0)} & \texttt{VALUE = 5.33333333333} & (1.5) \\
\texttt{(/ 17 3.0)} & \texttt{VALUE = 5.66666666667} &
\end{array}
$$

Now try using real numbers with some of the other arithmetic functions to see how they work.

TABLE 1.1. *NUMERICAL FUNCTIONS IN LISPVM*

Name	Operation	Input/Output Example
plus	Adds numbers or values of variables	(plus 3 4 12) = 19 (+ a b c)
difference	Subtracts the second number from the first	(difference 7 3) = 4 (− a b)
times	Multiplies numbers or values of variables	(* 5 7 12) = 420 (times a b c d)
quotient	Divides the first number by the second number.	(/ 6 2) = 3 (quotient a b)
remainder	Divides the first number by the second and returns the remainder.	(remainder 7 3) = 1 (remainder 8 2) = 0
divide	Divides the first number by the second and returns both the quotient and the remainder.	(divide 7 3) = (2 1) (divide 8 2) = 4 0)
minus	Changes the sign of its argument.	(minus 7) = −7 (minus −7) = 7
expt	Raises the first number to the power of the second.	(expt 5 2) = 25 (** 5 2) = 25
add1	Adds one to its argument.	(add1 5) = 6
sub1	Subtracts one from its argument.	(sub1 6) = 5
absval	Returns the absolute value of its argument.	(absval −7) = 7
max	Returns the largest of the numbers that follow.	(max 5 12 21 7) = 21
min	Returns the smallest of the numbers that follow.	(min 5 12 21 7) = 5
rnum2int	Converts its argument to an integer.	(rnum2int 3.45) = 3
fix	Identical to rnum2int.	(fix 3.45) = 3
int2rnum	Converts integer to real.	(int2rnum 3) = 3.0
float	Identical to int2rnum.	(float 3) = 3.0
nump	Returns its argument if it is a number, otherwise returns NIL (= false).	(nump 5) = 5 (nump x) = NIL
numberp	(same as nump)	
greaterp	Returns TRUE if the first number is greater than the second.	(greaterp 7 2) = TRUE (greaterp 2 7) = NIL
lessp	Opposite of greaterp.	(lessp 7 2) = NIL (lessp 2 7) = TRUE
equal	Returns TRUE if its two arguments are equal.	(= 1 3) = NIL (equal a a) = TRUE
zerop	Returns its argument if it is zero.	(zerop 0) = 0 (zerop 5) = NIL
minusp	Returns its argument if it is negative.	(minusp −6) = −6 (minusp 6) = NIL
plusp	Returns its argument if it is greater than or equal to zero.	(plusp −3) = NIL (plusp (− 7 9)) = NIL
intp	Returns its argument if it is integer.	(intp 7) = 7
rnump	Returns its argument if it is a real number.	(rnump 3.75) = 3.75 (rnump 3) = NIL
oddp	Returns its argument if it is an odd integer.	(oddp 15) = 15 (oddp 12) = NIL
evenp	Returns its argument if it is an even integer.	(evenp 4) = 4 (evenp 3) = NIL

TABLE 1.2. *NUMERICAL FUNCTIONS IN COMMON LISP*

Input Example	Output Value	Remark
(+ 3 4 12)	19	"plus", etc., not allowed
(+ 3.6 5 6.35)	14.95	mixed numbers
(+)	0	by convention
(+ 4)	4	
(− 17 6)	11	
(− 5 6 7)	−8	same as 5 − 6 − 7
(− 7.3 2)	5.3	
(*)	1	by convention
(* 2 3 4)	24	
(* 3 2.35)	7.05	
(/)	ERROR	
(/ 15 3)	5.0	
(/ 15 4)	3.75	
(/ 12 2 3)	2.0	
(/ 3 2 12)	0.125	
(/ 1 3)	3.33333F-01	= 0.333. . . . .
(truncate 16 5)	3 1	quotient and remainder
(rem 7 3)	1	remainder of 7/3
(rem 8 4)	0	
(mod 5 3)	2	
(mod 3.75 2)	1.75	
(− 7)	−7	changes the sign
(− −7)	7	
(expt 5 2)	25	
(expt 2 3)	8	
(1+ 5)	6	same as (add1 5) in Lispvm
(1− 6)	5	same as (sub1 6) in Lispvm
(abs −7)	7	absolute value
(abs (* 2 −3.6))	7.2	
(max 5 12 3 21 7)	21	the largest number
(min 5 12 3 21 7)	3	the smallest number
(zerop 0)	T (= TRUE)	test for zero
(zerop 5)	NIL (= FALSE)	
(zerop x)	ERROR	(unless x has a value)
(integerp 5)	T	test for integer
(floatp 3.0)	T	test for real number
(numberp 63)	T	test for number
(oddp 5)	T	
(evenp 12)	T	
(minusp −7)	T	test for negative number
(signum −345)	−1	a variant of the above
(plusp −7)	NIL	test for positive number
(signum 7)	1	same as above
(signum 0)	0	
(float 25)	25.0	change fix to real
(floor 25.0)	25	change real to fix
(= 5 5)	T	arguments are equal
(= 5 5 5 5)	T	
(= 5 5 7 5)	NIL	
(= 5 5.0)	T	

(continued)

TABLE 1.2.   NUMERICAL FUNCTIONS IN COMMON LISP (continued)

Input Example	Output Value	Remark
(= 5 5.0 (+ 2 3) (* 2 2.5))	T	
(/= 5 6)	T	not equal test
(< 5 7)	T	less than
(> 7 5)	T	greater than
(<= 5 7)	T	less than or equal
(>= 5 7)	NIL	greater than or equal
(> 9 8 6 5)	T	
(> 9 8 10 6)	NIL	
(equal 5 5)	T	
(equal 'a 'a)	T	
(eql 5 5)	T	

Equal, eql, eq, and = test for equality, but there are differences between them, which will be explained later in the text (see Section 4.3). = accepts numerical values only.

In Table 1.2, for numerical functions in Common Lisp, examples of the most common functions are given. At this point, the reader will be able to understand the form and use of these functions without much difficulty. In any case, there will be further examples with these functions as the need arises in the remainder of this text and, whenever necessary, additional explanations and examples will be given.

As in the case of Lispvm, there are many other numerical, logical, and geometric functions in Common Lisp, some of which will be encountered as the need arises. The reader should be reminded that not all dialects of Lisp have as many varieties of numerical functions as shown in Tables 1.1 and 1.2. For example, MacLisp and IqLisp cannot deal with real numbers, and their arguments for arithmetic operations are restricted to two. Furthermore, in IqLisp all input must be in capital letters.

The function **truncate** in Common Lisp is similar to **divide** in Lispvm, in that they both return the quotient and remainder of a division operation:

```
(divide 16 3)      VALUE = (5 1)      [Lispvm]
(truncate 16 3)    ==)  5   1         [Common Lisp]
```
(1.6)

There are, however, significant differences between the two. In addition to the above property, in Common Lisp, **floor, ceiling, truncate,** and **round** serve to round up or down a real number to an integer, in accordance with the examples in Table 1.3, and return the integral part and fractional part separately. Thus, **truncate,** with the argument 65.321, (truncate 65.321), will return two separate values, 65 and 0.321.

Another pair of useful numerical functions in Common Lisp are **incf** and **decf**, which take two arguments, and the first argument is increased (**incf**) or decreased

TABLE 1.3. *CONVERSION OF NONINTEGRAL VALUES TO INTEGERS.*

Argument	floor	ceiling	round	truncate
3.45	3 | 0.45	4 | −0.55	3 | 0.45	3 | 0.45
3.65	3 | 0.65	4 | −0.35	4 | −0.35	3 | 0.65
3.50	3 | 0.5	4 | −0.5	4 | −0.5	3 | 0.5
		(floor (round 3.65)) ⇒ 4 | 0		
		(round (floor 3.65)) ⇒ 3 | 0		

(**decf**) by the value of the second argument. If the second argument is null, the value of the first argument is increased or reduced by one. Thus, if we set the value of "n" to 5 by writing the function:

then,

$$
\begin{array}{ll}
\text{(setq n 5)} & ==\rangle\ 5 \\
\text{(incf n 3)} & ==\rangle\ 8 \\
\text{(incf n)} & ==\rangle\ 6 \\
\text{(decf n 3)} & ==\rangle\ 2 \\
\text{(decf n)} & ==\rangle\ 4
\end{array}
$$

(1.7)

Actually, however, if all of the above expressions were run in the sequence given, the results for the value of n would be 5, 8, 9, 6, and 5, because like **setq**, **incf** and **decf** globally change the value of a variable.

We have already seen, in at least one example, that the differences in examples in Table 1.4 may not be just in the nomenclature.

TABLE 1.4 *A COMPARISON OF SOME OF THE DIFFERING FUNCTION FORMATS BETWEEN "UNCOMMON" AND COMMON LISP DIALECTS*

Uncommon	Common
plus	+
difference	−
times	*
divide	truncate
quotient	/
remainder	rem
minus	− [for sign change]
add1	1+
sub1	1−
absval	abs
intp	integerp

1.4 EXERCISES

1. Write Lisp functions to evaluate the following expressions. Try these with a computer and obtain results. Recall that the following hierarchy of operators holds:

> Expressions within parentheses
> Exponentiation
> Multiplication or division
> Addition or subtraction

$$75 + 12 \times 10$$
$$25 \times (6 + 2 - 3) - 5$$
$$253 + 252 - (6 - 3)$$

2. Mary has purchased five pounds of apples to divide among six children. Assume that there is an average of four apples in a pound. Mary will give each child an equal number of apples, and eat the remainder, if any. Write a complete Lisp program to calculate how many apples each child will get, and how many apples, if any, will be left for Mary.

3. Evaluate the following Lispvm expressions (Hint: recall that, in Lispvm, certain 'predicate' (test) functions return a numerical value, rather than T or NIL):

```
(plus (minusp -6) 7)
(times (add1 6)(sub1 5))
(greaterp (intp 7)(minusp -8))
(atom (divide 6 2))
(atom (divide 7 2))
(atom (/ 6 2))
(divide (oddp 5) 2)
(quotient (* 3 2) (+ 2 1))
```

4. Convert the expressions in Exercise 3 to Common Lisp whenever possible.

5. Write a Lisp program to compute how long it will take to go from New York to Buffalo, a distance of 425 miles, at 55 miles per hour. Assume that there will be an additional hour and a half delay on the road.

6. Show that 5 plus 5 is equal to 2 times 5.

7. The area of a circle is computed by the square of the radius times pi (equal to 3.14). Write a function to compute the area of a circle with a radius of 5.75. *Note:* In Common Lisp, *pi* is a constant with a fixed value.

8. Show that 5 divided by 2 is not equal to 5 divided by 2.0, in some forms.

9. Recall that, in Common Lisp, comparisons can be made between a string of numerical elements, for example (= 5 5 5), (< 2 4 6 3), and so on. One use of this facility is to test whether a variable with some numerical value falls within a range, for example, whether the value of x occurs between 1 and 10. Write

expressions to assign a value to x and test its occurrence within the ranges of forms in $=$, $/=$, $>$, and so on.

10. In Common Lisp, both **equal** and **eql** are restricted to two arguments, but the following holds:

```
(equal 5 5) ==> T
(equal 5 5.0) ==> T
(eql 5 5) ==> T
(eql 5 5.0) ==> NIL
```

Can you explain the discrepancy?

1.5 DATA AND PROGRAM STRUCTURES AND FUNCTIONS

Throughout the preceding material, the terms *function* and *expression* have been used; let us now define these terms more explicitly. There are two types of structures in Lisp that should be mentioned now.

The first is an *atom* (or symbol), which consists of a single element. Here are eight examples of atoms:

> a
> abc
> Mary
> book
> book-of-verses
> 1
> 267584398032
> w45 + 6

The second type is a *list,* which consists of one or more atoms enclosed in a pair of parentheses. A list may contain other lists. Examples of lists are:

> (a)
> (J F K)
> (Mary has a book)
> (book of verses)
> (father (bill jim))
> (5 32 a (6 9) 1 34 (20 (10 11) g))

Note that the parentheses are significant in these structures, and they must always be balanced. There can also be an empty list, represented as ( ) or NIL, which is a list with nothing in it. NIL is a data structure in Lisp that is both an atom and a list.

An expression (or, more exactly in Lisp, an s-expression or symbolic-expression) is a structure consisting of one or more atoms or lists. Thus, all of the examples given so far in this chapter are expressions. An expression is called a *form* when it is meant to be evaluated. A function is an expression that provides instructions for the computer. All of the arithmetic examples and other examples that were given at the beginning of this chapter are functions.

A function has a name, and may have arguments and a body. In the expression (+ 5 8), " + " is the name of the function, and 5 and 8 are its arguments. A function may have inputs and must always have an output. In (plus a b), the values assigned to a and b are inputs, and the response, VALUE = . . . , is the output. In (plus 5 8), 5 and 8 stand for their own input values and the output is VALUE = 13.

The examples of functions that have been given so far are those that have been built into the Lisp system. These are called built-in, intrinsic, or system functions. Other functions can be constructed by the user for particular needs. To construct new functions, system functions, expressions, and other constructed functions can be used. We will call these new functions *defined functions,* or *d-functions* for short. It will be seen that there are several ways to define new functions. Here is one way. Suppose there is an application where there is a consistent need to add the number 5 to other numbers. Lisp provides a system function that adds 1 to a number, but not one that adds 5. So a new function can be defined:

$$(\text{defun add5 (n) (+ n 5)}) \tag{1.8}$$
$$\text{ADD5}$$

In Lisp, **defun** is a term that is used to "define a function"; **add5** is an arbitrary name; "n" is called the *parameter* of the function, it is a variable or slot for putting a value into (or, more technically, to *bind* it with a value); (+ n 5) is a form that is evaluated by adding 5 to the current value of n. When the function is written in Example (1.8), the output **add5**, the name of the new function, appears under it. Then this d-function can be *called* by writing, for example, (add5 10). This will then produce an output of 15. Note that (+ n 5) in Example (1.8) is the 'body' of the function. When the function is called, (add5 10), 10 is the *argument* of the function, and it is bound to the parameter "n".

The function **add5** will be available for the remainder of the log-on session (i.e., until log off). In Chapter 3, we will see how to save the work of a session and retrieve it at future sessions.

Suppose that there is a need, again and again, to triple numbers. The following will define a function to do this.

Then,
$$(\text{defun triple (n) (* n 3)}) \tag{1.9}$$
$$(\text{triple 4) ==> 12}$$

Many times, a function is needed that will do one thing to a certain input and a different thing to another input. It is possible to define such functions. What if a function is needed that doubles numbers that are less than ten and triples numbers that are greater than or equal to 10? The following can be defined:

```
(defun double-or-triple (n)
(cond ((< n 10) (* n 2))
      ((>= n 10) (triple n))))
DOUBLE-OR-TRIPLE
```
(1.10)

There are many things to observe in this example. There is a new word, **cond**, which will be explained shortly (in the meanwhile, can you guess what it is an abbreviation of?). Also, in defining this new function, **triple** was used—a function that was previously defined. Lisp is an ideal language for many applications, because it can be expanded by defining new words (function names) in terms of the words it already has, and in terms of other new words that have been created. Can you predict the outputs of

```
(double-or-triple 6)?
(double-or-triple 12)?
```

Let us look at another example:

```
(defun example1 (x)
    (cond ((equal x 0) nil)
          (t (1+ x))))
```
(1.11)

In this example, a function called **example1** has been defined. The parameter for this function is the variable "x". In the second line, a *cond*itional expression, **cond**, begins and tests to see whether the value of "x" is equal to zero. If so, the value NIL is returned as output and the function ends. If "x" is not equal to zero, control goes to the next line, where (in all cases (because t means true)) the current value of "x" is increased by 1 (recall that that is what 1+ does) and the new value of "x" is displayed as the output.

If any of the above functions fail to work, or result in error messages, try again. Check the parentheses. The most common error at this stage of progress is unbalanced or misplaced parentheses. Also note that the words **cond**, **equal**, **nil**, **t**, and 1+ are the names of system functions or forms that the Lisp system *understands*, and we have used these to construct new functions.

In the above examples, we saw that values can be assigned to variables by a 'function call.' For example, when the function in Example (1.10) was called the values of 6 and 12 were 'bound' to "n". A common way of assigning values to variables globally is through the use of **setq**:

```
(setq x 5) ==> 5
(setq names '(bill mary anne jim maxwell))
   ==> (BILL MARY ANNE JIM MAXWELL)
```
(1.12)

The first example assigns 5 as the value of x. The second example assigns a list of names as the value of **names**. Again, the quote mark will be ignored at present. The only thing to remember for the present is this: when a single number is assigned as a value of a variable, do not use the quote mark. At all other times, whether nonnumeric characters, words, or lists of any kind are assigned, the quote mark should be used. (In Lispvm, atoms can be assigned via **setq** without a quote mark, e.g., (setq name kate), but this is not true of many other dialects of Lisp, and it is better to get used to writing the quote mark for everything except a single number. We will see later that the use of quote mark is not restricted to **setq**.) Here are some more examples:

```
(setq fido 'dog)
(setq fido 15)
(setq numbers '(1 2 3 4 5))
(setq house '(rooms basement attic))
```

(Strictly speaking, the above forms are *procedures*. Recall that a function has an output; when we write (setq fido 'dog), the output is DOG, but there is a side effect: the current value of FIDO will be 'globally' changed to dog, so that if we input fido, DOG will be the output. However, when the assignment is changed to (setq fido 15), the value, or the content, of the 'slot' fido will be changed to 15.)

What if it was desirable not to assign a fixed value to an argument in the function, but to read a new value every time the function was called? Type the following:

```
(setq x (read))
```

The function will be put in a "hold" situation, and the Lisp system will wait for an input value at the keyboard to be bound to "x". Let us now try another example of a d-function. First, we will construct separate lists of democrats and republicans:

```
(setq democrats '(mary sara john felix))                    (1.13)
(setq republicans '(james andrew sophi henry))
```

Then, when John changes his party, the following function will update the lists:

```
(defun update (name L1 L2)
    (setq L1 (remove name L1))                              (1.14)
    (setq L2 (cons name L2)))
```

Details of the functions **remove** and **cons** will be discussed later. Here, it is necessary to realize that **cons** adds the value of the variable *name* to the front of the list L2. Instead of the function in Example (1.14), two separate forms: (setq democrats (remove 'john democrats)) and (setq republicans (cons 'john republicans)) could simply have been written, but the function in Example (1.14) is more general, in that it can be applied to any two lists and any name. The affiliation of John can be changed by inputting:

$$(\text{update 'john democrats republicans}) \qquad (1.15)$$

$$\Longrightarrow (\text{JOHN JAMES ANDREW SOPHI HENRY})$$

We will see later, however, that the function in Example (1.14), as written, does not permanently ('globally') change the two lists, while the alternative method makes a permanent change.

The format of the **remove** function in Example (1.14) is that of Common Lisp. In Lispvm, the item comes after the list, so that the second line in Example (1.14) would be written as (setq L1 (remove L1 name)). Thus,

```
(setq L1 (remove name L1))     [Common Lisp]
(setq L1 (remove L1 name))     [Lispvm]
```

When Example (1.15) is processed, John is bound to name, democrats and republicans are bound to L1 and L2, respectively. Ignore the quote mark in front of John for the present. For the last example in this section, try to figure out what example3 does:

```
(defun example3  nil
    (setq text (read))
    (cond ((equal (length text) 1) text)
          (t (sort text))))
```
$$(1.16)$$

Before leaving this section, take another look at the examples that we have had in this chapter so far. As noted before, in Lisp, unlike many other programming languages, there is no syntactic distinction between instructions and data or between program structures and data structures. Any expression can be a program. For example, the expression (a 5 7 12) is a data expression. However, if we input (setq a +) in Lispvm, then *a* will have the same value as + or **plus**, and (a 5 7 12) would then be a function, and would produce VALUE = 24. In **example3**, text is some data for sorting (in alphabetic or numeric order). The expression (setq text (read)) will cause the computer to pause for you to input the text as a list enclosed in parentheses. The next line tests to see if the text has only one word (equal (length text) 1); if so, the computer returns (displays on the terminal) the one-word text. The last line is for the case where the text is longer than one word; then the text is sorted and the result is displayed.

EXERCISE

Write functions to assign the following expressions as the values of variables "x", "y", and "z", respectively. Then write an expression that will combine the values of "x", "y", and "z" into one list, and assign it to "k".

```
(one foot up and one foot down,)
(that is the way)
(to London town.)
```

1.6 CONDITIONAL EXPRESSIONS

This is a good place to elaborate further on the structure of the conditional (**cond**) expressions. A conditional expression can be constructed by typing **cond**, followed by a series of condition-action pairs. The general structure of the conditional is, then, the following:

```
(cond (⟨condition⟩  ⟨action⟩)
      (⟨condition⟩  ⟨action⟩)
      (⟨condition⟩  ⟨action⟩)
                :
                :
      (⟨condition⟩  ⟨action⟩) )
```

(The data between angle brackets, $< \ldots >$, can be valid test and action expressions—see below)

If any one of the conditions is true (satisfied), the action associated with it is carried out and no other conditions are tested. The conditions are tested (or evaluated) in the order that they are listed. If one fails, the next one is tried. In writing a conditional expression, make sure that the last condition in the sequence is always true, so that the last action takes place, even if none of the others have. This will prevent the control from hanging up at the end and getting unexpected results. To make the last condition always true, t (or 't in Lispvm) is written as the last conditional. In Lisp, t is a term that always evalutes as *TRUE,* and the last action is always carried out. The complete structure of the conditional expression is, then, the following:

```
(cond (⟨condition⟩   ⟨action⟩)
                :
                :
      (t ⟨action⟩) )
```

In the last line, the last closing parenthesis closes the opening parenthesis of (cond; thus signifying the end of the conditional expression. The action part can

TABLE 1.5. *SIMPLE CONDITIONAL EXPRESSIONS*

Cond expression	Result
(cond ((numberp n) n))	5
(cond ((zerop m) 'yes))	YES
(cond ((equal (car L1) 'mary) 'y))	Y
(cond ((equal L2 '(a b c d))(last L2)))	(D) [D in Lispvm]
(cond ((> x y) (+ 7 5)))	12

be any expression. Table 1.5 contains some examples of simple conditional expressions; assuming n = 5, m = 0, L1 = (mary jim kay), L2 = (a b c d), x = 12, y = 6.

1.7 RECURSIVE FUNCTIONS

Many programming tasks involve repetitions, for which computers are extremely useful tools. Word processing programs (for example), which are valuable and popular, contain many examples of repetitive processes. Consider the question of determining whether a particular word belongs to a list of words. Such a function could be defined as follows: Let us name the function **find** and name its parameters *word* and *sentence*. First the function checks to see whether *word* is the same as, or equal to, the first item in sentence, and, if it is, to return the message "found". If *word* is not equal to the first item in sentence, then it tries to **find** the word in the rest of the sentence, the **cdr** of the sentence. This is the essence of the definition. Because it may be necessary to keep looking at **cdrs** of **cdrs** if the word is not found right away, it is also necessary to check often to see whether the sentence being searched has any words left in it or not; so, that question should be included in the function also. The procedure for doing these things can be described as follows:

Step 1. If the sentence is empty, print "not-found" and stop.
     2. If *word* is equal to the **car** of the sentence, print "found" and stop.
     3. Otherwise, try to find *word* in the **cdr** of the sentence.

The functions **car** and **cdr** (to be defined extensively in Chapters 2 and 4) return the first element and the remainder elements in a list, respectively. The remainder being the list minus its first element.

The above procedure is called an *algorithm*, because it always returns an answer and stops after a finite number of steps, in this case not more than the number of elements in the list. (The procedures for the functions in earlier sections were also algorithms.)

The function in Lisp can now be defined as:

```
(defun find (word sentence)
       (cond ((null sentence) 'not-found)              (1.17)
             ((equal word (car sentence)) 'found)
             (t (find word (cdr sentence)))))
```

An important difference between this function and those that have been defined in previous sections is seen in the fourth line. The function *uses itself.* This process of a function's calling itself is called *recursion,* and such a function is called a *recursive function.*

Now if we input (find 'how '(hello, how are you)), the function **find** will bind the argument *how* as the value of *word* and (hello, how are you) as the value of *sentence* and check to see whether *sentence* is empty. It is not, so **find** will check to see if *how* is equal to the **car** (the first word) of the sentence. The **car** of the sentence is *hello,* which is not equal to *how.* The function will then call **find** (itself) with the value of *word* still being *how,* but the value of *sentence* is now (how are you), the **cdr** of the original sentence. This time, *how* matches the **car** of sentence, and the message FOUND will be returned. Now try to run the function **find** with the following data:

1. (find 'how '(I am fine))
2. (setq names '(harry martin james charles terence))
   (find 'james names).

Because of the importance and elegance of recursive functions, several simple examples will be examined in detail.

Let's look at an arithmetic example. (+ 5 10 12 13) can be used to add four numbers, but if you had to add, say, 2000 numbers, it would be awkward to write a plus followed by 2000 different numbers! Even for shorter lists, it might be preferable to find another procedure if, say, it is desirable to be able to work with lists of varying lengths. In Lisp, there is a much more elegant way of performing this task. The sum of the numbers in a list can be obtained by adding the first number to the sum of the rest of the numbers. The sum of "the rest of the numbers" can be computed by adding the first of them to the sum of the rest of them, and so on. Now, if the list of numbers is empty (and eventually the list in the above procedure will become empty), the value of its sum will be given as 0. Then, the process can be written as follows:

Step 1. If the list is empty, its sum is 0
     2. If the list is not empty, add the first element of the list to the sum of the rest of the list.

The Lisp function for the above algorithm can be named **sum-of**, and the list of numbers *list-of-nums*, then the function will look like this:

```
(defun sum-of (list-of-nums)
    (cond ((null list-of-nums) 0)
        (t (+ (car list-of-nums)
            (sum-of (cdr list-of-nums))))))
```

(1.18)

Let us follow the details of this function: In the first line, the name of the function, **sum-of**, and its parameter, (list-of-nums), are defined. In the second line, a conditional expression is started, which states that if the *list-of-nums* is empty (null), return 0 for value. The third line is the TRUE case of the conditional; it adds the first element of the list, (car list-of-nums), to the sum of the remainder of the list, (cdr list-of-nums). Notice, however, that (in order to obtain the sum of the remainder of the list) the function calls itself, **sum-of**, in the last line of the above function. This process is repeated until the list is empty. At that point, sum is given the value 0 and this value is returned to the previous step.

Try the function **sum-of** now with the *list-of-nums* equal to (2 3 7). Input the function and then type:

```
(sum-of '(2 3 7))
```

The variable *list-of-nums* is bound to the value (2 3 7). The function **sum-of** looks at (2 3 7) to see whether it is empty. It is not; so **sum-of** prepares to add 2, the **car** of the list of numbers, to the **sum-of** (3 7). In order to do this, **sum-of** checks (3 7) to see whether it is empty. Again, it is not; so **sum-of** prepares to add 3, the **car** of (3 7), to the **sum-of** (7). This requires checking to see whether (7) is empty; it is not, so then **sum-of** prepares to add 7 to the **sum-of** ( ). This time, ( ) is empty; so the value 0 is *sent back* to the previous step. All of the previous steps have been waiting in a stack for a numerical answer, and finally there is one. So now, 7 is added to 0, giving the result of 7; and 3 is added to 7, giving 10; and 2 is added to 10, giving the result of 12, which is returned as the value of (sum-of '(2 3 7)). This process can be demonstrated graphically in Figure 1.1 (in this figure, *list-of-nums* is abbreviated to *lon*).

In Example (1.18), a variable or slot for the accumulation of the addition process has not been provided. Where is the output accumulated and finally presented? When a function is defined, such as **sum-of** in Example (1.18), its name is returned as the value of the function. So that, as in previous examples, if Example (1.18) were the input, **sum-of** will be the output of the function. When a function, such as (sum-of '(2 3 7)), is called, it is evaluated, and the name of the function takes the value of the output, so that what is output is really the final value of the name of the function.

Later on in the text, other ways of defining a function to add a list of numbers will be presented. In the meantime, try using **sum-of** again. Input:

```
(setq k '(1 3 7 34 81 25))
(sum-of k)
```

151 should appear as output.

First Cycle:	lon = (2 3 7)
	lon not null (empty)
	add 2 to sum-of (3 7)

Second Cycle:	lon = (3 7)
	lon not null
	add 2 + 3 to sum-of (7)

Third Cycle:	lon = (7)
	lon not null
	add 2 + 3 + 7 to sum-of ( )

Fourth Cycle:	lon = ( )
	lon = null
	add 2 + 3 + 7 + 0 = **12**
	Halt

Figure 1.1. Example of a recursive process.

We have seen that there are system functions for extracting the first, the last, and the remainder of the elements in a list of numbers or words. Here are some examples as reminders:

```
(setq L1 '(23 14 5 6 8 70))
(setq L2 '(noun verb adjective adverb))
(car L1)      23                                           (1.19)
(car L2)      NOUN
(cdr L2)      (VERB ADJECTIVE ADVERB)
(last L1)     (70) [70 in Lispvm]
```

It will be seen later that you can combine a series of **car** and **cdr** forms to get at any element in a list. The functions **car** and **cdr** are historical terms in all dialects of Lisp. Some dialects have added more obvious terms, such as *first*, *rest*, etc. (See Section 2.2, Chapter 2). A function can also be written to return, say, the *n*th element of a list. Here is a recursive function for doing that:

```
(defun my-nth (n L)
   (cond ((null L) 'empty-list)
         ((zerop n) nil)
         ((> n (length L)) 'cant-do!)                      (1.20)
         ((equal n 1) (car L))
         (t (my-nth (1- n) (cdr L) ) ) ))
```

For the time being, the reader can, as an exercise, try to figure out how this function works. (It is only observed here that the safeguards built into the first few lines are prudent.) Input it at the keyboard, and then input the following sequence of function "calls", the results will assist in your understanding.

```
(my-nth 5 ( ))
(my-nth 7 L1 )
(my-nth 0 L1 )
(my-nth 1 L2 )
(my-nth 3 L2 )
(my-nth 2 L1 )
(my-nth 4 L2 )
```

Note that, in these calls, ( ) represents an empty list, and it is assumed that L1 and L2 have been input as lists defined with **setq**, as shown above.

Now that we have learned how to write a function to find the nth member of a list, it can be told that there are built-in functions in Lispvm and Common Lisp that will give the nth member of a list. In Lispvm, this function is called **elt**. Thus, if "L" is a list and "n" is a positive integer, then (elt L n) will return the nth element of L. In Common Lisp, the form is called **nth**, so that (nth n L) will return the nth + 1 element of L (note the difference in order between Lispvm and Common Lisp forms), for example, if L = (a b c d e), then (nth 4 L) $\Rightarrow$ E. (nth + 1 is returned because the count starts from 0, so that (nth 0 L) will return A.)

```
(elt L n)      [Lispvm]
(nth n L)      [Common Lisp]
```

In Common LISP, there is another function called **nthcdr**, which returns the tail-end of a list:

```
(nthcdr 2 '(a b c d e f)) ==> (C D E F)
(nthcdr 5 '(a b c d e f)) ==> (F)
```

There will be many more examples and discussions of recursion in this text. One point to stress at the outset is that recursive functions need a "null" condition (or something that serves the same purpose) in order for them to stop, and a good place for this condition is at the beginning of the **cond**. It is very undesirable for functions to go on computing forever.

A classical example is the following (recursive) function for the addition of two arbitrary numbers ("m" and "n"), by subtracting 1 from "n" and adding 1 to "m", until "n" is equal to zero and "m" contains the summation.

```
(defun addition (m n)
    (cond ((equal n 0) m)
          (t (addition (1+ m)(1- n))))))        (1.21)
==> ADDITION
    (addition 5 6) ==> 11
```

(Recall that in all cases when 1+ and 1− forms are written in Common Lisp, **add1** and **sub1** should be used if Lispvm or other compatible dialects are being used.)

A very popular exercise is to write a function to obtain the factorial of any integer "n". The symbol in mathematics for factorial is !. It may be recalled that n! is the product of all of the positive whole numbers up to and including "n". For example, 5! = 5 × 4 × 3 × 2 × 1 = 120, and, by convention 0! = 1. The recursive procedure for computing factorials can be described by:

$$(1) \quad \text{If n = 0, then n! = 1} \qquad\qquad (1.22)$$
$$(2) \quad \text{Otherwise, n! = n * (n-1)!}$$

This can be written in Lisp:

```
(defun factorial (n)
    (cond ((zerop n) 1)                    (1.23)
          (t (* n (factorial (1- n)))))))
```

Try this and then input (factorial 3). What is returned as output? Stepping through the procedure in Example 1.22, we have:

```
3! = 3 x 2!
     3 x 2 x 1!
     3 x 2 x 1 x 0!
     3 x 2 x 1 x 1
     6
```

Similarly, stepping through the Lisp recursive function in Example 1.23, the following steps can be visualized:

```
        (factorial 3)
(* 3 (factorial 2))
(* 3 (* 2 (factorial 1)))
(* 3 (* 2 (* 1 (factorial 0))))
(* 3 (* 2 (* 1 1)))
(* 3 (* 2 1))
(* 3 2)
6
```

In the computation of (factorial 3), n is a *bound variable*; it is first bound to 3. Then, the function checks to see if n = 0; it is not. So it computes 3 * 2! In order to compute that, it must compute 2! So it uses the same function definition, binding 2 to n. 2 does not equal zero, and the function computes 2 * 1! and so on. When "n" is finally 0, there is a value for 0! (0! = 1), and the function can compute as shown above. As an exercise, trace the steps in the computation of (factorial 4).

Let us look at another text problem. For the next example, a function to search a text for any given keyword, and to print the sentences containing that keyword (a concordance program) will be described. Since the process of storing text as a file has not yet been discussed, the function will be written so that both the keyword and the text are input as the arguments of the function. First, the function that determines if a word occurs in a sentence needs to be defined. This function will be written as a general set membership function that determines whether a token is a member of a set or not.

```
(defun mem  (token set)
    (cond ((null set) nil)                        (1.24)
          ((equal token (car set)) t)
          (t (mem token (cdr set)))))
```

Now, if (mem 'up '(jack and jill went up the hill)) is called, T (true) will be returned. However, if (mem 'x '(a b c d)), is input, NIL will be returned. Note that this function is very similar to the **find** function, which was introduced in this section. There is also a system function called **member** in Lisp, which has the same effect as **mem**, although with a different output (the difference will be discussed in Section 2-3.) Now for the search, or concordance, function:

```
(defun search (word text)
    (cond ((null text) nil)
          ( (mem word (car text) )                  (1.25)
        (cons (car text)(search word (cdr text)) ))
          (t (search word (cdr text)) ) ))
```

The function **cons** is short for constructor, and is the name of a system function in Lisp that takes lists and/or atoms and makes a new list out of them. There will be more about this function in the next chapter. The search function expects the text to be a list, and every sentence in the text to be a sublist enclosed in a pair of parentheses. Thus, (car text) will give the first sentence, (last text) will give you the last sentence, etc. Notice that the function uses the d-function **mem**, which we constructed above, to decide if a given word is in the first sentence of the current list of text. If so, it starts constructing ("**cons**ing") a corpus of the sentences containing the keyword, by tacking the sentence in which the word is found onto the result of recursively calling the search function with the remainder of the text (cdr text). If a sentence does not contain the keyword, control goes to the last line of the function, where the function is invoked with the remainder of the text as its argument. Now, with:

```
(search 'books '((there are many good books in my library.)(I have read  some
of them.)(there are also  some books that are not so good.)(I haven't read
those.)(I like a good book to read.)(you can look at all my books.)))
```

as input, the following output will appear:

```
    ((THERE ARE MANY GOOD BOOKS IN MY LIBRARY.)(THERE ARE ALSO
SOME BOOKS THAT ARE NOT SO GOOD.))
```

Why didn't search return the last two sentences?

A variant of the search function in Example 1.25 is the following:

```
(defun search2 (word text)
    (cond ((null text) nil)
          ((member word (car text))
                (print (car text))
                     (search2 word (cdr text)))
          (t (search2 word (cdr text))))))
```
                                                                (1.26)

Now, if a text is defined as (setq passage '((b c a d)(k j l m)(f t a b)(i o a n)(t p c)(a b c d))), and **search2** is called as (search2 'a passage), the output will be in the following format:

```
(B C A D)
(F T A B)
(I O A N)
(A B C D)
```

Note that in Example (1.26) the system function **member**, instead of the d-function **mem** was used. Another interesting observation is that the functions **search** or **search2** can be called in the following manner:

```
(search (read) (read))
```

In this case, the computer will pause for a word and a text to be entered in the appropriate format.

1.8 EXERCISES

1.   Describe what the following functions do.

   (a)   ```
(defun temp (p)
    (cond ((> p 80) 'too-hot!)
          ((< p 50) 'too-cold!)
          (t 'ok)))
```

   (b)   ```
(defun ftoc (temp)
    (/ (- temp 32) 1.8))
Hint: (ftoc 100) ==> 37.77
```

```
(c)     (defun addition2 (x1 x2)
           (cond ((= x1 100) x2)
                 (t (addition2 (+ x1 1)(- x2 1)))))
        Hint: (addition2 0 0) ==> -100
```

2. Explain the following results:

```
(setq x '(* 2 3)) ==> (* 2 3)
x ==> (* 2 3)
(car x) ==> *
(eval x) ==> 6
(eval 'x) ==> (* 2 3)
(eval ''x) ==> X
```

3. Write a function that counts the number of elements in a list. (Don't use the **length** function.)

4. Write a function to compute the value of any integer "m" raised to the power of integer "n".

5. Write a function to count the number of articles (a, an, the) in a text.

6. Write a function to give the sum of numbers from 1 to 100 without doing sequential addition and without using any *plus* (or +) function. Hint: The answer should be 5050.

1.9 ITERATION

There is another approach to the repetition of a series of expressions, called *iteration*. Lisp provides several procedures for iteration. One of these is the **do** construct. Consider again the problem of finding the sum of a list of numbers where the list can be of arbitrary length, and look carefully at the following function:

```
(1)     (defun sum-of2 (lyst)
(2)        (do ((sum 0) (L lyst (cdr L)))               (1.27)
(3)            ((null L) (return sum))
(4)            (setq sum (+ sum (car L))))))
```

In sum-of2, **do** is a *macro*; that is, a single word that represents a group of computer instructions, which are generated at the time of the compilation or execution of codes. In its first expression, line (2), **do** defines local variables, gives them initial values, and describes what these variables should be replaced by each time around the loop. In line (2), sum and L are local variables; sum is initialized to 0 and L is initialized to the value of the variable *lyst*. The latter is the parameter of the function **sum-of 2**. The remainder of this line indicates that, in each cycle of the iteration, the value of L should be set to (cdr L). Line (3) provides the "loop termination test": If L is empty (that is, null), return the value of sum. In line (4), the instructions that are to be performed in each cycle of the loop are given: the first element of the current L is added to the current value of sum.

Now, if the above function were to be called by inputting: (sum-of 2 '(3 4 8 9)), the list (3 4 8 9) will be bound to *lyst* and that, in turn, becomes the initial value of L. Then the following iteration takes place:

```
sum = 0              L = (3 4 8 9)
sum = 0 + 3 = 3      L = (4 8 9)
sum = 3 + 4 = 7      L = (8 9)
sum = 7 + 8 = 15     L = (9)
sum = 15 + 9 = 24    L = ( )
VALUE = 24
```

In each step, sum is being increased by the first element of L, and L is being replaced by its **cdr**. The **do** macro sets up the cycle and transfers control to the beginning of the loop until the final result is obtained. The process is demonstrated graphically in Figure 1.2.

In general, the syntax (or structure) of do is:

```
(do ((⟨var-1⟩⟨initial-value-1⟩) (⟨replacement-expression-1⟩)
     (⟨var-2⟩⟨initial-value-2⟩) (⟨replacement-expression-2⟩)

                         .
                         .
                         .

     (⟨var-n⟩⟨initial-value-n⟩) (⟨replacement-expression-n⟩))
    ( (⟨end-test⟩) (⟨expression⟩) )
    (⟨expression⟩ ... ⟨expression⟩) )
```

In the above structure, the replacement-expression is optional; that is, if a replacement-expression is not given, the value *var* (variable) does not change with the cycle.

Many of the problems that have been solved recursively may also be solved using the **do** construct. For example, to raise the number "m" to the "n" power, we can initialize a variable *prod* to 1, a variable *counter* to "n", and write:

```
(defun power (m n)
    (do ( (prod 1) (counter n (1- counter)) )         (1.28)
        ( (zerop counter) (return prod) )
        ( setq prod (* m prod) )))
```

Now, (power 5 3) $\Rightarrow$ 125.

Note that raising "m" to the power "n" is equivalent to multiplying "m" by itself "n" times, and that is what the **power** function does. The use of **return** in the above example is optional in Common Lisp. Thus, line 3 of Example (1.28)

```
First Cycle      DO:   SUM = 0
                       L = (3 4 8 9)
                       L not NULL
                       SUM = 0 + 3 = 3
Second           DO:   SUM = 3
Cycle                  L = (4 8 9)
                       L not NULL
                       SUM = 3 + 4 = 7
Third Cycle      DO:   SUM = 7
                       L = (8 9)
                       L not NULL
                       SUM = 7 + 8 = 15
Fourth Cycle     DO:   SUM = 15
                       L = (9)
                       L not NULL
                       SUM = 15 + 9 = 24
Last Cycle       DO:   SUM = 24
                       L = ( )
                       L = NULL ⇒ SUM = 24
                       STOP
```

Figure 1.2. Example of a **do** macro process.

could have been written ((zerop counter) prod). Now try (power 2 3), and trace the steps in its evaluation in a manner similar to what is in Figure 1.2.

We can now compare the iterative function in Example (1.28) with the following recursive function, which obtains the same result.

```
(defun power2 (m n)
      (cond ((zerop n) 1)
            (t (* m (power2 m (1- n)))))))
```

To count the number of articles in a sentence using **do**, the following might be defined:

```
(defun count-arts (sent)
      (do ((count 0)
           (L sent (cdr L)))
          ((null L) (return count))                    (1.29)
          (cond ((member (car L) '(a an the))
                 (setq count (+ count 1)))))))
```

Try (count-arts '(now is the tme for a party)). There are some striking similarities between this function and the recursive version, and some subtle and interesting differences. (See Exercise 5 in Section 1.8.) The comparison of the evaluation processes would be a profitable exercise for the reader. There are a number of variants of the macros **do** and **prog** (seen later in this section) in Common Lisp. These variants, and other iterative forms, will be discussed in Chapter 5. In the last line of Example (1.29) we used the expression (+ count 1). Recall that this expression works in all dialects of Lisp. In Lispvm, (add1 count) can be used with the same effect, and in Common Lisp (1 + count) can be input.

```
(+ x 1)     [All dialects]
(add1 x)    [Lispvm]
(1+ x)      [Common Lisp]
```

In later chapters, recursive and iterative functions will each be used when they are most appropriate. Functions should be designed so that they are clear, elegant, and efficient.

Another iterative procedure for adding numbers in a list L of "n" numbers, where "n" is any arbitrary positive integer, is the following:

Step 1. Set sum = 0
    2. If L is empty, output sum and stop; otherwise go to the next step.
    3. Set sum = sum + the first element of L.
    4. Remove the first element of L.
    5. Go to step 2.

There is another form of Lisp iterative function that follows the above sequence of instructions. To define this function, a procedure called **prog** is used. The word **prog** marks the beginning of a block of instructions, and there are one or more **return** statements that produce outputs, and end the processing if the condition specified in the statement is met. In Lisp, **return** is a macro name that displays its argument. If **return** is used without any argument, the **prog** procedure terminates if the condition is met, and the current result of the **prog** is displayed. Here is a Lisp function, using **prog**, for the above problem:

```
(defun sum-of3 (lyst)                              (1.30)
    (prog ((sum 0))
  tag1  (cond ((null lyst) (return sum))
              (t (setq sum (+ sum (car lyst)))
                 (setq lyst (cdr lyst))))
              (go tag1)))
(sum-of3 '(2 3 5)) ==> 10
```

In this example, **prog** marks the beginning of a block within the function. Its general structure is:

```
(prog ( ((variable-1)  (value-1))
        ((variable-2)  (value-2))
                :

                :
```

$$(\langle variable\text{-}n\rangle \quad \langle value\text{-}n\rangle)\ )$$
$$\langle expression\rangle \quad ... \quad \langle expression\rangle \quad)$$

where *variable* is a local variable, and *value* is its initial value. Thus, in Example (1.30) *sum* is the local variable, and its initial value is set to zero (prog ((sum 0)). *tag1* is arbitrarily selected as a label, attached to one of the lines, and (go tag1) keeps transferring control back to that line until *lyst* is empty (null), when the accumulated value of *sum* is returned as the output. In the first expression of **prog**, the value of *sum* is zero.

The trace of (sum-of3 '(3 4 5 6)) is graphically represented in Figure 1.3.

The *prog* construct can be used to raise "m" to the power "n":

```
(defun power3 (m n)
    (prog ( (count 0) (prod 1) )
    loup (cond ((equal count n) (return prod))
               (t (setq prod (* prod m))
                  (setq count (+ count 1))
                  (go loup))))))
```
(1.31)

(power3 5 3) ==> 125

```
Prog SUM = 0
First Cycle      tag1:  SUM = 0
                        lyst = (3 4 5 6)
                        lyst not NULL
                        SUM = 0 + 3 = 3
                        lyst = (4 5 6)
Second Cycle     tag1:  SUM = 3
                        lyst = (4 5 6)
                        lyst not NULL
                        SUM = 3 + 4 = 7
                        lyst = (5 6)
Third Cycle      tag1:  SUM = 7
                        lyst = (5 6)
                        lyst not NULL
                        SUM = 7 + 5 = 12
                        lyst = (6)
Fourth Cycle     tag1:  SUM = 12
                        lyst = (6)
                        lyst not NULL
                        SUM = 12 + 6 = 18
                        lyst = ( )
Last Cycle       tag1:  SUM = 18
                        lyst = ( )
                        lyst = NULL ⇒ SUM = 18
                        STOP
```

Figure 1.3. The trace of a function call with a **prog** structure.

1.10 EXERCISES

1. Multiplication is defined as repeate adddition. For example, 5 × 4 means 5 + 5 + 5 + 5. Write a Lisp function using **do** that multiplies "m" by "n", using repeated addition.

2. Write an iterative function to decide whether a given word occurs in a given sentence.

3. What does the following function do?

```
(defun pw  (m n)      (prog (k)
            (setq k m)
            repeat  (setq n (- n 1))
                 (cond ((zerop n)(return m))
                       (t (setq m (* m k))))
                 (go repeat)))
```

4. Explain what the following functions in Common Lisp do:

```
(a) (defun plus (x y) (setq plus (+ x y)))
```

```
(b) (defun difference (x y)(setq difference (- x y)))
```

```
(c) (setq x '(+ 1 2 3) y (cons x nil))
```

```
(d) (setq x '(+ 1 (* 5 6)))
```

```
(e) (setq name 'fido kind 'dog sex 'female age 3)
```

5. Write a function to check whether a given word occurs in list (dictionary), and if it dosen't, to add the word to the list.

6. Compare the following function with the **sum-of** function in Example (1.18):

```
(defun multiply (nums)
    (cond ((null nums) 0)
          (t (* (car nums)(multiply (cdr nums))))))
```

Now, if (multiply '(2 3 7)) is called, what output will be returned? Why? What changes should be made in **multiply** to get 42 as the output of the call?

2

Operations on Lists

2.1 CONSTRUCTING LISTS

There are a number of system functions that can be used to construct lists. The most common of these are **cons**, **append**, and **list**. **Cons** is a function with two arguments. If the second argument is a non-list, the output is in the form of *dotted pair*. Otherwise, dots will not appear in the output. In any case, **cons** constructs a list in which the first argument becomes the first element (**car**) and the second argument becomes the rest (**cdr**) of the list. Examples are:

```
(cons 'a 'b)            VALUE = (A . B)
(cons 'a nil)           VALUE = (A . NIL)
(cons  'a '(b c d))     VALUE = (A B C D)
(setq L1 '(a b c d))    VALUE = (A B C D)
(setq L2 '(e f g h))    VALUE = (E F G H)              (2.1)
(cons (car L1)(car L2)) VALUE = (A . E)
(cons (cadr L1)(cdr L2))VALUE = (B F G H)
(cons 'j L1)            VALUE = (J A B C D)
(cons L1 'j)            VALUE = ((A B C D) . J)
(cons L1 L2)            VALUE = ((A B C D) E F G H)
```

Notice the difference in the output when the inputs to **cons** are two atoms, an atom and a list, a list and an atom, or two lists.

So far, the term *list* has been used loosely. With the introduction of the term *dotted pair*, a bit more precision is necessary. A dotted pair (or **cons** cell) is internally a pair of pointers. A pointer may point to NIL, to an atom, or to another dotted pair. Thus, the first pointer is the **car**, and the second pointer is the **cdr**, of the list. Here are some examples of internal representations constructed by **cons**:

$$
\begin{array}{l}
\texttt{NIL} \\
\texttt{(A . NIL)} \\
\texttt{((A . B) C . D)} \\
\texttt{(A .(B . NIL))} \\
\texttt{(A .(B .(C . NIL)))}
\end{array} \qquad (2.2)
$$

Strictly speaking, there is a difference in the internal representation between (a . b) and (a b), but this is of no concern for the present. These matters are touched on here simply to avoid confusion if dots are seen in the output lists. Later (in Chapter 4) there will be more details of the structure of lists in the computer's memory.

It was stated that **cons** has two arguments, but if more than two arguments are to be combined, a series of **cons'** can always be written:

```
(cons 'a (cons 'b '(c d)))   VALUE = (A B C D)                    (2.3)
(cons L1 (cons L2 '(i j k)))
                    VALUE = ( (A B C D) (E F G H) I J K )
```

However, in Lispvm there is a special function, called **consfn**, that will do the same thing:

```
(consfn L1 L2 '(i j k))   VALUE = ((A B C D)(E F G H) I J K)      (2.4)
```

Another useful function for building lists is **append**. It takes two or more arguments and combines them into one list. The arguments of **append** must be lists.

```
(append '(a b) '(c d) '(e f))                                     (2.5)
                    VALUE = (A B C D E F)
(append 'a 'b 'c '(d e f))  VALUE = (D E F)
```

Note that, in the last example, the first three arguments are atoms and they are ignored by the function. In the earlier dialects, as well as some recent dialects of Lisp written for personal computers with limited memory, **append** can take only two arguments, which must be lists. In Lispvm, there is also a function called **append2**, which takes exactly two lists as arguments.

A third list-building function is **list**. It can have one or more arguments, which can be atoms or lists, and returns a combined list of all of the arguments.

```
(list 'a 'b 'c 'd)    VALUE = (A B C D)
(list 'a)             VALUE = (A)                                 (2.6)
(list '(a))           VALUE = ((A))
(list L1 L2)          VALUE = ((A B C D)(E F G H))
```

Note that (list arg1 arg2 . . . argn) is equivalent to (cons arg1 (cons arg2 . . . (cons argn nil))). Thus, the above example could be written as:

```
(cons 'a (cons 'b (cons 'c (cons 'd nil))))
```

In Table 2.1 there are several examples (some repeats) of **cons, append,** and **list** functions, and some combinations of these for ready reference and comparison. In this table, it is assumed that values for variables "p", "q", and "r" have been assigned by the following forms:

```
(setq p '(x y z))
(setq q '(u v w))
(setq r '((2 3) 6 (a)))
```

Now, using the forms in Table 2.1, you can experiment on the computer with any number of other variations to see how these functions work.

TABLE 2.1. EXAMPLES OF LIST-CONSTRUCTING FUNCTIONS

Function Form	Output
(cons 'a 'b)	(A . B)
(cons 'a nil)	(A)
(append 'a 'b)	NIL
(append (list 'a) (list 'b))	(A B)
(append '(a) '(b))	(A B)
(append p 'a)	(X Y Z . A)
(list 'a 'b)	(A B)
(list '(a) '(b))	((A) (B))
(cons 'a p)	(A X Y Z)
(append 'a p)	(X Y Z)
(list 'a p)	(A (X Y Z))
(cons p q)	((X Y Z) U V W)
(append p q)	(X Y Z U V W)
(append q p)	(U V W X Y Z)
(list p q)	((X Y Z) (U V W))
(cons p q r)	((X Y Z) U V W)*
(append p q r)	(X Y Z U V W (2 3) 6 (A))
(list p q r)	((X Y Z) (U V W) ((2 3) 6 (A)))
(cons p (cons q r))	((X Y Z) (U V W) (2 3) 6 (A))
(cons 'a (append p q))	(A X Y Z U V W)

****cons** takes only two arguments. In Lispvm, the first two arguments are combined, and the rest are ignored. In Common Lisp, giving more than two arguments to **cons** would be an error.

2.2 ACCESSING LISTS

References have been made earlier to the functions **car** and **cdr**, which allow access to the first element and the remainder of a list, respectively.

Figure 2.1 is a graphic representation of a partial construction and breaking apart of a list L = (a b c d).

The functions **last** give the last element of a list. As already indicated, the names **car** and **cdr** (pronounced cutter or cudder) are historical names in Lisp. In almost all dialects of Common Lisp, in addition to **car** and **cdr**, there are also system functions called **first, second**, and (in some dialects) up to **tenth** forms defined. There is also a form called **rest** for **cdr**. The reader can also define his/her own names; for example, in Lispvm (setq first car), (setq rest cdr), and so forth can simply be written; or, if it is preferred, other functions can be defined, such as the following:

$$\text{(defun first (L) (car L))}$$
$$\text{(defun rest (L) (cdr L))} \tag{2.7}$$
$$\text{(defun final-element (L) (last L))}$$

The second element of a list is the **car** of the **cdr** of that list, thus:

$$\text{(defun second (L) (car(cdr L)))} \tag{2.8}$$

However, if the functions **first** and **rest** have already been defined, they can be used to define **second**:

$$\text{(defun second (L) (first(rest L)))} \tag{2.9}$$

Similarly, the third element is the **car** of the **cdr** of the **cdr** of L:

$$\text{(defun third (L) (car(cdr(cdr L))))} \tag{2.10}$$

Again, a previously defined function can be used to write this in a more elegant

$$\text{(defun third (L) (second(rest L)))} \tag{2.11}$$

```
                          a →  | L        | —(car L)→a
   (cons 'a '(b c d))          | a b c d  |
                    b c d →    |          | —(cdr L)→b c d
```

Figure 2.1. List operations.

These examples show how to define functions to change the names of some system functions.

We have seen that a number of **car** and **cdr** functions can be combined to get at any element of a list. For example, given the list L = (a b c d e f g h i j),

$$
\begin{array}{ll}
(\,car\ L\,) = a \\
(\,car\ (\,cdr\ L\,)\,) = b \\
(\,car\ (\,cdr\ (\,cdr\ L\,)\,)\,) = c \\
(\,car\ (\,cdr\ (\,cdr\ (\,cdr\ L\,)\,)\,)\,) = d
\end{array}
\qquad (2.12)
$$

And so on to the end. Note also that a list may have other lists embedded in it; for example, if L2 = ((a b) c (d (e f)) (g (h i))), then:

$$
\begin{array}{ll}
(\,car\ L2\,) = (\,a\ b\,) \\
(\,car\ (\,car\ L2\,)\,) = a \\
(\,car\ (\,cdr\ L2\,) = c \\
(\,car\ (\,cdr\ (\,cdr\ L2\,)\,)\,) = (\,d(\,e\ f\,)\,) \\
(\,car\ (\,car\ (\,cdr\ (\,cdr\ L2\,)\,)\,)\,) = d \\
(\,cdr\ L2\,) = (\,c\ (\,d\ (\,e\ f\,)\,)(\,g\ (\,h\ i\,)\,)\,) \\
(\,last\ L2\,) = (\,(\,g\ (\,h\ i\,)\,)\,)\quad [(\,g\ (\,h\ i\,)\,)\ in\ Lispvm] \\
(\,car\ (\,last\ L2\,)\,) = (\,g\ (\,h\,)\,)\quad [\,g\ in\ Lispvm]
\end{array}
\qquad (2.13)
$$

It is important to realize the levels of structure in these constructions. For example, L2 at the top level consists of the four substructures shown in the boxes in Figure 2.2.

Another way of representing the levels is to number the parentheses: each pair of parentheses with the same number represents a list, and the number represents the level of embedding. Thus, the example in Figure 2.2 can be represented as:

$$
\begin{array}{l}
L2 = (\ (a\ b)\ c\ (d\ (e\ f)\ )\ (g\ (h\ i)\ )\ ) \\
1\ 2\ \ \ \ 2\ \ \ 2\ 3\ \ \ 3\ 2\ 2\ \ 3\ \ \ 3\ 2\ 1
\end{array}
\qquad (2.14)
$$

It is possible to abbreviate a string of **cars** and **cdrs**. This is done by writing a string beginning with a "c" and ending with an "r"; in between, any number of "a's" for **car** and "d's" for **cdr** can be inserted. Thus, instead of writing (car(car(cdr(cdr(car(cdr L2)))))), one can simply write (caaddadr L2). It should be noted, however, that in most implementations of Lisp systems, there is a limit to the number of "a's" and "d's" that can be listed in such strings.

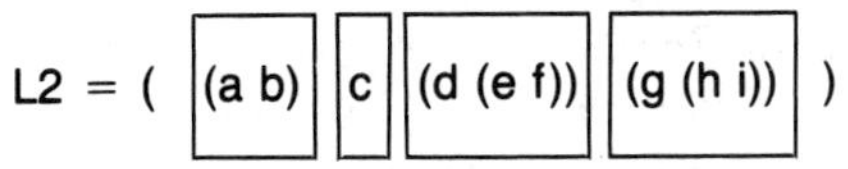

Figure 2.2. Top-level structure of a list.

Let us now examine the following sequence of interactions with a computer:

```
(setq x1 '(a b c d)) ==> (A B C D)
x1 ==> (A B C D)
(cdr x1) ==> (B C D)                                    (2.15)
x1 ==> (A B C D)
(setq x1 (cdr x1)) ==> (B C D)
x1 ==> (B C D)
```

Note that by inputting (cdr x1), (B C D) is returned, but the value (binding) of x1 is not changed; so that when x1 is again input, (A B C D) is displayed. To change the value of x1 to the value of its remainder, x1 must be *set* to (setq x1 (cdr x1)). Thus, **car** and **cdr** are not "destructive" functions (it will be seen in Section 2.10 that some forms are destructive). Overlooking this simple observation is often the cause of bewilderment for beginners. The following example somewhat dramatizes this point.

```
(defun count ()            ;; [bugged]
    (prog ((c 0))
    again  (+ c 1)                                      (2.16)
            (cond ((equal c 10) (return c))
                  (t (go again)))))
```

If the function **count**, as given above, is called by inputting (count), it will go into an infinite loop; that is, the processing will not stop. This is because, in each cycle of the loop, one is added to the value of "c", but this adding is not permanent and "c" is still set to 0 in the next cycle; thus, "c" will never reach 10. To remedy this situation, the line with the label *again* must be amended as:

```
again (setq c (+ c 1))
```

Another advantage of writing recursive functions is that there is no worry about this kind of error, because the necessary bookkeeping is done by the function automatically. Thus, the function in Example (2.16) can be written as a recursive function in the following way:

```
(defun count (c)
    (cond (((< c 10)(count (1+ c)))                     (2.17)
          (t c)))
```

(In Lispvm, the second line in Example (2.17) would normally be written as (cond ((lt c 10) (count (add1 c))), where "lt" is a form for 'less than'.) Now if (count 0) is called, 10 will be displayed as the output. Observe, however, that the **count** function in Example (2.17) is not quite the same as the one in Example (2.16). Invoking the latter does not require an argument; just input (count), and 10 will always be returned. The one in Example (2.17) requires an argument with the function call. As long as this argument is less than 10, the function will return 10. However, what will be returned if (count 15) is input? Why? The reason is in the last line in the recursive count function. It will return the value of "c" if the argument is larger than 10.

Let us now try a slightly more useful example. Recall that, in English, as in other natural languages, there are groups of words (idioms or phrases) that have specific meanings, which are not the same as the sum of the meanings of their individual words. Examples of such collocations are *how do you do*, *kick the bucket*, *how much*, *the buck stops here*, and *and so forth*. In the following example, a very simple function will be written to find the phrase *how much* in a text and print it. In later sections and chapters, this function will be generalized to do more.

```
(defun find-col (text)
    (cond ((null text) nil)
          ((equal (car text) 'how)
              (cond ((equal (cadr text) 'much)             (2.18)
                         (list (car text)(cadr text))))))
          ('t (find-col (cdr text))))))
```

Now the following function will read the text and call the above function:

```
(defun rd-text ()
        (setq text (read))                   (2.19)
        (find-col text))
```

When the **rd-text** function is called by inputting (rd-text), the computer will pause until a text in a pair of parentheses is input.

Two other functions available in Common Lisp for taking lists apart are **butlast** and **nbutlast**. The function **butlast** takes as arguments a list and an integer "n". It returns the list minus the "n" elements at the end of it.

```
(setq x '(a b c d e f))
  ==> (A B C D E F)
(butlast x 3) ==> (A B C)
x ==> (A B C D E F)
```

The above sequence shows that **butlast** is not destructive; that is, after applying **butlast**, the original list remains intact. If the integer argument of **butlast** is left out, the value is assumed to be 1.

```
(butlast x) ==> (A B C D E)
```

Note also that the last elements could be sublists:

```
(butlast '(a b c (d e f))) ==> (A B C)
```

nbutlast is the destructive version of **butlast**:

```
(nbutlast x 3) ==) (A B C)
x ==) (A B C)
```

The **ldiff** function in Common Lisp returns a list minus its sublist, provided that a sublist has been defined for the list:

```
(setq x1 '(a b c d e f g))
(A B C D E F G)
(setq x2 (cdddr x1))
(D E F G)
(ldiff x1 x2) ==) (A B C)
```

Thus, **ldiff** provides the difference between two sets (see Section 2.7).
The function **copy-list** makes a copy of a list:

```
(setq x1 '(a b c d))
(setq x2 (copy-list x1))
 x1 ==) (A B C D)
 x2 ==) (A B C D)
```

2.3 PROGRAM STYLE

It is perhaps time to say something about the style used in writing Lisp functions and programs, and about the single quotation mark. You have noticed that, in writing functions and expressions with more than one line, certain identations were used. This is solely for the purpose of making a function more readable and understandable. This consideration aside, the following styles represent exactly the same function, and both are valid:

```
(defun English-French (English French)
       (cond ((null English) nil)
            (t (cons (cons (car English)                          (2.20)
                              (list (car French)))
                   (English-French (cdr English)
                              (cdr French)))))))

(defun English-French (English French)
(cond((null English)nil)(t(cons(cons(car English)
(list(car French)))(English-French(cdr English)(cdr French)))))))
```

(If it could have been fitted on a page, the second version in Example (2.20) could have been written all on one line!) It is recommended that the user use the former style; it is also recommended that, for names and variables, the user select those which are indicative of what is being represented.

With regard to the quote mark, recall that, in Lisp, any expression or data structure can be a program or a function. There are, however, certain words that evaluate to codes performing certain functions. These are, for example, the names of the system functions or names of functions defined by the user (d-functions), or variables bound to some values. However, in Lispvm there are no reserved words (except NIL); the atom **car** can be the name of the function for accessing the first element of a list, it can be a data item with no evaluation other than itself, or it can have some other value assigned to it. Here are the three representations of **car** mentioned above:

```
(car '(a b c d)) ==> A
car ==> Error in Common Lisp/CAR in Lispvm
'car ==> CAR   [note the quote mark]                    (2.21)
(setq car 15) ==> 15
car ==> 15
```

There are, however, certain restrictions. In general, the rule of thumb is that, after each opening parenthesis, Lisp evaluates the first word as a function name and the other words within the scope of the parentheses as arguments of that function. Thus, in Lispvm (plus 12 (times 3 4)), first **times** is treated as a function name and 3 and 4 are treated as its arguments; then **plus** is treated as a function name and 12 and (times 3 4), or rather the result of the evaluation of (times 3 4), are treated as its arguments. According to this principle, if we write (setq x (3 4 5)), the Lisp system will try to evaluate 3 (after the opening parenthesis) as the name of a function, which is, of course, inappropriate, and will result in an error message. To prevent this situation, a single quote mark must be placed before the list of numbers that we want to assign to x: (setq x '(3 4 5)). Thus, any nonnumeric atom or list preceded by a single quote (or the word *quote*) is treated as data and evaluates to itself. Single numbers (numeric atoms) evaluate to themselves in Lisp and do not need a quote mark.

An almost unique characteristic of Lispvm is that all atoms evaluate to themselves and need not be quoted. Thus, in Lispvm if andrew were input, ANDREW will be returned, but in Common Lisp and most other dialects, an error message will result. However, in all dialects, including Lispvm, if 'andrew or (quote andrew) is input, ANDREW will be returned.

```
'andrew ==> ANDREW [all dialects]
andrew ==> ANDREW [Lispvm]
andrew ==> Error  [Common Lisp]
```

Thus, it is safe to use the quote mark in all dialects. Of course, function names and special forms that are a part of the vocabulary of Lisp should not be quoted if they are intended to perform operations. Some examples are:

```
(setq a 5) ==> 5     a ==> 5    'a ==> A
('setq a 5) ==> Error                                    (2.22)
'setq ==> SETQ
setq ==> Error (in Common Lisp);  SETQ (in Lispvm)
```

One function name with a special property is **setq**, in that the word immediately following it is understood to be a variable, and need not be quoted, but **set**, which has more or less the same function as **setq**, must have a quote mark for the atom following it, if the atom is to be treated as a variable to be assigned some values (see Section 5.12 for further explanations). Examples:

```
(set 'names '(john mary dick))
(JOHN MARY DICK)                                         (2.23)
(set (car names) (cdr names))
(MARY DICK)
```

Now, inputting john will output (MARY DICK) as its value.

Another characteristic of Lispvm is that it has only one reserved word: **nil**, which has several roles in the language. It stands for the logical false opposite of **t** (true), for an empty list ( ), or for an atom. Other values cannot be assigned to **nil**, but values can be assigned to other words in the vocabulary:

```
(setq t 'false) ==> FALSE; t ==> FALSE
(setq car plus) ==> PLUS; (car '(2 3 4))==> 9!           (2.24)

(setq plus difference); (plus 5 3) ==> 2
```

But (setq nil 'false) $\Rightarrow$ Error

```
┌──────────────────────────────────────────────────┐
│  (setq nil 5) ==> Error   [all dialects]          │
│  (setq t 5) ==> 5         [Lispvm]                │
│  (setq t 5) ==> Error     [Common Lisp]           │
└──────────────────────────────────────────────────┘
```

Because **t** can have other values in Lispvm, when it is used as the last condition in a conditional expression (see Section 1.6), it is always evaluated; and if no other value has been assigned to it, it evaluates to true. To avoid this additional process, it is a good practice in the style of Lispvm to put a quote in front of **t**:

```
(cond ((Equal x y) 'same)
      ('t 'not-same))
```

There is no harm in putting a quote mark in front of **t** in similar circumstances in Common Lisp as well.

The dichotomy in Lisp is not so much between **nil** and **true** as it is between **nil** and non-**nil**. Some further details of this will be given in the next section.

In general, it is useful to recall (as was stated in Chapter 1) that the top-level Lisp expressions always operate in what is called a *read-eval-print* cycle; that is, every element must be *read*, *eval*uated, and then given as output (*print*). Anytime an element is to evaluate to or stand for itself, a single quote mark must be put in front of it. Thus, in (set 'names '(john mary james)), neither *names* nor the list (john mary james) are to be *eval*ed as anything other than themselves; therefore, quote marks are placed in front of them. In (setq names '(john mary james)), the function **setq** supplies the quote for *names*. After *names* has received a value in either of the above expressions, it can be used without a quote to allow its *eval*uation, thus:

```
'names       VALUE = NAMES
names        VALUE = (JOHN MARY JAMES)
```

The English-French function defined in Example (2.20) expects, as input, a list of English words and a corresponding list of French words, where the latter are translations of the former arranged in the same order. The function then produces a list consisting of pairs of corresponding English and French words. A similar function, defined previously for reading texts, can now be used to read the list of English and French words and then call the English-French function:

```
(defun rd-text2 nil
       (setq English (read))                    (2.25)
       (setq French  (read))
         (English-French  English French))
```

Note that, because English-French has already been defined as a function in this example, it is not to be quoted; similarly, the word **read** is a function name in Lisp, and it should *eval*uate to its codes. The words English and French in the last line of Example (2.25) were assigned values by the second and third lines, and quote marks should not be placed in front of them.

A final remark in this section concerns *comments*. It is often desirable to attach notes to a computer program explaining some aspects of the program as a reminder for the programmer or for the benefit of the user. These notes and comments should not enter into the processing of the program. In Lisp, any input line preceded by one or more semicolons (;) is treated as comment. The line will be printed in the listing of the program, but it will not enter into the processing. The reader should be aware, however, that when a line is entered by pressing the ENTER key on the keyboard, that marks the end of the line, and, if the next line is to be another comment line, it must begin with a ; mark. Comments can be inserted anywhere in a program. As an example:

```
;a predicate function (see Section 2.4) for
;depth search:
       (defun my-memberp (item L)
```

TABLE 2.2. EXAMPLES OF PREDICATE FUNCTIONS

Function	Dialect	Output
(atom 'a)		T(RUE)
(atom '(a))		NIL
(boundp 'x)		T (if x has value)
(characterp 'a)	CL	T (character test)
(charp a)	LVM	A (character test)
(digitp 6)	LVM	6 (digits, 0-10, test)
(eq 5 5)/(eq 'a 'a)		T(RUE)
(eq 5 5.0)/(eq 'a 'b)		NIL
(eql 5 5)	CL	T
(eql 5 5.0)	CL	NIL
(equal 5 5.0)		NIL
(equal 'a 'a)		T(RUE)
(= 5 5.0)		T(RUE)
(= 'a 'a)	CL/LVM	Error/TRUE
(evenp 8)	CL/LVM	T/8
(floatp 3.45)		T
(ge 7 5)/(ge 5 5)	LVM	TRUE
(greaterp 7 5)	LVM	TRUE
(gt 7 5)/(gt c a)	LVM	TRUE/Error
(>= 7 5)/(>= 5 5)	CL	T
(> 7 5)/(> 5 5)	CL	T/NIL
(integerp 12)(intp 12)	CL/LVM	T/TRUE
(le 5 7)(le 5 5)	LVM	TRUE
(<= 5 7)(<= 5 5)	CL	T
(lessp 5 7)	LVM	TRUE
(lt 5 7)	LVM	TRUE
(< 5 7)	CL	T
(listp '(a b c))		T(RUE)
(memb 'a '(j k a b c))	LVM	(A B C) [uses eq]
(member 'a '(j k a b c))	LVM	(A B C) [uses equal]
(member 'a '(j k a b c))	CL	(A B C) [uses eql]
(minusp −7)	CL/LVM	T/−7
(ne 5 6)(/= 5 6)	LVM/CL	TRUE/T
(null ( ))		T(RUE)
(numberp 5)	LVM/CL	5/T
(nump 5)	LVM	5
(oddp 15)	LVM/CL	15/T
(pairp '(a b))	LVM	(A B)
(pairp ( ))	LVM	NIL
(plusp 6)	LVM/CL	6/T
(stringp "a b c")		T(RUE)
(zerop 0)	LVM/CL	0/T
(zerop 'a)	LVM/CL	NIL/Error

```
;the name of function
;;and its parameters
        (cond ((equal L item) t)
;if L=item, return T.
        ((atom L) nil)
;if L is an atom return NIL.
;else apply the function to the CAR or CDR of L:
        (t (or (my-memberp item (car L))
        (my-memberp item (cdr L))))))
```

In Lisp, **member** is a system function that applies to the top level of a list and searches to see whether a given item is a member of the list (see the next section). The function **my-memberp** will search through any level of a list. Compare the following:

```
(setq L '(x y (b (c a)) d))
(member 'a L) ==> NIL
(my-memberp 'a L) ==> T
```

2.4 PREDICATE FUNCTIONS

Predicate functions are forms in Lisp that test some expression and return NIL (false) or non-NIL (true) as output. The names of some of these functions end with letter **p** (for predicate). Some further examples of predicate functions in both Lispvm and Common Lisp will follow. In Table 2.2, the functions in Lispvm and other compatible dialects are marked with LVM, those in Common Lisp and its compatible dialects with CL, and those that are identical in both dialectal families are left blank. (See also Section 4.3 for a further explanation of the equality predicates.)

2.5 EXERCISES

1. Describe the following functions:

    (a) (defun erase (N L)
             (cond ((null L) nil)
                   ((zerop N) L)
                   ((GT N (length L)) L)
                   ((equal N 1) (cdr L))
                   ('t(cons(car L)(erase(sub1 N)(cdr L)))))))

    (b) (defun belongsto (x L)
             (cond ((null L) nil)
                   ((equal x (car L)) t)
                   ('t(belongsto x (cdr L))))))

```
(c)  (defun my-subst (x y L)
        (cond ((null L) nil)
              ((equal y (car L))
                 (cons x (my-subst x y (cdr L))))
              ('t (cons (car L)
                     (my-subst x y (cdr L)))))))

(d)  (setq names '(john mary nick sue))
     (setq relations '(husband wife son daughter))
     (defun kinship (names relations)
        (cond ((null names) nil)
              (t(cons(list(car names)(car relations))
                   (kinship (cdr names)
                       (cdr relations)))))))
```

2. Function (a) in the first Exercise is written for Lispvm. Define forms **gt** and **sub1** for Common Lisp so that this function can also run in Common Lisp without any change (see Section 2.6).

3. Write a function to search through a text of multiple sentences and count the number of occurrences of any particular word.

4. Write a function to scan a list of numbers and return those divisible by 3.

2.6 COMPATIBILITY

Most of the functions defined so far in this book can run on most dialects of Lisp, but there have also been some differences, as well. For example, in Common Lisp, the operators $>, <, > =, / =$, etc. are used for comparison, whereas in Lispvm, **greaterp**, **gt**, **lessp**, **lt**, **ge**, **ne**, etc. are used. In Franz Lisp, both of these sets of forms are acceptable. In both Common Lisp and Lispvm, the operators $+$, $*$, and so forth take any number of arguments (operands), whereas in MacLisp and IqLisp, the arguments are restricted to two, and they can only be integers. Furthermore, in IqLisp, all input must be in capital letters. We have also noted that, in most cases, the user can define a function in one dialect to be compatible with another. In this section, some of the latter facility in Lisp will be repeated, in order to bring together under one heading all aspects of this very important characteristic of Lisp.

In Lispvm, because of its special handling of atoms and other facilities, it is very easy to define function names that exist in other dialects. For example, the system function **rem** in Common Lisp is the equivalent of **remainder** in Lispvm. To define **rem** for Lispvm, all that has to be done is to write (setq rem 'remainder), and then (rem 5 3) $\Rightarrow$ 2 will apply to both dialects. It is important, however, to be cautious about such definitions, because the underlying implementation of **rem** and **remainder** may not be exactly the same in the two dialects. For example, the system function **mod** in Common Lisp behaves like **rem** with certain arguments, but it is really a modulus function in the mathematical sense, so that if it is defined in Lispvm as (setq mod remainder), the output will be (mod 13 4) $\Rightarrow$ 1 in both dialects, but for (mod − 13 4), it will be 3 in Common Lisp and − 1 in Lispvm.

The situation is not that simple in Common Lisp; that is, the form cannot simply be written (setq plus ' +) in order to define the word **plus** in the vocabulary of Common Lisp, but a function such as (defun plus (x y)(+ x y)) can be defined. Note, however, that "+" in Common Lisp can take any number of arguments, including none (see Table 1.2), but the function **plus**, as presently defined, must have exactly two arguments in Common Lisp, whereas **plus** in Lispvm can take any number of arguments. (See Section 5.7.2 for the solution to this problem.)

These cautionary warnings aside, some examples of "pseudo-compatability functions" will be given below for conversions in both dialects. (Again CL will be used for Common Lisp, and LVM for Lispvm—compare Tables 1.1 and 1.2.)

```
CL:  (defun remainder (x y)(rem x y))
          (remainder 7 2) ==) 1
CL:  defun times (x y)(* x y))
          (times 5 6) ==) 30
CL:  (defun divide (x y)(truncate x y))
          (divide 16 5) ==) 3 1
CL:  (defun add1 (x) (1+  x))
          (add1 5) ==) 6
CL:  (defun rnump (x)
        (cond ((floatp x) x)(t nil)))
          (rnump 3.75) ==) 3.75
          (rnump 3) ==) NIL
LVM: (setq first 'car)
          (first '(a b c d)) ==) A
LVM: (setq rest 'cdr)
          (rest '(a b c d)) ==) (B C D)
LVM: (defun signum (x)
        (cond ((minusp x) -1)
              ((plusp x) 1)
              ((zerop x) 0)
              ('t nil)))
```

2.7 LOGICAL OPERATORS

Let us reconsider the function **find-col**, given in Section 2.2, repeated below for ready reference.

```
(defun find-col (text)
    (cond ((null text) nil)
          ((equal (car text) 'how)
            (cond ((equal (cadr text) 'much)
                  (list (car text) (cadr text)))))
          ('t (find-col (cdr text)))))
```

Notice that there is an embedded conditional in this example. The sequence of conditional expressions is the following:

```
If the text is empty (null) then return nothing.
If the first word of the text (car text) equals how
        then if the first word of the remainder
            of the text (cadr text) equals much
                then list [and output] the two
                words.
Else call the function (find-col) again with the
      remainder of the text (cdr text) as its argument.
```

Another way of stating the complex conditional expresison is to say something like this: *"If* the first word of the text is *how, and* the next word is *much,* then list. . . ."* It turns out that this can be done in Lisp:

```
(defun find2 (text)
      (cond ((null text) nil)
            ((and (equal (car text) 'how)                    (2.26)
                  (equal (cadr text) 'much))
                      (list (car text)(cadr text)))
            ('t (find2 (cdr text))))))
```

The standard 'logical operators' in Lisp are **and, or,** and **not,** with the following truth values, assuming *a* and *b* are two propositions:

a and *b* = T, if both *a* and *b* are true.
a or *b* = T, if one of the propositions is true.
not *a* = NIL (false), if *a* is true.

Recall, however, that such expressions are written in Polish notation in Lisp; so, we must write (and a b), (or a b), and (not a).

In both Lispvm and Common Lisp, the operator **and** can take an arbitrary number of arguments and will return the value of the last argument if all of the arguments have non-NIL values; otherwise, it will return NIL. Similarly, **or** can take any number of arguments and will return the value of the first non-NIL argument that it finds in a left to right evaluation of the list of its arguments. To understand all of this, the following examples should be examined carefully and run on a computer. (In Example (2.27) the Lispvm notation has been used; the programmer should convert these to Common Lisp for exercise, whenever there is a difference.)

```
(cond ((and (zerop 0)(null nil))
        (print 'ok)))            VALUE = OK
(and (gt 7 3) (oddp 7))          VALUE = 7
(and (gt 8 5) (+ 5 6))           VALUE = 11
```

```
(and (gt 8 5) (zerop 0) (oddp 8))    VALUE = NIL
(* (and (gt 8 5) (+ 5 6)) 7)         VALUE = 77
(and (gt 8 5) (le 46 67))            VALUE = TRUE
;;Recall that for (le 46 67), VALUE = TRUE.
(and (gt 8 5) (le 46 67) (max 8 5))  VALUE = 8              (2.27)
(or (gt 8 5) (le 46 67) (max 8 5))   VALUE = TRUE
;;here the returned value is the value of the first
         expression (gt 8 5), which is true.
(or (gt 5 10) (atom '(a b)) (lt 12 15))  VALUE = TRUE
(and (equal 'a 'a) (or (equal 'a 'b) (ge 5 5))) = TRUE
(zerop 0)  VALUE = 0
(zerop 5)  VALUE = NIL
(not (zerop 0))  VALUE = NIL
(not (zerop 5))  VALUE = TRUE
```

In Lisp there are also operations on sets. The function **union** will return a list consisting of the unique elements of two lists, and the function **intersection** returns a list consisting of the elements that are common to two lists:

```
(setq names1 '(dick liz sally bill))
(setq names2 '(max john liz bill clide))
(setq numbers '(3 5 7 9 10))
(union names1 names2) ==>  (DICK LIZ SALLY BILL MAX       (2.28)
                                 JOHN CLIDE)
(union names1 names1) ==>  (DICK LIZ SALLY BILL)
(intersection names1 names2) ==>   (LIZ BILL)
(intersection names1 numbers) ==>  NIL
```

The function **set-difference** (**setdifference** in Lispvm) has two list arguments and returns the elements (at the top level) in the first list that are not included in the second list:

```
(set-difference names1 names2) = (DICK SALLY)
```

(See Section 4.5.6 for an expanded use of the functions in this and the next section.)

2.8 SEARCHING, SORTING, AND UPDATING LISTS

In this section, we will discuss some system functions and develop some d-functions for list manipulations.

```
(member 'a '(a b c d)) ==> (A B C D)
(member 'b '(a b c d)) ==> (B C D)          (2.29)
(member 'c '(a b c d)) ==> (C D)
(member 'e '(a b c d)) ==> NIL
```

Recall that **member** has two arguments: an item and a list, and it searches the list to see whether the item is included in the list. If so, it returns the portion of the list starting with the first occurrence of the item. It should also be recalled that lists can have many levels of embedding. The **member** search is carried out at the top level only. It should also be reemphasized that these operations do not change the structure of the list in storage. Thus,

```
(setq names '(jay carry mike henry))
names ==>  (JAY CARRY MIKE HENRY)
(member mike names) ==>  (MIKE HENRY)                    (2.30)
names ==>  (JAY CARRY MIKE HENRY)
(setq names (member mike names))
names ==> (MIKE HENRY)
```

Also note:

```
(setq x '(a b (c d (f g)) k l))
(member k x) ==>  (K L)                                 (2.31)
(member d x) ==> NIL   ;[d is not on the top level]
```

Now we will define a function that will search a list for an item, and if the item is there, it will return TRUE, otherwise it will return NIL (cf. **member**). We will call this function **setmember**.

```
(defun setmember (item L)
   (cond ((null L) nil)                                 (2.32)
         ((equal item (car L)) 'true)
         (t (setmember item (cdr L) ))))
```

Now, with the value of "x" as set under Example (2.31), the following results will appear:

```
(setmember k x) ==> TRUE
(setmember d x) ==> NIL
```

(For the Common Lisp Function **member-if**, which requires an additional test for membership, see Section 5.15).

The function **concat** in Lispvm, if applied to strings, concatenates the strings; if applied to lists, it behaves like **append**.

```
(concat a b c)    VALUE = "ABC"
(concat 'a 'b 'c) ==>  "ABC"
(concat water fall) ==>  "WATERFALL"
(concat '(a b c) '(e f g)) ==>  (A B C E F G)
(concat '(a b c) 'd) ==>  (A B C . D)
```

(There is a form **concatenate** in Common Lisp, which functions differently; it will be discussed in Chapter 5.)

The function **reverse** takes a list as argument and returns the list in the reverse order:

```
(reverse '(a b c)) ==) (C B A)
(reverse '(3 2 1 0)) ==) (0 1 2 3)
```

The function **remove** in Lispvm can have three arguments: a list, an atom, and a possible third argument. Some examples are:

```
(setq s '(b c a d a a a g))
(remove s a)==)(B C D A A A G) ;the first a is removed
(remove s a 2)==)(B C D A A G) ;the first two a's are removed
(remove s a k)==)(B C D G) ;when the third argument
        ;; is anything other than a positive integer, all of
                ;; the a's are removed]
```

The **remove** function in Common Lisp is demonstrated by the following examples:

```
(remove 'a s) ==) (B C D G)
(remove 'a s :count 1) ==) (B C D A A A G)
(remove 'a s :count 1 :from-end t)==)(B C A D A A G)
```

(See Section 5.15 for **remove-if**).

Let us now write a function that deletes all occurrences of a given item in a list without specifying a third argument. This function will be called **erase1** (see Exercise 1(a), Section 2.5).

```
(defun erase1 (a s)
    (cond ((null s) nil)
          ((equal a (car s))
                (erase1 a (cdr s)))          (2.33)
          (t (cons (car s)
                (erase1 a (cdr s)))))))
(erase1 x '(a b x x z y x c)) ==) (A B Z Y C)
```

There is a function **delete** in Common LISP that has the same effect as **erase1** in Example (2.33): (delete x '(a b x x z y x c) $\Rightarrow$ (A B Z Y C), but it is destructive (see Section 2.10, and also Section 5.15, for **delete-if**).

Some other searching, sorting, and updating functions are listed in the following paragraphs.

The **sort** function takes a list as argument and returns the list in numerical and alphabetical order:

```
(setq letters '(c d f a e b g))
(setq digits '(0 9 3 5 2 4 1 7 6 8))
(sort letters) ==) (A B C D E F G)
(sort digits) ==) (0 1 2 3 4 5 6 7 8 9)
(sort (append letters digits)) ==)
          (0 1 2 3 4 5 6 7 8 9 A B C D E F G)
```

In Lispvm, there is also a function called **sortby**, which sorts on a specified element of a list. Compare the following:

```
(sort '((2 b) (1 c) (3 a)))==) ((1 C) (2 B) (3 A))
(sortby 'cadr '((2 b)(1 c)(3 a)))==) ((3 A)(2 B)(1 C))
```

The function **addtolist** in Lispvm adds an element to the end of a list, if the element is not already in the list. In Common Lisp, **adjoin** does the same, except that the item is added to the beginning of the list.

```
(addtolist '(the evil that men do lives after) them)==)
         (THE EVIL THAT MEN DO LIVES AFTER THEM)
(addtolist '(jack shall have jill) jill) ==)
         (JACK SHALL HAVE JILL)
         ; not added because Jill is already there.
```

The function **adjoin** adds an element to a set, if the element is not already there:

```
(adjoin 'a '(b c d e)) ==) (A B C D E)
(adjoin 'a '(x y a b c)) ==) (X Y A B C)
```

```
(addtolist ⟨list⟩ ⟨item⟩ ) [Lispvm]
(adjoin ⟨item⟩ ⟨list⟩)       [Common Lisp]
```

The functions **rplaca** and **rplacd** replace the **car** and **cdr** of a list, respectively, with a given element or list:

```
(rplaca '(5 2 3 4) 1)  ==)  (1 2 3 4)
(rplacd '(10 2 3 4) '(20 30 40)) ==) (10 20 30 40)
```

A function that will replace any given (*n*th) element of a list is the following:

```
(defun my-repl (nth-element lyst new-element)
      (cond ((null lyst) nil)
            ((zerop nth-element) lyst)
            ((> nth-element (length lyst)) lyst)
            ((equal nth-element 1)
                     (cons new-element (cdr lyst)))        (2.34)
            ('t(cons (car lyst)(my-repl
                     (1- nth-element)(cdr lyst)
                                  new-element)))))
(my-repl 3 '(easy come let go) 'easy) ==>
                     (EASY COME EASY GO)
```

Notice the difference between the function **my-repl** and the function **my-subst**, given in Section 2.5.

```
(my-subst 'easy 'let '(easy come let go)) ==>
                              (EASY COME EASY GO)
(my-subst 2 'a '(a b c a d a)) ==> (2 B C 2 D 2)
(my-subst '(1 2 3) 'a '(a b c a d a) ==>
                     ((1 2 3) B C (1 2 3) D (1 2 3))
```

The function **my-subst** is useful for making global corrections in a text. Suppose the word *infer* has been misspelled as *inffer* throughout a text; **my-subst** can be used to correct all occurrences of *inffer*:

```
(my-subst 'infer 'inffer text)
```

There are functions **substitute** and **subst** in Common Lisp, and **subst** in Lispvm, which can produce the same results as **my-subst**.

2.9 EXERCISES

1. Assuming that the functions **union** and **intersection** were not system functions, write functions to perform the same operations as these functions. These functions must be given some other appropriate names, because **union** and **intersection** are already known words in Lisp.

2. Explain the following: (remove 3 '(1 2 4 1 3 5) :test '>) $\Rightarrow$ (4 3 5).

3. Write a function or functions that delete(s) the last word in any sentence and replace(s) it with three dashes (---).

4. Two courses, CL4 and CL6, are scheduled to meet on Thursday afternoons at 2:00—4:00. Write a Lisp program to do the following: (a) If there are any students registered in both the courses, output a message saying that the time of CL4 should be changed [hint, use (print '(change time CL4))]. (b) For all students in CL4, send the message: CL2 is a prerequisite for CL4. (c) For all students in CL6, send the message: CL5 is a prerequisite for CL6. (d) For all students registered in both CL4 and CL6, the message should be: CL2 and CL5 are prerequisites. Avoid sending identical messages to the same person.

5. Given two lists: (John Mary Andy Sue) and (daughter son wife husband), write a function that will produce the following list: ((husband (John Mary)) (wife (Mary John)) (son (Andy John)) (son (Andy Mary)) (daughter (Sue John)) (daughter (Sue Mary))).

6. Write a function that will reverse the order of elements in a list. This function cannot be called **reverse**, since there is already a system function by that name in Lisp.

7. A book dealer announces a sale as follows: Purchases of up to five books cost $3.00 each. Each book above five costs $2.00. Write a function to read the number of books purchased and compute the amount to be paid. Run the function against the purchases of 3, 5, and 12 books.

2.10 DESTRUCTIVE FUNCTIONS

Some functions and operations in LISP permanently change the structure of a list. Reconsider the following sequence of operations:

```
(setq foo '(a b c d)) ==> (A B C D)
foo ==> (A B C D)
(cdr foo) ==> (B C D)
foo ==> (A B C D)
(setq foo (cdr foo)) ==> (B C D)
foo ==> (B C D)
```

Thus, it is said that the **setq** form is destructive, but **cdr** is not. Similarly, **sort** is destructive:

```
(setq foo '(d b a c f)) ==> (D B A C F)
(sort foo) ==> (A B C D F)
foo ==> (A B C D F)
```

The programmer should always be careful about the side effects of destructive functions. We saw in Example (2.16) that a function could go into a so-called infinite loop because of lack of attention to these matters. In Chapter 4, graphic representations of data structures, as affected by destructive and nondestructive operations will be given. Whenever in doubt use tests similar to the examples given above.

Among the system functions given so far in this chapter, the following are destructive: **delete**, **rplaca**, **decf**, **incf**, **rplacd**, **set**, **setq**, **sort**, **subst**, and **substitute** (the last two depending on implementation). Other destructive forms will be noted as they are encountered.

2.11 LIST MAPPING OPERATORS

Let us look again at Exercise 7 in Section 2.9. A function to decide the cost of "n" books could be written, and then run three times—once with the input 3, then again with the input 5, and finally with 12—or a special operator in Lisp that is able to apply the cost function to each element of a list of numbers, and then run the function on the the list (3 5 12) could be used. The name of this operator is **mapcar**. If the cost function is called **cost**, then (mapcar 'cost '(3 5 12)) would return the value (9 15 29), which contains the costs of 3, 5, and 12 books, respectively. The operator **mapcar** will apply **cost** first to the **car** of the list, then to the **cadr** of the list, then to the **caddr** of the list, and so on until **cost** has been applied to each element of the list. The operator **mapcar** will return a list of the values obtained by applying **cost** to the elements of the list.

For another example of the use of **mapcar**, suppose that a function **fact**, which computes the factorial of a number has been defined, and is now to be used, to compute 4!, 6!, 9!, and 3!. The function **fact** can then be applied to each element of the list of numbers (4 6 9 3) by inputting (mapcar 'fact '(4 6 9 3)). Lisp will return (24 720 362880 6).

The general format (syntax) for **mapcar** is:

```
(mapcar ⟨function-name⟩
        ⟨list-1⟩ ⟨list-2⟩ ... ⟨list-n⟩ )
```

The function-name must be preceded by a single quote mark in Common Lisp. Note that the above formula indicates that a function can be applied to the elements of more than one list, if it is appropriate. For example, if there are three lists of numbers and we want to add the first number in list-1 to the first number in list-2, and the first number in list-3, and the second numbers in each list to each other, and the third numbers, and so on, then (mapcar plus list1 list2 list3); or in Common Lisp (mapcar '+ list1 list2 list3) would be used.

Suppose the lists are (1 2 3), (4 5 6), and (7 8 9). The result of (mapcar '+ '(1 2 3) '(4 5 6) '(7 8 9)) will be (12 15 18). The function **mapcar** applies plus to the **cars** of the lists, and so adds $1+4+7$, then it applies plus to the **cadrs** of the lists and adds $2+5+8$, and then it applies plus to the **caddrs** of the lists and adds $3+6+9$. It returns a list of the results of these three applications of *plus*. If the lists are of unequal lengths, **mapcar** will stop applying *plus* (or whatever the function was) as soon as one of the lists is exhausted. For a silly but suggestive exercise, try the following:

```
(setq names '(john mary terry susan mike))
(setq verbs '(likes wants hates sees hits kisses))        (2.35)
(setq objects '(candy diamonds dogs stars babies))
(mapcar 'list names verbs objects)
```

The results can be predicted. Note that the list of verbs is longer than the others, and so nouns and objects wil be used up before verbs. Consequently, no one kisses anything.

In the following example, a function is defined and given arguments as part of the application of **mapcar**:

```
(mapcar '(lambda (x y)
          (cons x y))
        '(5 7 12 3) '(1 2 9) )            (2.36)
   ==) ((5 . 1) (7 . 2) (12 . 9))
```

Tracing through this function and its result is left as an exercise for the reader. Recall that (cons 5 1)$\Rightarrow$(5 . 1). The term *lambda* in Example (2.36) is part of what is called the *lambda expression*. Lambda expressions will be discussed in some detail in Chapter 5, but it can be informally said here that lambda expressions are a sort of nameless function, so that in:

$$(lambda (x y) (cons x y))\qquad(2.37)$$

the list (x y) following lambda is the list of parameters of the unnamed function and (cons x y) is its body. However, Example (2.37) cannot be called as given, because lambda is not a form; it is not a function name. It can, however, be run by supplying it with arguments to be bound with its parameters:

```
((lambda (x y) (cons x y)) '(5 7 12 3) '(1 2 9))     (2.38)
   ==) ((5 7 12 3) 1 2 9)
```

This is what is embedded in the function in Example (2.36), where another function name was not necessary. The different output in Example (2.36) is the result of the effect of **mapcar**. Another example of a lambda expression is the following:

$$((lambda (x) (* x x)) 5) ==) 25\qquad(2.39)$$

Example (2.39) can, of course, be defined as a named function:

$$(defun square (x) (* x x)) ==) SQUARE\qquad(2.40)$$

Example (2.39) is appropriate where computing a function only once is needed, whereas Example (2.40) can be called any number of times, with different arguments for its parameter *x*.

An operator similar to **mapcar** is **mapc**. It will also apply a function to the **cars**, **cadrs**, **caddrs**, etc. of the lists that follow function names. However, **mapc** in Lispvm and Common Lisp returns, as its value, the first list: (mapc plus '(1 2 3) '(4 5 6) '(7 8 9)), which will return VALUE = (1 2 3). (In other dialects of Lisp, the value returned may be NIL, the second list, etc.) The operator **mapc** performs the same addition procedure that was described above for **mapcar**, but the result is not displayed; in fact the result is thrown away, as it were. It might be asked, then, what is the use of this function? The operator **mapc** runs more efficiently than **mapcar**. It is useful when the result of an operation is to be incorporated into another function, or when it is necessary to see the trace of the application of the operator on the display screen, but the final result does not matter. To see the trace, a **print** function can be included in writing a **mapc** expression. Here are some examples:

```
(mapc '(lambda (a b c)
          (print (+ a b c)))
           '(1 2 3) '(4 5 6) '(7 8 9) )

12
15
18
(1 2 3)
```

```
(mapc '(lambda (x y) (print (cons x y)))          (2.41)
       '(5 7 12 3) '(1 2 9))
(5 . 1)
(7 . 2)
(12 . 9)
(5 7 12 3)
```

```
(mapc '(lambda (x y) (print (+ x y))) '(5 7) '(10 12))
15
19
(5 7)
```

In the following example, the result of **mapc** is incorporated in another function:

```
(mapcar '+ '(10 10 10)
     (mapc '+ '(1 2 3) '(4 5 6)))          (2.42)
==> (11 12 13)
```

Compare this with the following example:

```
(mapc 'print (+ 5 6 7 3)) ==> 21
(mapc '+ 5 6 7 3) ==> 5
```

As can be seen from the examples, **mapcar** and **mapc** apply to the **car, car** of **cdr, car** of **cdr** of **cdr**, etc. of a list or lists. There is a pair of mapping operators that apply to the **cdr, cdr** of **cdr**, and so on. These operators are **maplist** and **map**. Examples:

```
(setq list1 '(a b c)) ==> (A B C)
(setq list2 '(1 2 3)) ==> (1 2 3)
(maplist 'append list1 list2)
    ==> ((A B C 1 2 3) (B C 2 3) (C 3))
(maplist 'length '(a b c d)) ==> (4 3 2 1)

(maplist '(lambda (x y)
            (list x y))
               '(1 2 3) '(4 5 6) )
==> ( ((1 2 3)(4 5 6)) ((2 3)(5 6)) ((3)(6)) )
```

$$(2.43)$$

In the first example in Example (2.43), list1 is first appended to list2, then the **cdr** of list1 is appended to the **cdr** of list2, and finally **cddr** of list1 is appended to the **cddr** of list2. In the second example, the length of the list (a b c d) is originally 4, but as it is reduced to its successive **cdr**'s, the length becomes 3, 2, and finally 1.

The **map** operator does the same thing as **maplist,** except that (like **mapc**) it does not show the result; it outputs the value of the first list. In all dialects of Lisp, from its beginnings, the term **map** is used. In Common Lisp, this term has been changed to **mapl**.

```
LVM:   (map print '(a b c d))
    (A B C D)
    (B C D)
    (C D)
    (D)
    VALUE = (A B C D)

CL:    (mapl 'print '(a b c d))     [same output as above]
```

$$(2.44)$$

The function **mapcan** is similar to **mapcar**, but it accumulates the results into one list. Compare the following:

```
(setq list1 '(a b c)) ==> (A B C)
(setq list2 '(1 2 3)) ==> (1 2 3)
(mapcar 'list list1 list2)
    ==> ((A 1) (B 2) (C 3))
(mapcan 'list list1 list2)
    ==> (A 1 B 2 C 3)
```

The function **mapcon** is similar to **maplist**, but again accumulates the result in one list:

```
(maplist 'list list1 list2)
  ==) ( ((A B C)(1 2 3)) ((B C)(2 3)) ((C)(3)) )
(mapcon 'list list1 list2)
  ==) ( (A B C) (1 2 3) (B C) (2 3) (C) (3) )
```

2.12 EXERCISES

1. Explain the following functions:

    (a) ```
         (defun insert-number (n numbers)
           (cond ((null numbers) (list n))
                 (((< n (car numbers))(cons n numbers))
                 (t(cons (car numbers)
                     (insert-number n (cdr numbers))))))))
         ```

    (b)  ```
         (defun repeat-list (L)
           (cond ((null L) nil)
                 (t (cons (car L)(append
                             (cons (car L)(list (car L)))
                       (repeat-list (cdr L)))))))
         ```

    (c) ```
         ((lambda (x y) (cons x y)) 'a '(b c d))
         ```

    (d)  ```
         (setq names '(max mary joe phil tom))
         (and (member 'max names)
              (member 'mary names)
              (member 'joe names)
              (member 'phil names)
              (member 'tom names) )
         ==) ?
         ```

    (e) ```
         (defun list-numbp (L)
           (cond ((null L) t)
                 ((numberp (car L))(list-numbp (cdr L)))
                 (t nil)))
         ```

    (f)  ```
         (mapcar '(lambda (L)
             (cond ((numberp L) t) (t nil)))
               '(a 6 3 b c 7 2) )
         ==) ?
         ```

```
(g)  (defun sum-list (L)
       (prog ((sum 0))
        label1 (cond ((null L)(return sum))
                     (t (incf sum (car L))
                        (setq L (cdr L))
                        (go label1)))))
```

2. Reconsider **find-col** in Example (2.18). Write a function that can read any arbitrary pair of words in a multiple sentence text, and print the sentences that contain the pair of words occurring together. The text can be treated as a list of lists, in which every sentence is a sublist.

3. Write a function that will take a predicate sentence in English as input, and will output the question form of the sentence. Examples:

```
John is here ==> is John here?
Your French book is on the table ==> Is your French ...
Both the adults and children in the party were
exhausted ==> Were both the adults and ...
```

4. Write a function to compute the accumulation of interest on a sum of money "m" at the rate of "p" interest for a period of "y" years. Assume that once every three months the principal is compounded.

3

Editing Lisp

3.1 INTRODUCTION

Until now this text has been concerned with writing functions and trying them out. When you logged off the machine after a session, the functions were lost, and you have not been told how to correct errors. If the program had logical errors, erroneous or unexpected results were obtained. If there were syntactic errors, that is, if a function or expression was improperly formulated, error messages were printed. In each case, the reader had to retype the whole program, even if only one minor mistake was made. Actually, as the reader must have noticed, the situation is a bit more complicated than that. When an error occurs in writing a function in Lisp, the system puts the program into what is called an error-correcting loop. To get out of this loop, in Lispvm, the user must input **unwind** or **fin**, followed by a digit; for example, (unwind 4) or (fin 3). The program would get out of the loop, but it had to be retyped, and the user would not have taken any advantage of the error-correcting facilities in the system. Similarly, in Common Lisp, depending on the implementation, the user may press *CONTROL*, *Ctrl*, and *C* keys, or the *Ctrl* and *G* keys, simultaneously, to get out of the error loop (see Appendix A).

In this chapter, procedures will be presented for making files and saving them, as well as for making corrections in, or updating, an existing file under the "edit mode." Among the other topics to be discussed in this chapter are procedures for loading files and running programs stored in them, other aspects of editing components of Lispvm and Common Lisp, and input/output facilities. Further discussions for creating and manipulating files directly under Common Lisp are given in Chapter 5.

An edit program is a facility attached to a programming language or system that allows the user to write, edit, correct, update, link, save, print, and load a program. Most of the functions and expressions that are described for Lispvm and Common Lisp in this text are more or less applicable to many other modern Lisp dialects. However, edit programs are generally specialized, and are dependent upon the implementation of a particular computing or programming system. Thus, the Lispedit program discussed in this chapter is designed specifically for Lispvm. As mentioned before, Common Lisp already has many implementations or subdialects. In this chapter, editing facilities of the version called Golden Common Lisp (GCLisp), developed by Gold Hill Computers at Cambridge, Massachusetts, will be discussed. This is a particularly popular version, with special implementation for personal computers. Editing in Common Lisp is simpler and easier for a beginner than the facilities in Lispvm; nevertheless, Lispedit of Lispvm will be discussed first because of its comprehensiveness. The reader who does not have access to Lispvm should, nevertheless, skim through this portion to get some idea of elaborate editing facilities, which are similar to some other "uncommon" dialects, and then go to Section 3.7 for a simpler approach in Common Lisp. It is recommended, however, that the user have access to the reference manual or other instructions for the particular dialect or version of Lisp that he or she is using. Alternatively, the user can find what works and what doesn't by the simple process of trial and error!

3.2 DEFINING AN OBJECT WITHIN LISPEDIT

Lispedit is an editing program that is a component of the Lispvm system, and operates under the VM/CMS operating system in IBM computers. To demonstrate this facility, a simple example will be developed with the editor, and then it will be saved, changed, and so forth. For this exercise, a mini-example of the earliest approach in machine translation will be replicated.

This example will start with the compilation of a dictionary of English words and their Spanish equivalents. In later chapters, we will discuss how to attach parts of speech and other features to words, but for the present, single words with only one, unambiguous translation for each will be given. To compile the dictionary, Lispvm must be entered by inputting *Lispvm* under the VM prompt (see Appendix A) and pressing the *Enter* key. A divided screen, as shown in Figure 3.1, will appear:

NIL

Lispedit level 0 — — — — — — — Default id: NIL
LISP/VM version ⟨x⟩.
[more essages . . .]
PF: 1 ? 2 " 3 QUIT 4 B   5 S   6 D   7 −1   8 +1 . . .
⇒

Figure 3.1. The divided screen of the "command mode."

The arrow ⇒ at the bottom of the screen points to the *command line*. So far, if in Lispvm, it was assumed that the functions and expressions were written at this line, where they were directly evaluated and executed. This is sometimes called the *interactive mode*. The dictionary will be developed in the *edit mode*. To do this, the dictionary will be called DICTIONARY:

> e dictionary

"e" is for *edit* (note that, in Lispvm, *edit commands* are not enclosed in parentheses), and now DICTIONARY is the name of the dictionary that is to be developed, and it will appear at the upper left corner of the top screen. The bottom screen is called the *message area*, and will contain information that will be ignored for the present. The cursor will now be blinking at the command line. Input "i" (and press the *ENTER* key) to put the system in the *input mode*. The system is now ready for the entry of the dictionary items. Enter the following line:

$$((\text{how como}) (\text{are esta}) (\text{you usted})) \qquad (3.1)$$

Notice that the above line is a list with three sublists. Each sublist consists of a pair of words: English and Spanish. The whole line need not be entered at once. For a large dictionary, part of it can be entered in each line, until the whole dictionary is entered. When the definition of the dictionary is finished, the *function-key-3* (*PF3*, or *F3* on many keyboards) must be pressed to indicate the end of the input mode. The cursor will then be returned to the command line. Then input "assign" and press the ENTER key. If this procedure has been followed so far, a check on what has been created can be made by inputting DICTIONARY. In the message area of the divided screen, a copy of the command will appear, and:

> DICTIONARY = ((HOW COMO) (ARE ESTA) (YOU USTED))

3.3 SAVING AN OBJECT IN AN INDEXED FILE

Let us assume that the "object," the dictionary, has no errors, and is to be saved for future use. Normally, objects are saved in files, so that they can be loaded and the objects in them can be accessed. Such files in Lispedit are called *indexed files* (xf), because the system maintains a directory of the objects in each file. Each object can then be accessed by calling its name. Objects, of course, are databases, such as the above DICTIONARY, and programs that may be saved in the same file.

A file for storing objects must also have a name, so that it can be loaded by calling its name. If a name is not assigned to an indexed file, Lispedit will assign it a default name: LISPWORK. Normally, however, a file should have some other name. The file for this current exercise will then be called TRANS (file names in this system cannot be longer than eight characters). To change the file name from LISPWORK to TRANS, input:

```
xf trans
```

A message will appear in the message area of the screen indicating the change of the file name to TRANS. If the file TRANS was created after the creation of the above DICTIONARY, the message area will also indicate that DICTIONARY is a "member" of the file. Now, to save the dictionary, input:

```
save
```

The divided screen may disappear, and at the bottom of the screen the message: More . . . (or Holding) may appear. This means that the screen is full, and waiting for additional space. To get out of this situation, the screen must be "scrolled" (moved). On some keyboards, the function key *PA2* and then the *ENTER* key must be pressed. On some IBM keyboards, this can be simulated by pressing the *Alt* and *F6* keys simultaneously. In any case, this is a common occurrence, and the reader must find out how scrolling is done on the particular keyboard used. In this example, when the *Alt-F6* keys are pressed, the divided screen is returned with ((HOW COMO) (ARE ESTA) (YOU USTED)) at the top of the screen. This indicates that the object that was being edited (that is, DICTIONARY) was saved.

To recapitulate, the following sequence was input during this terminal session:

```
1.  e dictionary
2.  i
3.  ((how como)(are esta)(you usted))
4.  F3
5.  assign
6.  xf trans
7.  save
8.  Alt-F6 (or PA2 and ENTER on some keyboards)
```
(3.2)

Instructions given in the edit mode are called *edit commands*. In Example (3.2), line 1 commands the computer to enter the edit mode (e) and prepare for the creation of an "object" called DICTIONARY. Line 2 tells it to accept data as input (i). Line 3 is the definition or content of the object. Line 4 tells the computer that the object definition is finished. Line 5 assigns the input data as the current object. Line 6 changes the default name of the Lispedit indexed file to TRANS. Line 7 saves the object in the file. Line 8 indicates the completion of the save process.

3.4 EXERCISES

1. Define and save an English-French dictionary called DICTIONAIRE, containing English and French equivalents for several words. Save DICTIONAIRE in the indexed file TRANS.

2. Write functions that compute the mean, the standard deviation, or other statistical computations for a list of numbers, and store them in an indexed file called STATISK.

3.5 LOGGING-ON AND LOADING AN INDEXED FILE

The save procedure in Section 3.3 saves a file permanently in the allocated disk space. During the next session in the system Lispvm, the file can be *loaded*, in order to add to or make changes in the DICTIONARY, or to add other programs to complete the translation project. To load the file into the current Lisp environment, input the following on the command line:

```
load trans *
```

This will retrieve all of the objects stored in the indexed file TRANS (it is the * that causes *all* of the objects to be loaded). The message area will then indicate LOAD: TRANS*A DICTIONARY. The *A indicates that the file has been stored on the A disk (The disk label may vary depending on the computer set up).

To load one object (say, DICTIONARY) in a file containing many objects, input:

```
load trans dictionary
```

In general, if *indfile* is the name of an indexed file, and *indobj* is the name of an object in that file, the **load** command can be one of the following:

```
load indfile *       (which causes all of the objects
                      in the indfile to be loaded)
load indfile indobj  (which causes only the indobj
                      to be loaded)
```

In order to edit an *indobj*, input: e indobj.

3.6 EDITING OBJECTS IN A FILE

This section will begin by defining another object and saving it in the file TRANS. To continue with the translation project, a function that reads a sentence to be translated is necessary. Let us call this function **reader**. The function cues the user to input a sentence by printing the message: PLEASE TYPE A SENTENCE, ENCLOSED IN PARENTHESES, and then binding the input sentence to a variable called *sentence*. Under the procedures discussed in previous chapters, the function would be written as follows:

```
(defun reader nil
    (print                                                    (3.3)
      "please type a sentence, enclosed in parentheses")
        (setq sentence (read)))
```

This will now be done under edit mode:

```
e reader
i
(lambda nil
(print
 "please type a sentence, enclosed in parentheses")
(setq sentence (read)))
F3
assign
```
(3.4)

The end of the Lispedit input mode is indicated by pressing the function-key *F3*, and the cursor moves back to the command line. Notice that, in the edit mode, it is not necessary to put a quote mark before the **lambda** expression, and it is not necessary to begin with (defun. Also observe that, when in the edit mode (Lispedit), the **print** command (as shown above) can be used with the message in double quotes. However, when not in the edit mode, this format will not work for Lispvm. The message must then be put in two double quotes, or in parentheses with a single quote in front: (PRINT '(PLEASE TYPE A SENTENCE, EN-CLOSED IN PARENTHESES)). Whenever in doubt, use the latter format; it works in all cases.

To see the function reproduced on the computer screen, input (print reader), and the function will appear as:

```
(LAMBDA NIL (PRINT "PLEASE TYPE A SENTENCE, ENCLOSED
IN PARENTHESES") (SETQ SENTENCE (READ)))
```

To see the function printed in the indented style that we have been using, input (prettyprint reader).

To see what the function **reader** will do, invoke it by inputting (reader). The screen will be cleared except for the following message printed across the top of the screen: PLEASE TYPE A SENTENCE, ENCLOSED IN PARENTHESES. At this point, if a sentence is input, it will become the "value" of **reader** but nothing else will happen, because a function for translation has not, as yet, been defined. To save the definition of **reader** in the file TRANS, input:

```
xf trans
save
```

Since the definition of **reader** is still the object that the editor has been working on, it will be saved in the file. A function for "translating" English sentences into Spanish, using the DICTIONARY, will now be developed. (*translating* is put in quotations because all that is being done is to replace English words by their equivalent Spanish words, as listed in the dictionary.)

```
e transfer
i
(lambda (sentence)
(cond ((null sentence) nil)
('t (cons (look-up (car sentence) dictionary)
(transfer (cdr sentence))))))                                    (3.5)
F3
assign
xf trans
save
Alt-F6    [This is not always necessary; use only when
                the message MORE ... or HOLDING appears]
```

Figuring out how the function **transfer** works is left as an exercise for the reader. If the function **transfer** is **prettyprinted**, it will be more readable. Note, however, that this function calls another function which is called **look-up**. This latter function looks up the words in the input sentence in the dictionary. The function **look-up** will now be defined (cf. Examples (1.25) and (1.26) in Section 1.7).

```
e look-up
i
(lambda (word wordlist)
(cond ((null wordlist) word)
((equal word (caar wordlist)) (cadar wordlist))
('t (look-up word (cdr wordlist)))))                             (3.6)
F3
assign
xf trans
save
Alt-F6
```

Note that *word* and *wordlist* have been used as parameters in Example (3.6) to show that parameters in each function can be different. When **transfer** calls **look-up**, *word* and *wordlist* will be bound to SENTENCE and DICTIONARY, respectively. Also observe that, the way that the above function is written, if a word in the input sentence is not in the dictionary, the word will appear in the original form in the translation.

Four objects have now been defined and saved in the file TRANS: DICTIONARY, **reader**, **transfer**, and **look-up**. To make the translation project work, an expression must be added to the definition of **reader** to call **transfer**. At the same time, some corrections and additions will be made to the DICTIONARY. There are editing commands that will allow this to be done. First, however, the attention of the editor must be focused on the part of program that is to be altered.

3.6.1 Focus

While objects were being defined under the editor, you may have noticed that, sometimes, part or all of an object was highlighted or appeared in another color on the top of the screen. As you input the definition of an object, the attention of the editor shifts to the item just entered. This may be a list that is a member of another list, or an atom. The place in the structure that has the attention of the editor is the "current focus," and it usually appears highlighted or in a different color. On exiting the input mode (by pressing *F3*), the focus of the editor shifts to the entire expression on the screen. There are commands that can be used on the command line (or for which function keys have been defined) that will narrow the focus, shift it forward or backward item by item at the current level, or widen the focus to a higher level of the list structure. The definition of the **reader** will be used to practice shifting the focus. To bring **reader** to the screen, type:

```
load trans *
e reader
```

The screen will appear as in Figure 3.2.

In Figure 3.2, the focus is on the entire **reader** function. To shift the focus on the first element of the expression, input **smaller** on the command line, or press *FUNCTION-KEY 5* (*F5*). The focus will be on **lambda**. The next item on the same level is NIL. To shift the focus on NIL, input **next** or press *F8*. The next item on the same level is NIL. To shift the focus on NIL, input **next** or press *F8*. The next item at the same level as **lambda** and NIL is (PRINT "PLEASE . . . PARENTHESES"). To focus on this list, *F8* or **next** can again be used. Similarly, another use of *F8* will shift the focus on (SETQ . . . (READ)). The focus at this point is on the list (SETQ SENTENCE (READ)). There are levels of structure in this list. The focus can be shifted to sublists by inputting **smaller** (or *F5*). Suppose we want to focus on (READ); the following sequence will achieve this: **smaller next next**. Now, to focus on **read**, input **smaller** again. To return the focus to (READ), input **bigger** (or press *F4*). This command focuses on the list *containing* the current focus. Continuing to input **bigger** will eventually return the focus to the entire **reader** function. There is also a single command

```
(LAMBDA NIL
    (PRINT
        "Please type a sentence, enclosed in parentheses")
    (SETQ SENTENCE (READ)) )


Lispedit level 1  – – – – – – – – – – – Default id: READER
[messages . . . ]
⇒
```

Figure 3.2. The focus is on the entire expression.

that will take the focus to the top level of a function. The command is **top** (abbreviated **t**). Note that, when the focus is at the top level, the commands **bigger**, **next**, and **previous** will not have any effect. Similarly, when the focus is on an atom, the command **smaller** has no effect.

An alternative way of moving the focus is to move the cursor under the item or expression that is to be focused, and then pressing *F10*. This is called "select." (Provided that *F10* is set on your terminal for this function.)

It is important to master control of the focus before trying to correct or change definitions within the editor. Otherwise, objects may be changed that were not intended. Unfortunately, the highlighting of the focus is not always reliable on some monitors. Often what is highlighted is bigger than the actual focus. It is necessary to keep track of the focus.

Exercise: Type the following list under edit mode and then use the above commands to shift the focus on every sublist and every atom in the list:

$$(a\ b\ c\ (d\ (e\ f\ (g)\ h)\ i\ )\ k\ (l\ (m\ (n)))\ o\ p).$$

In the above discussion, **previous** was mentioned as an edit command. The **previous** command shifts the focus back towards the head of the list at the same level as the current focus. The opposite of this is **next**, which shifts the focus towards the tail of the list.

The commonly used edit commands that cause a shift in the focus are summarized in Table 3.1.

It should be pointed out that keyboards and communication software vary, and some keyboards may not have the function keys defined, or will have different function keys for the commands in Table 3.1. However, inputting the commands in their written forms should work for any keyboard.

Most of the commands in Table 3.1 can also be followed by a positive whole

TABLE 3.1. EDIT COMMANDS FOR FOCUS SHIFTING

Command	Function-Key	Effect
bigger	*F4*	Shifts the focus to the expression containing the current focus.
smaller	*F5*	Shifts the focus into the first subexpression of the current focus.
next	*F8*	Shifts the focus to the next item at the same level.
previous	*F7*	Shifts the focus back towards the head of the list.
top		Shifts the focus to the top level of the expression.
(move the cursor to the object desired to be focused and press)	*F10*	Shifts the focus to the selected object.

number, to achieve more than one move in the shift. For example, if BIGGER 3 is input, the focus will move out three levels in the list (provided that there are three levels to move).

3.6.2 Other Lispedit Commands

Other important commands in LISPEDIT are **change**, **delete**, **insert**, **insert-before**, **locexpr**, **prefix**, **replace**, **restore**, and **erasex**. Some of these will now be used to make changes in the four programs that are saved in the TRANS file. After that, some further descriptions of these commands will be given.

Let us return to the function **reader** in Figure 3.2, repeated below:

```
(lambda nil (print     "Please type a sentence,
                        enclosed in parentheses")
           (setq sentence (read)) )
```

Recall that this function prompts the user to type a sentence to be translated. However, the function must also call the translation routine, which has been called **transfer**. To do this, the name of the translation function and its parameters must be inserted as the last subexpression in the structure of **reader**. The following sequence of commands will do the job:

```
smaller
next
next
next
insert (transfer sentence)
```

This is the same as:

```
smaller
next 3
insert (transfer sentence)
```

The result will be the following:

```
(LAMBDA NIL (PRINT "Please type a sentence, enclosed
in parentheses") (SETQ SENTENCE
(READ)) (TRANSFER SENTENCE))
```

The command **insert** adds an expression after the current focus of the editor and then shifts the focus to the new expression. In the example above, the focus was moved to the subexpression (SETQ SENTENCE (READ)) and then the **insert** command was executed. After (transfer sentence) is inserted, it becomes the current focus. In order to save this revised function for **reader**, just input **assign** followed by **save**. The new version will replace the old one.

A "translation" system now exists, but it can only translate one sentence! Try it:

```
(reader)
PLEASE TYPE A SENTENCE, ENCLOSED IN PARENTHESES
(how are you)
(COMO ESTA USTED)
```

and again:

```
(reader)
PLEASE TYPE A SENTENCE, ENCLOSED IN PARENTHESES
(how are you and your brother)
(COMO ESTA USTED AND YOUR BROTHER)
```

Let us now make some changes in the dictionary:

```
e dictionary
((HOW COMO) (ARE ESTA) (YOU USTED))
```

Observe the following sequence of commands and the changes in the dictionary in each case (printed in caps). The focus is on the top level, the entire list. On the command line, type:

```
change esta estan
((HOW COMO) (ARE ESTAN) (YOU USTED))
change usted ustedes
((HOW COMO) (ARE ESTAN) (YOU USTEDES))
```

Shift the focus to the sublist (HOW COMO) and type a **replace** command:

```
smaller
replace (why porque)
((WHY PORQUE) (ARE ESTAN) (YOU USTEDES))
```

Then add another item to the dictionary:

```
next 2
insert (here aqui)
((WHY PORQUE) (ARE ESTAN) (YOU USTEDES) (HERE AQUI))
```

If you type **assign** at this point, (why are you here) can be translated. Now add to the dictionary (HOW COMO), which was replaced before:

```
previous 3
insert (how como)
((WHY PORQUE) (HOW COMO) (ARE ESTAN) (YOU USTEDES)
(HERE AQUI))
```

Now save the dictionary:

```
assign
save
Alt-F6  (this is to get back to edit screen)
```

A number of other sentences can now be translated. Try them. (Incidentally, the pairs of words in the DICTIONARY could have been entered in any order.)

Given the way that the **reader** function is written, to translate a number of sentences, **reader** must be invoked. This is awkward. It would be preferable for the control to go back to **reader** after each translation, and prompt the user for a new sentence. This is left as an exercise for the reader (see Exercise 3, in Section 3.11).

Returning to edit commands, a list of those mentioned earlier, together with a brief explanation for each, will be presented in the following paragraphs. Note that most of these command names can be abbreviated. The abbreviated form will be given after each name, in parentheses. All commands must be typed on the command line of the divided screen of the editor, and all commands are effective within the scope of the current focus. Unlike Lisp expressions, edit commands in Lispedit are not enclosed in parentheses.

replace (**rep**): may be followed by zero or more expressions. The expressions, when given, replace the expression under the current focus, and the focus shifts to the last expression inserted.

Examples: Given the expression (out of sight in of mind) and the focus on *in*:

```
rep out ==) (OUT OF SIGHT OUT OF MIND)
Given the expression (a b (f g) h) with focus on (f g):
rep c d e f g ==) (A B C D E F G H) with focus on G.
```

When **replace** is used with no argument, the focus is placed in the command line. At this line, any expression can then be written. Pressing the *enter* key will then replace the old focused expression with the new command line expression.

change (**ch**, **c**, or **cng**): The command **change** must be followed by two expressions, and the effect of it is to change the first expression for the second. A positive number "n" may follow the name of the command, in which case "n" expressions are changed. If an asterisk (*) is placed instead of "n", all expressions will be changed.

Examples: Before executing each command,

```
start with the list (a b c d e a b f g a b c d h i):
      ch a b ==) (B B C D E A B F G A B C D H I)
      ch a b 2 ==) (B B C D E B B F G A B C D H I)
      ch a b * ==) (B B C D E B B F G B B C D H I)
```

In the above examples, it is assumed that the three **ch** commands are applied independently to the original list; otherwise ch a b * will have the same result as ch a b 3 or as applying ch a b three times in a sequence.

The difference between **replace** and **change** is that **replace** assumes that the item to be replaced is the current focus; **change** starts with the current focus and searches through all levels until the end of the entire expression, for as many occurrences of the item as have been specified to be changed.

delete (**del**): The command **delete** erases the item under focus. It may be followed by a positive or negative number, or a positive or negative asterisk (*) for deleting more than one item on the right or left of the current focus.

Examples: Before executing each command, start with the list ((a b) c d (e f) (g h) i j) and focus on the sublist (g h):

```
del ==> ((A B) C D (E F) I J)
del 2 ==> ((A B) C D (E F) J)
del * ==> ((A B) C D (E F))
del -3 ==> ((A B) C I J)
del -* ==> (I J)
```

Another way of doing the above exercise without starting with the original list each time is to use **restore** after each application of **delete**:

```
del ==> ((A B) C D (E F) I J)
rest
del 2 ==> ((A B) C D (E F) J)
rest
etc.
```

Note that the **delete** command changes the focus to the item after or before the item deleted (depending on whether forward or backward deletion has been used). The **restore** command can be used to recover from, or undo, the most recent **del** or **rep** (see further on).

insert (**i**, **in**, **ins**): The command **insert** adds one or more expressions after the current focus, and moves the focus to the last expression inserted.

Example: Given the list (a b (c d) e f) with the focus on the sublist (c d):

```
i (k l) (g h) 5 ==> (A B (C D) (K L) (G H) 5 E F)
```

with the focus on 5.

When used alone, not followed by any expression, **insert** (*I*) changes the mode of the editor to the *input* mode, in which all expressions subsequently input on the command line are inserted after the previous one. The focus shifts after each such input to the most recent entry. This is how the editor has been used to define functions and other objects. To leave the input mode, press *F3* and then input **assign**. However, under the input mode, Lispedit commands will be recognized if they are prefixed with $, for example $next.

insertbefore (**inb**): The command **inb** can be followed by one or more expressions, and it inserts the expression(s) *before* the current focus. Unlike **insert**, **insertbefore** does not change the focus.

Examples: Given the list ((a b) (c (d e f)) g) and the focus on (a b):
inb list ⇒ (LIST (A B) (C (D E F)) G) with the focus still on (a b). If the focus of the list is changed to "g", the following can result:

$$\text{inb 5 ==} \rangle \;\; (A\;B)\;(C\;(D\;E\;F))\;5\;G)$$

For another example, given the list ((how como) (are estan) (you ustedes)), with the focus on (how como) and the following sequence of commands: **inb** (why porque), **in** (here aqui), will result in ((WHY PORQUE) (HOW COMO) (HERE AQUI) (ARE ESTAN) (YOU USTEDES)). What will be the output if the order of the two insert commands is reversed?

locexpr (/, **loc**, **lex**): This command shifts the focus to the expression within or to the right of the current focus that matches the expression following the command. It provides a quick way of shifting the focus to a particular element without the repeated use of **smaller**, **next**, etc. The search for the expression is depth-first and left to right; that is, given the expression (a (b (c d)) e (c d) f) and the command /(c d), the focus will shift to the first (c d).

prefix (**pref**, **prefi**): This command can be followed by one or more expressions. If the focus is a list, then the expressions are inserted at the head of the list, and the focus is on the entire new list. On the other hand, if the focus is on an atom, then the atom is linked to the expressions in a dotted pair form (see Chapter 4). Examples:

$$\text{Given the list (1 2 3 5):}$$
$$\text{pref digits ==} \rangle \;\; (DIGITS\;1\;2\;3\;5)$$

Now, if the focus is on 5 (an atom) and pref 4 is input, the resulting list would be (DIGITS 1 2 3 (4 . 5)). If the focus is on a single atom john, then pref big will produce (BIG . JOHN) with the focus on the whole dotted pair list.

restore (**rest**): This command restores the most recent **delete** or **replace** operation. Thus, in the previous example under **replace**, after producing (OUT OF SIGHT OUT OF MIND), if **rest** is input, (OUT OF SIGHT IN OF MIND) will be the output. Similarly, given the expression ((a b) c d (e f) (g h) i j) with the focus on (g h), observe the following changes:

$$\text{del -* ==} \rangle \;\; (i\;j)$$
$$\text{rest ==} \rangle \;\; ((A\;B)\;C\;D\;(E\;F\;)\;(G\;H)\;I\;J)$$

erasex (**erx**): This command is for erasing an entire indexed file or a member (object) in it. For example, if erx xf trans is input, the entire translation file will be erased. To erase just the dictionary, input erx trans dictionary. After each one of these commands, it is necessary to press the *ENTER* key to confirm the command.

There are a number of other edit commands in Lispedit; the following among them are the most useful.

listx (**lx**): This command can be used to obtain a listing on the screen of the contents of an indexed file. Thus, the command

```
lx trans
```

will list the names of the four objects in the example file.

The following two commands are useful for correcting inappropriate nested parentheses. For example, suppose (a b c d e f g) was input, when the appropriate input was (a b c (d e f) g). Parentheses can not be inserted using any of the insert commands discussed above. The error could, of course, be corrected by *replacing* or by *deleting* and *inserting*, but there is an easier way to do this in Lispedit: the **wrap** command, which embeds list objects in another level of list structure, can be used. In the above example, we can move the focus to d and type:

```
wrap 3
```

The result will be the desired (a b c (d e f) g). Note that three items, starting with "d", where the focus was, are combined into a new sublist within the original list. Let us take another example. Suppose that, in defining **transfer** (Example (3.5) in Section 3.6), the word **cond** was omitted, and the following was input:

```
(lambda (sentence)
        ((null sentence) nil)
        ('t (cons ((search (car sentence) dictionary)
                (transfer (cdr sentence))))))
```

It would require a lot of work to correct the omission without the use of the **wrap** command. However, using **wrap**, the process would be quite simple. With the focus on the list ((null sentence) nil), all that needs to be done is to input:

```
wrap 2 cond
```

Lispedit would take **cond** and the two sublists, starting with the focus, and create a new list, so that the following will result:

```
(lambda (sentence)
        (cond ((null sentence) nil)
                ('t (cons ((search (car sentence)
                                dictionary)
                        (transfer (cdr sentence)))))))
```

Note the additional closing parenthesis added at the end to balance the new parenthesis in front of **cond**.

The **wrap** command wraps one or more items into a list. It can also insert items at the head of a list. On the other hand, the **flatten** command removes a level of list structure from the focus. Thus, given a list ((a b c) ((d e) f g) h), with the focus on (d e), the **flatten** command will result in the following list ((a b c) (d e f g) h) with the focus on (d e f g). Additional information on these two commands is given in the following paragraphs.

wrap (w, wr, fof): The command **wr** may be followed by a number, "n", and by other expressions. "n" items, starting with the focus, will be formed into a list and the expressions following the "n" in the command, if any, will be inserted at the head of the list. If "n" is negative, the items to be wrapped start from the focus and go left. If "n" is *, then the focus and all items to the right of the focus at the same level are wrapped. If "n" is −*, then the focus and all items to its left at the same level are wrapped. Examples:

Given the list ((a b) (c (d e f) g)) with the focus on c:

wr 2 bird $\Rightarrow$ ((a b) (bird c (d e f)) g)) with the focus of (bird c (d e f)). If the focus is moved to e, the following result can be obtained:

$$\text{wr } -* ==) \text{ ((a b) ((bird c ((de) f)) g)).}$$

flatten (fl): The command **fl** cannot be followed by any other expression. This command is only effective when the focus is at a sublist of another list. It removes one level of list structure and the items in the focus become elements of the list that contained the focus. The new focus is on the first element of the flattened list. Example:

```
Given the list ((a b) (c (d e f)) g)
   with the focus on (d e f):
fl ==) ((a b) (c d e f) g) with the focus on c.
```

3.7 EDITING IN COMMON LISP

All of the operations that have been discussed so far in this chapter for the editing facility of Lispvm (Lispedit) are available in Common Lisp. However, as mentioned before, many of the procedures are simpler in Common Lisp, because in the 'edit mode' of Common Lisp the cursor can be moved into the body of expressions or programs and do deletion, insertion, replacement, change, wrap, flatten, and so forth the same as is done in word processing. To develop an example, we will first define two terms frequently encountered in GCLisp (Golden Common Lisp): *Keychord* refers to a series of keys on the keyboard, which must be pressed simultaneously; for example, the instruction to press Ctrl and *C* keys together is given as keychord Ctrl-C; other examples are Ctrl-E, Alt-A, etc. *Key sequence* refers to a sequence of keys or keychords that must be pressed one after another; for example: *Ctrl-X K*; *Ctrl-X Ctrl-E;* etc.

For a demonstration of editing facilities in Common Lisp, a simple database of information (the so-called knowledge base) about a toy block world will be developed. Figure 3.3 is an example of a toy block world, consisting of various toy blocks of various sizes, shapes, colors, etc.

A Lisp program, consisting of several functions, can be produced for adding data to the block world and answering questions about them. We will develop this program in the edit mode (see Appendix A). At the C:\GCLISP> prompt, enter *gmacs* to get into the Common Lisp editor. A *buffer* must then be allocated to develop, test, and eventually save the program in some permanent memory.

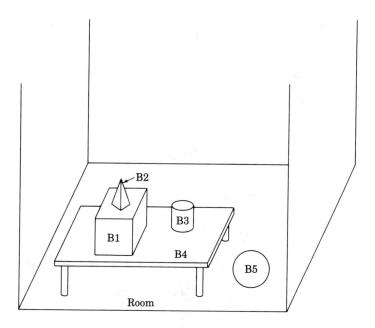

Figure 3.3. A block world.

This buffer must have a name, and the same name can be used for the file in which the data is saved. The process is similar to the Indexed File discussed for Lispvm in Section 3.3. The command (ed "play") will allocate the buffer with the name PLAY. To repeat, the following sequence of commands will provide for logging into the editor and allocating the buffer, which will appear on the terminal screen as in Figure 3.4:

```
C:\GCLISP)_ gmacs
[messages . . . ]
Top-Level
*_ (ed "play")
```

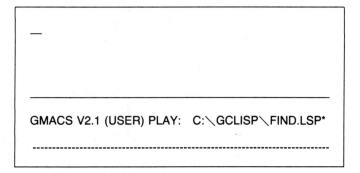

Figure 3.4. The editing buffer named PLAY. The empty space in the bottom is the message area and also echoes the edit commands.

Imagine now that all of the following material is developed within the top frame of Figure 3.4. This example will start with a database for the blocks by entering data in predicate calculus formulas (this format is, of course, entirely optional—there are various other ways to represent the data); for example, (in x y) denotes that x is in y, (shape x w) denotes that x has the shape of w, (isa x z) denotes that x is a z, and so forth.

```
(setq dbase1 '((color b1 red)(shape b1 cube)
  (on b1 table)(under b1 b2)(over b2 b1)
  (shape b2 prism)(color b2 blue)(size b2 small)          (3.7)
  (isa b4 table)(in b4 room)(size b4 large)
  (shape b3 cylinder)(on b3 table)(color b3 black)
  (left-of b1 b3)(color b5 maroon)(shape b5 sphere)
  (on b5 floor)))
```

The following functions will apply to the above database:

```
(defun show (query)                                       (3.8)
  (match query dbase1))
```

```
(defun match (x dbase)
  (cond ((null dbase) nil)
        ((and
          (or (equal (car x) '?)
              (equal (car x)(caar dbase)))               (3.9)
          (or (equal (cadr x) '?)
              (equal (cadr x)(cadar dbase)))
          (or (equal (caddr x) '?)
              (equal (last x) (last (car dbase))))))
        (cons (car dbase)(match x (cdr dbase))))
        (t (match x (cdr dbase))))))
```

The argument for **show** will be a triplet with a question mark in any one or all of the positions. It will then call **match** with the triplet and the DBASE1 in Example (3.7) as its arguments. **match** will find the matching triplet in dBASE1 and output it; so that the **query** triplet (on ? table) asks what objects are on the table and gets the right answer. Example (3.10) shows some computer input and output for the above exercise.

```
(show '(color b1 ?)) ==> ((COLOR B1 RED))
(show '(left-of b1 ?)) ==> ((LEFT-OF B1 B3))

(show '(color ? red)) ==> ((COLOR B1 RED))
(show '(shape ? ?)) ==>                                    (3.10)
        ((SHAPE B1 CUBE)(SHAPE B2 PRISM)
         (SHAPE B3 CYLINDER)(SHAPE B5 SPHERE))
(show '(? ? ?)) ==> [will output the entire DBASE1]
```

If Examples (3.7) through (3.9) were done within the framework of the buffer PLAY, any changes or corrections could be made by simply moving the cursor to the point of change and making insertions, deletions, or other changes. For example, to add some additional formulas to the database in Example (3.7), move the cursor to the last line in the text and delete the last two parentheses by pressing the *BACKSPACE* key. Input (isa b6 box1) (in b7 box1), and then replace the two parentheses (the cursor could also have been moved to the next to the last parenthesis and the new text inserted without deleting and retyping parentheses). When data entry into edit buffer is finished and every time changes are made in the data the buffer must be saved. The data can be saved at any time in the edit mode by pressing the *F9* key. As mentioned before, a file with the same name as the name of the buffer will be saved in the permanent storage. The data in the saved file, PLAY, can be retrieved for processing or further editing. Programs in the edit mode are not in the interactive or interpretive mode, and do not evaluate and produce results. To run a program, one must exit the edit mode by pressing *F1*. The program must then be loaded by inputting, for example, (load "play"). The functions can then be called in the standard way, for example, (show '(on ? table)). However, there is also a way of evaluating a program (to make sure that it contains no errors) without exiting the editor: When the cursor is in the range of an expression, if the key sequence Ctrl-X Ctrl-E is pressed, the expression will be evaluated without leaving the editor.

Table 3.2 contains a summary of the editing commands discussed above.

A stored file can be deleted under the DOS environement. If the installation set up is as assumed in Appendix A, at the DOS prompt C:\GCLISP> the following can be entered:

```
erase <file-name>
```

Within Common Lisp, there are three useful system functions for file handling: **delete-file**, **probe-file**, and **rename-file**. The argument for each of these is the same <filename.filetype>. In DOS, filetype is an arbitrary three-character symbol, which is optional; for example, the file name for the manuscript of this chapter

TABLE 3.2. EDITING COMMANDS UNDER GMACS

Operation	Command
To create a new buffer and file	(ed "⟨file-name⟩")
To evaluate a current function	Ctrl-X Ctrl-E
To evaluate an expression to the right of the cursor	Esc !
To save the buffer (file)	Ctrl-X Ctrl-S or *F9*
To exit the editor	Ctrl-X Ctrl-C or *F1*
To return to the buffer	Ctrl-E
To kill a buffer	Ctrl-X K
To load a file in the interpretive mode	(load "⟨file-name⟩")
To edit an existing file	(ed "⟨file-name⟩")

is Lisp3.msc. In Common Lisp, filetype .lsp is the default value assigned by the system to all file (buffer) names, so that the following three forms

```
(probe-file  'play.lsp)
(rename-file  'play.lsp  'foo.xyz)
(delete-file  'foo.xyz)
```

in the sequence given, will first confirm that the PLAY file, created above, exists; it will then rename it to FOO.XYZ; and finally it will delete the file!

There are many more important and interesting editing commands in GMACS. Some of these will be encountered later, but the full list and descriptions are clearly enunciated in the GCLisp manual. The above is enough to give the reader some appreciation of editing facilities in Common Lisp. In Chapter 5, Section 5.13, further details about file handling directly under Common Lisp will be discussed.

Before leaving this section, as an exercise, type and store the following functions as "utility programs" in our PLAY file. Note, incidentally, that the following functions, as well as those already in the PLAY file, are not system-dependent, and can run under any modern Lisp dialect. Example (3.11) is a predicate function that returns T if a given triplet is in a database, and returns NIL if it is not.

```
(defun matchp (x dbase)
   (cond ((null dbase) nil)
         ((and (equal (car x)(caar dbase))
               (equal (cadr x)(cadar dbase))                (3.11)
               (equal (last x)(last(car dbase)))))
          t)
         (t (matchp x (cdr dbase)))))
```

```
(defun add-dbase (item dlist)
   (cond ((matchp item dlist)      ;Uses MATCHP to test    (3.12)
           'already-there)          ;Item is there, stop
         (t (adjoin item dlist))))  ;Add to database
```

Note: In Lispvm, instead of **adjoin** in Example (3.12) we can use **append** which will work in all dialects. Examples:

```
(add-dbase '(a b c) '((e f g)(a b c)(k l m)))
   ALREADY-THERE
(add-dbase '(a b c) '((e f g)(k l m)))
   ((A B C)(E F G)(K L M))
```

Recall that in Common Lisp **adjoin** will add an item to a list if the item is not there, but it would not work for our purposes. Examples:

```
(adjoin 'a '(b c a d)) ==> (B C A D)
(adjoin 'a '(b c d)) ==> (A B C D)
```

```
(adjoin 'a '((a b c)(e f g))) ==) (A (A B C)(E F G))
(adjoin '(a b c) '((a b c)(d e f)))
                        ==) ((A B C)(A B C)(D E F))
```

Hence the new function **add-dbase**.

3.8 INPUT/OUTPUT COMMANDS AND PROCEDURES

We have already seen the use of **read** and **print** as input/output forms in Lisp. A Lisp programmer can live with these two forms for all of his/her needs, but there are other forms and functions that make life more interesting or easier. In this section we will give some variations of these commands as well as a few other input/output (I/O) procedures. Additional details for the I/O procedures will be given in Chapter 5.

3.8.1 Output

To observe the variations in print functions, consider the following cumbersome and clumsy function, which nevertheless demonstrates the various printing forms.

```
(defun print-commands (x y z)
  (prog ()
  tag1  (cond ((zerop x) (go tag2))
              (t (print 'hello)
                 (setq x (- x 1)) (go tag1)))
  tag2  (cond ((zerop y) (go tag3))
              (t (prin1 'goodbye)
                 (setq y (- y 1)) (go tag2)))         (3.13)
  tag3  (cond ((zerop z) (terpri) nil)
              (t (princ 'thanks)
                 (setq z (- z 1)) (go tag3)))))
```

Now, if (print-commands 3 3 3) is input, the following output will appear:

```
HELLO
HELLO
HELLO
HELLOGOODBYEGOODBYEGOODBYETHANKSTHANKSTHANKS

NIL
```

The (terpri) form in Example (3.13) causes a move to a new print line or the insertion of a blank line, so that in the above output NIL appears two lines below the previous line. If (terpri) is inserted in the line beginning with tag1 between (zerop x) and (go tag2), and a similar one in the line beginning with tag2, the output will look like this:

```
HELLO
HELLO
HELLO
GOODBYEGOODBYEGOODBYE
THANKSTHANKSTHANKS

NTI
```

We have seen three forms of print primitives: **print**, **prin1**, and **princ**. These print forms take a single argument. In **print**, when the argument is printed, a 'new-line', like a carriage-return in typewriter, is executed. In the other two, as can be seen from the above outputs, there are no returns and no spaces between the repeated outputs. Of course, if there are spaces in the body of the single argument, they will be preserved. For example, if the argument for a **princ** form is "This is a message" and the function requires it to be printed twice, the output will be:

This is a messageThis is a message

But there are other differences as well between the three print forms. The following example demonstrates these:

```
(defun print-commands2 ( )
    (print "This is message ONE")
    (print '(This is message TWO))
    (terpri)
    (prin1 "This is message THREE")
    (terpri)
    (prin1 '(This is message FOUR))
    (terpri)
    (princ "This is message FIVE")
    (terpri)
    (princ '(This is message SIX))
    (terpri nil) )
```
(3.14)

The output of Example (3.14) is the following:

```
"This is message ONE"
(THIS IS MESSAGE TWO)
"This is message THREE"
(THIS IS MESSAGE FOUR)
This is message FIVE
(THIS IS MESSAGE SIX)

NIL
```

Note the differences in the preservation of parentheses, preservation or discarding of quote marks, and capitalization.

The above examples for print forms are for Common Lisp, Lispvm, and other dialects have similar forms, but the names may vary. For example, in Lispvm **print** behaves pretty much the same as in Common Lisp, but the other two are called **prin0** (with zero at the end, not letter oh) and **prinm**. If a function to print *hello* three times is written, the output for these three forms would be the following:

```
Print:   HELLO
         HELLO
         HELLO
Prin0:   HELLO HELLO HELLO
Prinm:   HELLOHELLOHELLO
```

Note that **prin0** inserts a space between each argument of repeated printing. **prinm** does not print the top level parentheses:

```
(print '(type a sentence)) ==) (TYPE A SENTENCE)
(prinm '(type a sentence)) ==) TYPE A SENTENCE
```

Actually, if any of the print forms are used independently, as in the above examples, the argument is printed twice. (See Section 3.8.2 for explanation.)

We have already seen that **terpri** causes a "line break or 'carriage return' in printing. It can also be used for printing double-spaced lines, as the printing of NIL in the output of Example (3.14). **terpri** has another important function in clearing printing buffers. When any of the print forms is executed, its argument is collected in a buffer before the message is displayed on the screen. In some dialects, the argument is not cleared from the buffer regularly. For example, if a print function using **print** is written and run, and then the editor is used to change the form **print** to, say, **prinm**, and run it with the same data, we may not get the expected output. The use of **terpri** in a printing function will clear the buffer before each collection.

Another print form that has been mentioned is **prettyprint** in Lispvm for displaying functions in an indented format for ease of reading and understanding. Unfortunately, **prettyprint** does not have the same name in all dialects (**prettyprint**, **pp**, **pprint**, etc.). In the Common Lisp dialect that has been discussed in this chapter (GCLisp), **pprint** is used in the manner demonstrated in the following examples.

```
(a) (setq text '((You should guard
      against errors)(The hole gushed with water)
      (The girl wants to make herself known to you)
      (I marvel at your patience)(This is a job well done)     (3.15)
      (His life is full of woes)(This cellar is full of
      water) ) )
```

```
(b)  (defun phrase-finder (p tx)          ;preliminary
                                          ;version
      (cond ((null tx) nil)
            ((not (null (intersection p (car tx))))
                  (cons (car tx)(phrase-finder p (cdr tx))))
            (t (phrase-finder p (cdr tx)))))
```

```
(c)  (phrase-finder '(gushed with) text)
```

```
 ==> (THE HOLE GUSHED WITH WATER)
     (phrase-finder '(job well done) text)
 ==> (THIS IS A JOB WELL DONE)
     (phrase-finder '(full of) text)
==> ((HIS LIFE IS FULL OF WOES)(THIS CELLAR IS FULL OF WATER))
     (phrase-finder '(hammer at) text)
==> NIL
```

```
(d)  (pprint 'text) ==> ((YOU SHOULD GUARD AGAINST  ERRORS)(THE
HOLE GUSHED WITH WATER)(THE GIRL WANTS TO MAKE  HERSELF KNOWN TO
YOU)(I MARVEL AT YOUR PATIENCE)(THIS IS A  JOB WELL DONE)(HIS
LIFE IS FULL OF WOES)(THIS CELLAR IS FULL  OF WATER))
```

```
     (pprint 'phrase-finder) ==> PHRASE-FINDER
     (pprint phrase-finder) ==> Error
```

```
     (pprint (symbol-function 'phrase-finder)
        (LAMBDA (P TX)
          (COND ((NULL TX)
            NIL)
          ((NOT (NULL (INTERSECTION P (CAR TX))))
          (CONS (CAR TX) (PHRASE-FINDER P (CDR TX))))
          (T
          (PHRASE-FINDER P (CDR TX)))
          ))
```

The function **phrase-finder** in Example (3.15) calls on the logical operator **intersection** (see Section 2.7). Recall that **intersection** returns a set (list) consisting of common elements of two sets. The reader may have noticed that the use of **intersection** in the context of **phrase-finder** has some problems. The most serious one is that the function will return a sentence even if only one word of the phrase matches with one word of the sentence, so that it is not an accurate search for finding sentences containing a whole phrase and only those. This can be improved upon by adding another conditional expression to the function asserting that the output of the intersection of the phrase with the sentence is identical to the input phrase.

The output of a print form is normally displayed on the screen of the terminal.

To print a copy of anything displayed on the screen, use the *PRINT-SCREEN* key on the keyboard (*SHIFT-PRTSC* on some keyboards). Under DOS, a file can be printed on the printer with the command C:\>print <file-name> >pt1 (provided that the printer is attached to the appropriate port); for example, C:\> print play>pt1. If connected to a mainframe, there are procedures for sending files to the central printer, but the procedures are dependent on the set up at the computer center.

In addition to **terpri**, Lispvm has a form called **skip**, which inserts a blank line after the current print line. The form **skip** can be followed by an integer; for example (skip 5) will insert five blank lines before the next printing is done.

3.8.2 Input

We have encountered several examples of **read**. Recall that it causes a pause, waiting for data to be input, read, and processed. Another example is given here to complete this section. The example is the following simple exercise: Given a sentence in a simple progressive form in English, write a function that will produce the negation of that sentence. For example, if the sentence is *I was listening to the lecture.* The function should turn it to *I was not listening to the lecture.* Recall that printing forms can take only one argument; the following function shows one way of combining several pieces of data into one argument for print.

```
(defun negation nil     ;preliminary version
   (princ "Please enter a progressive
              sentence, enclosed in parentheses")
   (terpri)            ;skip a line
   (setq sentence (read))         ;pause to enter         (3.16)
      (print (append (list (car sentence))
                     (list (cadr sentence))
                     '(not)
                     (cddr sentence)))
   (terpri nil))
```

The following interaction can then be recorded:

```
(negation)           ;input
   Please enter a progressive sentence,
           enclosed in parentheses    ;output [pause]        (3.17)
   (You were listening to the concert)        ;input
      (YOU WERE NOT LISTENING TO THE CONCERT)     ;output
      NIL               ;output
```

It will be seen later that there are more elegant and realistic ways of writing the function in Example (3.16). For example, a search can be done through the sentence to find any form of the verb *to be* (is, are, was, were, etc.) anywhere (instead of only in the second position), and then to insert *not* after it. However, there are a few points of interest in Example (3.16) that are worth reviewing.

The use of **princ** with double quotes for the message allows the message to be printed in upper-lower, or mixed, case without quote marks or parentheses. This message, instructing the user to type a sentence, is called a *prompt*. When using the **read** form, the computer pauses for input, but the screen is blank. It is a good practice to use a prompt, telling the user what is expected to be done. The output of the function, however, will come out in capitals enclosed in parentheses irrespective of what print form is used, because that is the output from the **append** form.

In Section 3.8.1, it was stated that, if you use a print form not embedded in a function, its argument will be displayed twice. The situation is a bit more complex: In Example (3.16), if you omit the last line, (terpri nil), the output (e.g., YOU WERE NOT LISTENING TO THE CONCERT) will also be displayed twice. When a function is run, it evaluates to a value that becomes the value of the function. For example, when NEGATION is run, it will display the output as required by the print command. However, the value of the function is the result of the **append** form, which is also displayed, so that the output is displayed twice. By inserting NIL at the same level as the function definition, we make the final value of the function NIL, which will be displayed. The form **terpri** causes this NIL to be displayed below the output of **print**, which is of main interest in this function. This is also one of the reasons that, in functions containing conditional expressions, such expressions as ((zerop x) nil), ((null y) nil), and so forth are written. These expressions simply say that, when the work of the function is completed, its value is NIL. This will avoid the displaying of other confusing messages.

There are other input forms that are more implement-dependent. One that is common in most versions of Common Lisp is the use of the pound-sign (or sharp-sign), #, for a conversion of data in reading. For example, #b1101 will be read as binary (base 2) number 1101, and converted into decimal (base 10) 13; #\a may be converted into the numeric representation (ASCII code) of character a. Table 3.3 contains some further examples.

TABLE 3.3. EXAMPLES OF USES OF #

Input	Output	Remarks
'#\a	97 or "a"	depending on implementation
'#\b	98 or "b"	
'#b1010	10	binary 1010 = decimal 10
'#o12	10	Octal (base 8) 12 = decimal 10
'#xa	10	hexadecimal (base 16) a = decimal 10

(See Chapter 5 for further details.)

3.8.3 Formatting

The form **format** is a system function in Common Lisp and several other dialects of Lisp, which allows the output to be formatted in various ways. The general syntax of the **format** function is:

$$(\text{format } \langle \text{destination} \rangle \ \langle \text{format string} \rangle \ \langle \text{arguments} \rangle) \qquad (3.18)$$

In Lisp, a *string* is a character string in double quotes. For example, "This is a string" but (This is a list). A simple application of **format** is to use it as a printing command to display a string without any arguments, examples:

```
(format t "A simple string")==)A simple string
(format nil "A simple string") ==)                    (3.19)
"A simple string"
```

As the instances in Example (3.19) show, if the value of the *destination* is "t", the format string is displayed on the same line without quotations, but the format function will evaluate to nil. If the value of destination is nil, the string is displayed on the next line with quotations, but the function will evaluate to the value of the string. Consider the following examples:

```
(setq x (format t "Test"))==)Test NIL
       x ==) NIL

(setq y (format nil "test"))

       ==) "Test"
     y ==) "Test"
```

The *destination* characters direct the output to a *stream*, which could be the standard input-output streams, as in the above examples, but it could also be directed, for example, to a destination specified by the user. An illustration will be given for the latter in Example (3.20), without any further explanation for the present (see Chapter 5 for more details).

```
(setq my-output (make-string-output-stream))
    (format my-output "John") ==) NIL
    (format my-output " and Mary") ==) NIL                (3.20)
    (format my-output " are contrary!") ==) NIL
    (get-output-stream-string my-output)
        ==) "John and Mary are contrary!"
```

In addition, there are special format *directives* that can be inserted in the format string. These directives consist of a tilde (˜) followed by a special character. The most common among these are ˜a and ˜s (as usual, a and s could be in capitals

TABLE 3.4. COMMON FORMAT DIRECTIVES IN LISP

Name	Utility
ˉa	Prints argument without escape character
ˉs	Prints argument with escape character
ˉ%	Break line (can generate blank lines)
ˉ&	Start a new line, unless already at a new line
ˉb	Converts input to a binary number
ˉd	Converts input to a decimal number
ˉo	Converts input to an octal number
ˉx	Converts input to a hexadecimal number

or lower case). These two directives act somewhat like variables, which can be replaced by the arguments of the function. For the present purposes, ˉa and ˉs are interchangeable. In general, however, ˉs can be thought of as outputting, as in **prin1**, whereas ˉa prints as in **princ**. Examples:

```
(format nil "~s took ~s to ~s." 'john 'mary 'lunch)
   ==) "JOHN took MARY to LUNCH."

(format t "~s loves ~a" 'john 'mary)JOHN loves MARY
NIL
```

In Table 3.4 a list of some of the directives discussed in this book are given.

In Example (3.21) various examples for the use of the directives in Table 3.4 are given.

```
(a)  (format t "~& Both ~s and ~s love ~s, ~%
          but ~s loves only ~s." 'fred 'mike 'july
             'july 'fred)
   ==)  Both FRED and MIKE love JULY,
        but JULY loves only FRED.

(b)  (format nil "~d is ~b in binary, ~o in octal,        (3.21)
          and ~x in hexadecimal numbers. ~% So there!"
          125 125 125 125)
   ==) "125 is 1111101 in binary, 175 in octal, and
          7D in hexadecimal numbers.
      So there!"
   (format nil "~d" #b1111101)
 ==)"125"
```

(c) The following format will insert an error message in
a function.

```
(defun doubling (x)
    (cond ((numberp x) (* 2 x))
          (t (format nil "~a is not a number" x))))
```

(d) The following assignment expression and function can be
used to print a roster of student names and courses in a
desired format.

```
(setq roster '((aeschylus drama)(einstein math)(newton physics)
               (carter archeology)(bach music)))


(defun record (L)
    (cond ((null L) nil)
          (t (format t "~& Student Name:   ~a ~%   Course: ~a"
               (caar L) (cadar L))
             (record (cdr L)))))
          (record roster) ==>
          Student Name:    AESCHYLUS
                Course:    DRAMA
          Student Name:    EINSTEIN
                Course:    MATH
          Student Name:    NEWTON
                Course:    PHYSICS
          Student Name:    CARTER
                Course:    ARCHEOLOGY
          Student Name:    BACH
                Course:    MUSIC
```

Note the spaces in the format statement in the **record** function. The spaces are
measured to provide the output in the above format. There is a ¯t *format direc-
tive* in Lisp which, if implemented, can enable the user to specify the number of
spaces between output columns for alignment purposes.

For another exercise, consider the following Lisp program to solve the intri-
guing problem of the *Tower of Hanoi*, with a **format** function to print the solution.
The game consists of a board with three pins and a number of disks piled on the
first pin (see Figure 3.5). The charge is to move the disks from the first pin to
the second pin, using the third pin as a spare for temporary holding. What makes
the task difficult is the following provisions:

1. The disks are all of different sizes and they are initially arranged on
   the first pin so that no bigger disk is on the top of a smaller disk.
2. Only one disk can be moved at a time and no bigger disk must ever
   be placed on the top of a smaller disk.

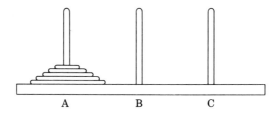

Figure 3.5. The Tower of Hanoi Game.

It is said that in some ancient times a group of monks set about to play this game with 64 disks on the first pin. According to their legend, when the succession of monks succeed in completing the game, the universe will come to an end. Estimated calculations show that the time required for this task, assuming that the monks work in nonstop relays, is way over 500 billion years. So there is no immediate danger of catastrophy for us mortals!

In the following solution, the pins are labeled A, B, and C; with the disks initially on pin A to be moved to pin B. The disks will be numbered, with 1 for the smallest on top and some number "n" for the largest at the bottom. If there were only two disks, the solution would be trivial:

> Move 1 from A to C
> Move 2 from A to B
> Move 1 from C to B

We want to solve this for any arbitrary "n" disks. A program for solving this can be written with the functions that have already been discussed, but the solution will be more elegant if we use two new system functions: **if** and **progn**.

The function **if** is a conditional function like **cond**, but it is more restricted. Its general format is

$$(\text{if} \ \langle\text{test}\rangle \ \langle\text{then}\rangle \ \langle\text{else}\rangle).$$

The test is boolean; it returns either true or false (non-nil or nil), the then-clause can be any Lisp expression, and the else-clause is optional. Examples:

```
(a)  (if() 5 3) 5) ==> 5
(b)  (if (equal x 'male) 'male 'female)          (3.22)
(c)  (defun type-finder (x)
          (if (oddp x) 'odd 'even))
```

The function **progn** can be followed by a number of expressions. The expressions will be evaluated, but the value of **progn** will be the value of the last expression. The other evaluations are done for the side effects. Examples:

```
(a)  (progn (+ 5 6) (* 2 3) (- 4 2)) ==> 2
(b)  (progn (setq x 5) x (setq y (1+ x)) (setq z (1+ y))) ==> 7
```
(3.23)

```
   x ==> 5    y ==> 6    z ==> 7
```

We can now begin working on the Tower of Hanoi problem:

```
(a)   (defun tower-of-hanoi (n)        ;n is the number
                                       ;of disks

         (hanoi n 'a 'b 'c))

(b)   (defun hanoi (n from to spare)
         (if (= n 1) (move-disk 1 from to)
                (progn                                (3.24)
                   (hanoi (- n 1) from spare to)
                   (move-disk n from to)
                   (hanoi (- n 1) spare to from))))

(c)   (defun move-disk (disk from to)
         (format t "~& Move disk ~a from ~a to ~a."
                disk from to))
```

There are three functions in example (3.24). The first one in (a) has the parameter "n," which will be bound with the number of disks in the function call. This function calls the second function, called **hanoi**, with the arguments "n" and the names of the pins A, B, and C. The function **hanoi** in (b) has four parameters "n," which will be bound by the *number* of disks; and *from, to,* and *spare,* which are variables, and will be bound to the pins A, B, or C in the evaluation of the clauses in **progn**. The function **hanoi**, in turn, calls the function **move-disk** in (c). This function prints the moves of the disks, which are the solution to the problem. Thus, to solve the problem for three disk, The function can be called with the argument 3.

```
(tower-of-hanoi 3)
    ==>  Move disk 1 from A to B.
         Move disk 2 from A to C.
         Move disk 1 from B to C.
         Move disk 3 from A to B.
         Move disk 1 from C to A.
         Move disk 2 from C to B.
         Move disk 1 from A to B.
         NIL
```

3.9 EXERCISES

1.   We have seen that dialects may use different names and procedures for pretty-printing. Write a function for dialects that use **pprint** to be able to use **prettyprint** also, with the same results.

2.   Write a function for dialects that use **prettyprint** to use **pprint** also.

3.   Create a database containing records of information about automobiles: license number, color, make, owner, etc. Then write a function or functions that retrieve information from this database. For example, given the license number, the name and address of the owner should be retrieved. Make the project as elaborate and comprehensive as you can.

4.   Prove that the following formula represents all natural numbers (quoted by Penrose, 1989, p. 71):

$$1/2((a + b)^2 + 3a + b)$$

5.   Write a function to add a list of numbers. But check every element in the list; if an element is not a number, issue a warning message and skip over it.

3.10 DEBUGGING LISP FUNCTIONS

There are two types of errors for a computer program, which may be referred to as *syntactic* and *logical*. Syntactic errors occur in Lisp when an expression is input in a way that violates the structure or rules of the language. For example, (5 a b c) will produce an error message, because it violates the rule that an expression must either begin with a quote mark to indicate data, or the first symbol following the open parenthesis must be a function name. The number 5 is not a function name. The so-called logical error is more difficult to detect, because the program may run and produce a result without any error message, but the result may not be what was expected. For example, if a function to add the elements in a list of numbers is called with the argument '(5 3 4), but got 0 as output, there is obviously something wrong with the function.

In this Section, both of these error types will be reviewed, and procedures provided in the editing facility of Lisp for detecting and correcting these errors will be discussed. Like all editing operations, error analysis and correction are dependent on the particular implementation of a dialect. However, what is presented here is the basic approach and principles that prevail in all modern Lisp dialects. For illustration and convenience of exposition, we will again explain some details of the facilities in Golden Common Lisp and in Lispvm, as representatives of Common Lisp and "Uncommon" Lisp dialects. However, even between these two specific implementations there are overlaps and common procedures, which make the differences superficial and terminological variations.

Recall that the activity of Lisp consists of going through a continuous cycle of reading expression, evaluating them, and ouputting the values or results. This is the read-eval-print loop mentioned before, and it occurs at the top level of Lisp operation. If an error occurs in an evaluation, control moves to another level of read-eval-print, which is called the break-level or error-loop. Lisp systems have many error levels, so that if another error is made at one error level, control moves to the next error level. In most dialects, the levels are numbered. The top-level is level 0 and other succeeding levels as 1, 2, ... In the following series of illustrations, it will be assumed that the prompt for Common Lisp at the top level is * with a blinking — for the cursor and, as you move into break or error loops, the prompt becomes 1>, 2>, . . .

```
      Top-Level
  *   (defun foo (n a b)
          (cond ((zerop n) nil)
             (t (incf a) (incf b) (setq x (+ a b))
                               (print (list n a b x))
             (foo (decf n) a b))))                    (3.25)
      FOO
  *_
```

```
      (foo 5 3 2)
          (5 4 3 7)
          (4 5 4 9)
          (3 6 5 11)                                  (3.26)
          (2 7 6 13)
          (1 8 7 15)
          NIL
```

Now let us call **foo** with a wrong number of arguments:

```
  *  (foo 3 2)
  ERROR: Not enough arguments for the function: FOO

  1)  (foo 5 3 2 4)
  ERROR: Too many arguments for the function: FOO

  2)  (my-foo 5 3 2)
  ERROR: Undefined function: MY-FOO

  3)  (Ctrl-C)
  Top-Level
  *_
```

The jumping from Top-Level to levels 1, 2, and 3 is called a *break*. At level 3, we pressed the control (Ctrl) and *C* keys together, where the control jumped back to the top level. A break occurs every time an error is encountered, but the user can also cause a break by inputting the function (break). In Example (3.27), a **break** expression with a **format** message is inserted in the **foo** function.

```
        Top-Level
    *   (defun foo2 (n a b)
          (cond ((zerop n) nil)
                (t (incf a)(incf b)(setq x (+ a b))            (3.27)
          (break "pause with a = ~s, b = ~s, x = ~s, and n = ~s"
                              a b x n)
                (foo2 (decf n) a b))))
        F002
```

Now if **foo2** is called, the following interaction can take place; demonstrating the processing of **foo2** in each cycle of its evaluation.

```
        (foo2 6 4 3)
        Pause with a = 5, b = 4, x = 9, and n = 6
        1) (contniue)
        Pause with a = 6, b = 5, x = 11, and n = 5
        1) (continue)                                          (3.28)
        Pause with a = 7, b = 6, x = 13, and n = 4
            :

            :
        Pause with a = 10, b = 9, x = 19, and  n = 1
        NIL
```

Note that, in every break loop in which (continue) is input, the next cycle is evaluated. Note further that in Examples (3.25) and (3.27) the system functions **incf** and **decf** have been used, which add one or subtruct one from their arguments, respectively. The functions **incf** and **decf** are macros (see Chapter 5 for more details), which can be thought of as miniprograms that generate codes into another program at the time of execution. Thus, in Common Lisp, (incf a) and (defc n) expand to their underlying structures (SETQ A (1+ A)) and (SETQ N (1− N)), respectively. Let us now replace **incf** and **decf** in Example (3.25) as in the following illustration:

```
        (defun foo3 (n a b)
          (cond ((zerop n) nil)
                (t (+ a 1) (+ b 1) (setq x (+ a b))            (3.29)
                  (print (list n a b x))
                  (foo3 (- n 1) a b))))
        F003
```

Now, if FOO3 is called with arguments (5 3 2), the following will appear:

```
(foo3 5 3 2)
(5 3 2 5)
(4 3 2 5)
(3 3 2 5)
(2 3 2 5)
(1 3 2 5)
NIL
```

(3.30)

No error message is received, but the output is perhaps not what was expected. The program in Example (3.29) has what is called a "logical error." Logical errors will be discussed presently, but let us first consider other ways of tracing or stepping through a program to follow its processing.

3.10.1 Trace

The function **trace** actually traces through a program and displays the input and output for each expression in the program. Thus, if any expression has an error, the error would be localized and easily detectable. The format of **trace** is (trace <function name>). This will return "T." The function can then be called with some arguments to examine the steps in its evaluation. Once a function is **traced**, it remains traced for the duration of the session, so that you can try it with different arguments, make changes and corrections and try again, and so forth. When finished, the function can be **untraced** by inputting (untrace <function name>). If (untrace) is used without giving a function name, all traced functions will be untraced.

Examples:

```
* (trace *)      ;; traces the function *
  T
* (+ (/ 6 2) (* 3 (- 10 (* 3 2)))))        ;input
  ENTERING: *, ARGUMENT LIST: (3 2)      ;output
  Exiting: *, VALUE: 6
  ENTERING: *, ARGUMENT LIST: (3 4)       ;(- 10(* 3 2))=4
  EXITING: *, VALUE: 12
  15.0                       ;value of the entire function
* (untrace *)
  (*)

*_
```

(3.31)

In Example (3.31), there were two instances of the * (multiplication) function; they were traced, and then the value of the evaluation of the entire expression was printed. You can now trace any of the **foo** functions in Examples (3.25) through (3.29) and observe their evaluation.

3.10.2 Step

Another procedure that visually demonstrates the processing of a function is **step**. The format of the **step** function is:

$$(step \ (\langle function \ name \rangle \ \langle argument\text{-}1 \rangle \ ... \ \langle argument\text{-}n \rangle))$$

When you call the **step** function, the arrow keys on the keyboard can be used to go forward, backward, left, and right in 'small' or 'large' steps in the processing of the function, which is the argument of **step**. In the following example, only the down arrow will be used to move from one step to another. Thus, every line in the example is printed as a result of pressing the down arrow once. The reader is urged to try this with a more complex function (for instance, **foo** in Example (3.25)), using all four of the arrow keys to appreciate the working of this function. (Of course, all dialects do not use arrows for movement, but the process is the same whether you have to use arrows, function keys, or spell out commands).

```
*  (step (+ 5 (* 6 5)))          ;input
(+  5 (*  6  5))                    ↓
    5                               ↓
      5 = 5                         ↓
      (*  6 5)                      ↓
      6                             ↓
        6 = 6                       ↓          (3.32)
      5                             ↓
        5 = 5                       ↓
      (*  6 5) = 30                 ↓
    (+  5 (*  6 5)) = 35            ↓
  35                                ↓
  *  _
```

3.10.3 Debugging in Lispvm

Lispvm and other similar dialects have tracing and stepping functions containing much the same procedures as discussed earlier for Common Lisp. The differences may be in terminology or the use of particular keys on the keyboard. However, we will present some details of an elaborate system in Lispvm to get some general insight into error detection and correction.

Among the several aids for debugging, perhaps the most popular is the interactive evaluator HEVAL. It is used in the Lispedit environment, and allows for the step-by-step examination of the evaluation of a function (the size of the steps can be varied). In this process, if you get an incorrect result at any step in the evaluation, you are still in Lispedit, and can modify the definition of the function so that it will behave as expected. We will demonstrate how HEVAL can be used to test newly defined functions, to detect errors (even potential infinite loops), to interrupt evaluation, to correct errors, and to resume evaluation.

We will now construct a set of functions to take a sentence that begins with a name, substitute Henry for the name in the sentence, and add on the word "too" at the end of the sentence. Thus, the function should take, for example, (John loves Mary) and return (Henry loves Mary too). Let us call the main function **copy-cat**, as defined below.

```
(defun copy-cat nil    ; [bugged]
    (print '(type a sentence, enclosed in
             parentheses, that begins with a name))
    (setq sent (read))                                    (3.33)
    (setq name (car sent))
    (substitute 'henry name sent)
    (add-on 'too sent))
```

(An alternative way of writing **copy-cat** is to delete (setq name (car sent)), and rewrite the next line as (substitute 'henry (car sent) sent). But the way we have written it is more convenient for the following discussion on stepping through the function.)

Buried in Example (3.33) is a very common error. We will see later what it is. The way **copy-cat** is defined, we will also need a function to substitute Henry for the name in the sentence (called **substitute** in the above definition), and another function to attach the word "too" at the end of the sentence (called **add-on**). There are system functions for what has been called **substitute** and **add-on**, but we will write our own (see also exercise 1. (c) in Section 2.5). The **substitute** function has the structure (substitute <item1> <item2> <list>). It replaces every occurrence of item2 by item1 in the list; for example: (substitute 'a 2 '(1 2 3 1 2 3)) ⇒ (1 A 3 1 A 3). We will also make the **add-on** function general enough to insert any item specified at the end of any list; so that (add-on 'yesterday '(i went shopping)) should result in (I WENT SHOPPING YESTERDAY).

```
(defun substitute (I1 I2 L)
    (cond ((null L) nil)
          ((equal I2 (car L))
             (cons I1 (substitute I1 I2 (cdr L))))
          ('t (cons (car L)
                    (substitute I1 I2 (cdr L))))))          (3.34)
```

```
(defun add-on (x L)                                        (3.35)
    (reverse (cons x (reverse L))))
```

Recall that **reverse** is a system function that reverses the order of its list argument; for example (reverse '(a b c)) ⇒ (C B A).

The **add-on** function can be tested by entering (add-on) 'x '(1 2 3)); (1 2 3 X) will be returned, so we know that it works. The **substitute** function also works; it has been tried before (as **my-subst** in Section 2.5). Now let us try the **copy-**

cat function. If (copy-cat) is called and, in response to the prompt, (Claire went to Norway), is entered (CLAIRE WENT TO NORWAY TOO) will be returned. It didn't work! The name Claire was not changed to Henry. There must be some trouble in the **copy-cat** function. Let us evaluate the function step by step to locate the trouble spot. Note that, while in HEVAL, the brightened focus serves as an evaluation pointer (EP), pointing to the expression that is going to be evaluated next or has just been evaluated. If the highlighting on the monitor is unreliable, you can keep track of the focus with the assistance of the messages displayed in the message area of the divided Lispedit screen. Now enter:

```
e copy-cat
```

to draw the editor's attention on the function and then input

```
heval
```

to initiate the interactive evaluation of the function. The evaluation pointer (EP) will be at the (print . . .) expression, because this is the first item in the definition that can be evaluated. If HEVAL had been invoked while the focus of the editor was not at the top of the definition, the evaluation pointer would have been set at the item that the focus was on. Note, incidentally, that some of the function keys have different settings under HEVAL. *F3* (or *PF3*) now indicates a **stop** of the evaluation. *F9* stands for **run**, whose effect is to complete the evaluation of the expression that EP is pointing at, without any further interaction with the user, and to move the EP to the next expression. *F12* stands for **step**. Its effect is to evaluate the current item and to move EP to the next item to be evaluated. The values computed by each evaluation are displayed in the message area. When EP enters a list, it points to the first element of the list. If the element is an atom, it is evaluated with the result displayed in the message area, and then EP points to the next atom or expression. If EP is at the last element of a list, that element is evaluated, and any other expressions requiring this value are evaluated, with the values displayed. The HEVAL operations are summarized in Table 3.5.

Note that, as shown in Table 3.5 HEVAL must be followed by the function arguments, if any. In the use of HEVAL with **copy-cat**, we did not use any arguments, because **copy-cat** had no parameters.

Let us now use **step** and **run** to find the mistake in **copy-cat**. The EP is at the (print . . .) expression, as noted before. Press *F9*. The entire print expression will be evaluated. The divided screen of Lispedit will disappear, and the prompt TYPE A SENTENCE, ENCLOSED IN PARENTHESES, THAT BEGINS WITH A NAME will appear on the screen. This means that the **print** expression has been evaluated and it works. After that, EP moves to (setq sent (read)). If *F9* is pressed again, the message in the bottom corner of the screen would be VM Read. Lisp is waiting for us to input a value for **sent**. Now type (claire is going to norway). It will be echoed on the top of the screen. Then, in the message area, (CLAIRE IS GOING TO NORWAY) will appear, and EP will move to (setq name (car sent)). This expression can be evaluated more slowly, since the problem was

TABLE 3.5. A SUMMARY OF
HEVAL PROCEDURES

e ⟨function-name⟩
heval ⟨function-arguments⟩

Function-Key	Effect
F3	**Stop**
F9	**Run**
F12	**Step**

with the name. Press *F12*. All that happens is that EP moves. Press *F12* again and again. Now the following display appears in the message area:

```
STEP
SENT = (CLAIRE IS GOING TO NORWAY)
(CAR SENT) = CLAIRE
(SETQ NAME (CAR SENT)) = CLAIRE
```

Press *F9,* and the message area will contain . . . = (HENRY IS GOING TO NOR-WAY)! We should go through the next part very slowly, because so far everything seems to work as desired. Press *F12* three times. Now the messages are:

```
SENT = (CLAIRE IS GOING TO NORWAY)
(ADD-ON 'TOO SENT) = (CLAIRE IS GOING TO NORWAY TOO)
```

The command **add-on** did its job, but to the old value of SENT. The error is that the value of *sent* was not changed. Now, an examination of the function **copy-cat** will show that the value of *sent* was not changed after the name Henry was substituted for Claire. The expression (substitute 'henry name sent) does not change the value of *sent* outside of the **substitute** function. Variables that appear as arguments of a function are *local variables* and resume their original values when the function is executed. To make a variable *global,* so that its value is retained, **setq** (or **set**) must be used. Our mistake in the **copy-cat** function is what we dubbed a "logical error." In this case, a very common programming error. To correct it, we note that the message says that we are about to leave HEVAL. Press *F12* once more to get out of HEVAL and back to Lispedit so that the function can be corrected. We need to change (substitute 'henry name sent) to (setq sent (substitute 'henry name sent)). To do this, move the focus to (substitute 'henry name sent) and then input:

```
wrap 1 setq sent
```

(The 1 is optional, since it is the default value for "n" in the **wrap** command—see the **wrap** command in Section 3.6.2). The function **copy-cat** should work now. Input (copy-cat) and then, when the prompt appears, input (claire is going to norway). (HENRY IS GOING TO NORWAY TOO) will be returned. Try it again with (john loves mary). In fact, whatever anyone does, Henry will do it too.

Another way of stepping through a program is the use of the edit command **trap**. Do this now at the terminal, using the **substitute** function that was defined earlier. You must first "trap" the function, then call it in the usual way:

```
trap substitute
(substitute 'a 1 '(1 2 3 1 2 3))
```

The command **trap** must be used in the edit mode on the command line of the divided screen. When a function is trapped, it will be evaluated interactively every time it is used, until the **untrap** command is used (compare with **trace** and **untrace** in Common Lisp). Let us continue with the above exercise. We can step through the evaluation of **substitute** by repeated application of the **step** command (*F12*). We will see messages along the way indicating the following developments: L = (1 2 3 1 2 3), and is therefore not null; Y = 1; (CAR L) = 1, therefore (EQUAL Y (CAR L)) is TRUE. Then we get to (SUBSTITUTE X Y (CDR L)) and see the values of X and Y, and that (CDR L) = (2 3 1 2 3). Next, the evaluator begins the evaluation of the whole expression (SUBSTITUTE X Y (CDR L)), and because **substitute** is a trapped function, this substitution will also be done interactively; so will each of the many substitutions needed to complete the evaluation. When the last one is done, that is, (SUBSTITUTE 'A 1 '(3)) = (3), we can watch the function do the **cons**ing to build up the final value (A 2 3 A 2 3). Incidentally, this is a convenient way to observe recursion and become familiar with it. If you prefer not to go through all of the details of the evaluation, at any point the **run** command (*F9*) can be used instead of **step** (*F12*). The command **step fast** will suppress the interactive evaluation of the trapped functions contained in the expression at which the EP is pointing. On the other hand, if you wish to see more of the details, you can use the **stepfine** command, which allows the evaluation to be observed in finer detail. There are no standard function keys for **step fast** and **stepfine**. (Keys can be reset for these or any other function, but that is not our concern at present. For now, you can simply spell out the words as given above.)

It is possible to trap more than one function during a session in Lispvm. On the command line, simply input:

```
trap (function-name)
```

for each function that you wish to trap. To trap all of the functions in an indexed file, type:

```
trap xf *
```

where xf stands for the indexed file name. Any time a trapped function is called, either directly by you or by another function being evaluated, the function will be evaluated interactively. If you wish to suppress the interactive evaluation of a function during the interactive evaluation of another trapped function, the **step fast** command can be used.

In this section, you have been introduced to the interactive evaluator HEVAL, which can be invoked from within Lispedit by either of two commands: HEVAL followed by the arguments of the function, or **trap** followed by the name of the function and then by a call to the function. You can then step through the evaluation, using **run** (*F9*), **step** (*F12*), **stepfine**, or **step fast**. When the functions have been checked, and they are performing correctly, you should **untrap** them. It should be pointed out once again that the function keys (e.g., *F9* or *PF9*, etc.) mentioned above may not be the same on all keyboards and systems, but the spelled-out commands (**step**, **run**, etc.) should work for all implementations.

3.11 EXERCISES

1. System function **member** returns non-NIL if the item is found on the top level of a list. For example:

```
(member 'a '(x y a b c)) ==) (A B C)
(member 'a '(x y (a b) c)) ==) NIL
```

Write a function called **memberp**, which will return T if the item is found at any level of a list. For example:

```
(memberp 'a (x y (b (c a)) d)) ==) T
```

2. Write a function that will keep prompting for inputting individual sentences, and will call another function to find whether a given fixed phrase occurs in any sentence, and will print the sentences that contain the phrase. The process should stop when you input a null line or some other message for ending.

3. The following function has a couple of procedures that have not been mentioned so far. Can you explain what the function does? Hint: (if (< = 5 i 15) t) returns T, if i lies between 5 and 15.

```
(defun explain ()
    (terpri) (setq i (read))(setq j (read)) (terpri)
    (cond ((null i) nil)
          ((or (not (numberp i))
               (not (numberp j)))
           (error "~s and ~s must be numbers" i j))
          (((<= 0 i j) (print (list i j)) (explain))
          (t (format t "~& ~s and ~s are not in the right
                    sequence" i j)
             (explain)))))
```

4. **step** through the following functions:

```
((lambda (x) (* x x)) 5)
(maplist '(lambda (x y) (list x y)) '(1 2 3) '(4 5 6))
```

4

Data Structures

4.1 INTRODUCTION

This chapter is concerned with memory organization and the internal structure of data in a computer. For those who are studying Lisp as their first computer language, and who have followed the text so far with little difficulty, the detailed discussions and technicalities presented in this chapter may seem to be unnecessary complications. However, later in the chapter, when various data representations, property lists, and other more advanced topics are studied, it will be found that a general knowledge of data structures and memory organization is useful. Furthermore, at the end of this chapter, the undertaking of a term project will be recommended, and some suggestions for selecting such projects will be given. It will be found that the material in this chapter and the next are helpful in making such projects substantial, efficient, and more elegant than simplistic computer exercises.

Earlier in this book, expressions with dots in them, such as (BIG . JOHN) and (A . (B . C)), were encountered. These expressions were referred to as *dotted pairs;* **cons** *cells* were also mentioned. These structures have special significance in the internal (inside the computer) representation of Lisp objects. In this chapter, the organization of computer memory, the internal representation of Lisp objects, and some of the important types of data structures that can be used in constructing Lisp functions and expressions will be discussed.

4.2 MEMORY ORGANIZATION

The memory of a computer is like an extended system of pigeonholes, each of which contains a 0 or a 1 (actually a no-pulse or a pulse). A single binary digit (otherwise known as a *bit*) cannot hold much information by itself, so bits are grouped into *bytes* and *words,* usually of some standard length, such as 8, 16, or 32 bits, each of which can be referred to by an *address* (like the street address of a house). Inside the machine, information is then coded into strings of binary bits; information that represents some object that the user is working on, and information relating to the internal working of the computer. Sometimes, the information contained in a word is the address of some other information, a *pointer.* In Lisp, a **cons** cell is a memory location that is organized to hold two pointers. Conventionally, a **cons** cell is externally represented as a rectangle with two slots, as in Figure 4.1.

Figure 4.1. A **cons** cell.

In this figure, arrows represent pointers. In a normal Lisp "list structure," the left arrow points to the **car** of a list, and the second arrow points to the **cdr.** This is, however, recursively constructed, so that if the list is (a b c d), its structure looks like Figure 4.2A:

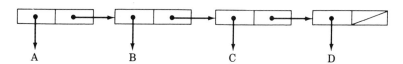

Figure 4.2A. The structure of (a b c d).

The last slot in Figure 4.2A points to NIL, since the **cdr** of a list with one element is NIL. Conventionally, in the diagrams, NIL is represented by a line drawn across the slot. Some authors place the **car** of a pair or a list inside the first box, so that Figure 4.2A would then look like Figure 4.2B:

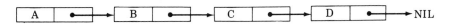

Figure 4.2B. Alternate representation of (a b c d).

Recall that a list may contain other lists, so that the list ((a b) c (d e)) would be represented as shown in Figure 4.3:

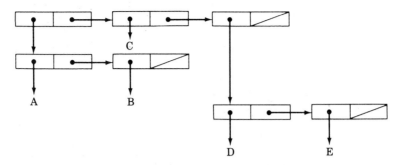

Figure 4.3. The representation of ((a b) c (d e)).

If both of the pointers in slots of a **cons** cell point to atoms, the representation shown in Figure 4.4, which is of a dotted pair (a . b), is appropriate.

Figure 4.4. 'l ne representation of (a . b).

Recall that this structure is produced by (cons 'a 'b). You can now see the difference in the representation of (a . b) and (a b). The latter has the following representation shown in Figure 4.5:

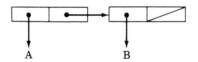

Figure 4.5. The representation of (a b).

One other important observation here is that in many Lisp dialects (e.g., Lispvm) atoms are stored only once, while lists with different names can be duplicated. Thus, the list (a b a c b) will have representation shown in Figure 4.6:

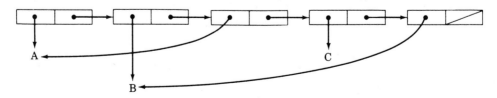

Figure 4.6. The representation of (a b a c b).

On the other hand, (setq x '(a b c)) and (setq y '(a b c)) will be represented as two lists (a b c) in the memory (see below, however). (setq x 'a) and (setq y 'a) will store only one "a" in the memory. In the graphic representation, if the list has a name, we attach the name to an arrow going to the first cell, as in Figure 4.7.

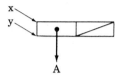

Figure 4.7. The representation of (setq x 'a) (setq y 'a).

Note that any list can be represented in dotted pair notation. For example, (a b c d) can be written as (a . (b . (c . (d . nil)))), but in printing or display on the terminal, it will appear as (a b c d). On the other hand, the list (a . (b . (c . d))) does not have the same structure, and will appear as (a b c . d).

To repeat then, **cons** is the basic pair-creating function in Lisp. It creates a divided cell whose left half contains a pointer to the first argument of **cons**, and whose right half contains a pointer to the second argument of **cons**. This is represented as shown in Figure 4.8.

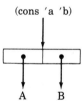

Figure 4.8. The representation of (cons 'a 'b).

In Figure 4.8, the second pointer does not point to a divided cell, but rather to an atom. The result is then expressed as (A . B). When **cons** is applied to an atom and a list, the left half points to the atom, and the right half points to the list (i.e., to the divided cell that points to the **car** of the list and the **cdr** of the list). For example, (setq x (cons 'a '(d e))) sets up a cell whose left half points to A, and whose right half points to the first cell in the representation of (D E), as shown in Figure 4.9.

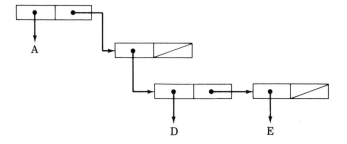

Figure 4.9. The representation of (setq x (cons 'a '(d e))).

Compare this with the structure for y = (a d e), shown in Figure 4.10:

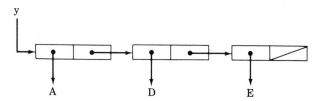

Figure 4.10. The representation of (setq y '(a d e)).

Also compare the representation of (setq x 'a), given in Figure 4.7, with (setq x '(a)), shown in Figure 4.11:

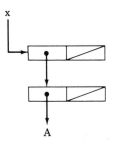

Figure 4.11. The representation of (setq x '(a)).

and compare (cons 'a '(b)), in Figure 4.12, with (cons 'a 'b), in Figure 4.8.

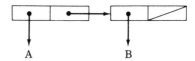

Figure 4.12. The representation of (cons 'a '(b)).

Not every expression containing parantheses and dots is a legitimate Lisp object, and one must be careful in their use. Even using periods to mark the ends of sentences to which Lisp functions are applied may cause unexpected trouble.

4.3 EQUALITY FUNCTIONS

Functions testing equality are predicate functions in that they return T (true) or NIL. We have already seen the functions = (equal to), which in Common Lisp takes any number of numerical arguments, and **equal**, which takes two data objects for arguments. There are two other equality functions, **eq** and **eql**, which are widely used in Lisp dialects. The functions **eq**, **eql**, and **equal** are listed here in order of decreasing efficiency. The function **eq** is the most efficient, and **equal** is the least efficient, in terms of the computing time taken for checking various comparisons of type, form, and so forth. However, while they all check equality, they all have differences, which are important in some applications. The study of pointers and storage criteria in this chapter makes it possible to demonstrate the differences in these equality functions with graphic examples.

In general, **equal** returns true if its two arguments are equal in the intuitive sense of having equivalent values. The functions **eq** and **eql** return true if their arguments point to the same atom or to the same divided cell. Let us consider some examples for further elaboration.

$$
\begin{array}{ll}
(\texttt{setq test1 (list 'hi 'there)}) & \\
(\texttt{setq test2 (list 'hi 'there)}) & (4.1) \\
(\texttt{setq test3 test1}). &
\end{array}
$$

The results will look something like those shown in Figure 4.13:

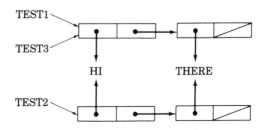

Figure 4.13. The representation of the three lists.

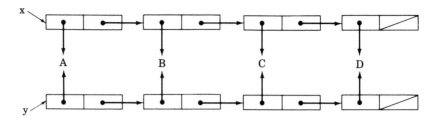

Figure 4.14. Two lists sharing the same data.

Now (equal test1 test2) will return true, but (eq test1 test2) and (eql test1 test2) will be NIL, because TEST1 and TEST2 point to different cells. On the other hand, (eq test1 test3) and (eql test1 test3) are both true. Similarly, (eq (car test1) (car test2)) and (eql (car test1) (car test2)) are true because they point to the same atoms. Another example is given in Figure 4.14:

$$(\text{setq } x \text{ '(a b c d))} \qquad (4.2)$$
$$(\text{setq } y \text{ '(a b c d))}$$

In the following examples from the structure in Figure 4.14, results from **equal** and **eq** will be shown. The results from **eql** are the same as those of **eq**.

```
(1)  (equal x y) ==> T
(2)  (eq x y) ==> NIL
(3)  (eq (car x) (car y)) ==> T           (4.3)
(4)  (eq (cdr x) (cdr y)) ==> NIL
(5)  (eq (cadddr x) (cadddr y)) ==> T
(6)  (eq (cdddr x) (cdddr y)) ==> NIL
```

In (5), the value is D, which is an atom, whereas in (6) the value is (D) which is a list.

The function **equal** is the equality function most commonly used by many Lisp programmers. However, as mentioned above, the differences may be significant, and the reader should be aware of them because, as we will see later, they play a role in the structure of some system functions. In the following series of examples, the differences between the four equality system functions can be reviewed.

```
(eq 'a 'a) ==> T
(eql 'a 'a) ==> T
(equal 'a 'a) ==> T                       (4.4)
(= 'a 'a) ==> Error (TRUE in Lispvm)
(eq '(a b) '(a b)) ==> NIL
(eql '(a b) '(a b)) ==> NIL
```

```
(equal '(a b) '(a b)) ==) T
(eq 5 5) ==) T
(eql 5 5) ==) T
(equal 5 5) ==) T
(= 5 5) ==) T
(eq 5.0 5.0) ==) NIL ;;Common Lisp stores real numbers separately.
(eql 5.0 5.0) ==) T
(equal 5.0 5.0) ==) T
(eq 5 5.0) ==) NIL
(eql 5 5.0) ==) NIL
(equal 5 5.0) ==) NIL
(= 5 5.0) ==) T
(= .5 (/ 1 2)) ==) T
(eq .5 (/ 1 2)) ==) NIL
(eql .5 (/ 1 2)) ==) T
(equal .5 (/ 1 2)) ==) T
```

Some of the illustrations in Example (4.4) may be confusing. As stated before, **equal** is the most general; it returns true if the two objects of its comparison have the same print or display value. In other words, **equal** does not care if its objects do not have the same storage, as long as they evaluate to the same value and type. On the other hand, **eq** (which is the most specific) returns true if and only if its objects are identical and have the same storage; in other words, if the pointers of its objects point to the same cell. However, there is a further complication for **eq** in Common Lisp in that (for numerical values) Common Lisp, unlike other dialects, allows implementations where identical numbers are stored in different cells. Thus, for (setq x 5) and (setq y 5) the representation shown in Figure 4.15 may be the case:

Figure 4.15. An example of copy implementation.

rather than the standard implementation of single atomic storage, as in Figure 4.16:

Figure 4.16. An example of single atom representation.

In the former case, (eq 5 5) will return NIL. In the illustrations in Example (4.4), an implementation of Common Lisp in which integers are not copied, but real numbers are is assumed, so that (eq 5 5) $\Rightarrow$ T, but (eq 5.0

5.0) ⇒ NIL. On the other hand, **eql** returns true if its numeric arguments are of the same type and have the same value. The = (equal to) predicate is true if its numeric arguments have the same value, irrespective of type, so that (= 5 5.0) ⇒ T.

If there is still confusion, **equal** (for the present) should be used if there is no concern for the finer points of equality!

4.4 EXERCISES

1. (a) Assign a list of numbers as the value of NUMBERS. (b) Assign a list of colors as the value of COLORS. (c) Write a function that will combine the above two lists into a new list called ADJECTIVES, which has the form (ONE WHITE TWO BLUE TEN BEIGE . . .). The processing should stop when one of the lists, (a) or (b), is exhausted.

2. Write a function to show that one-half of the length of ADJECTIVES is equal to the minium or the lesser of the lengths of NUMBERS and COLORS. Do you use **equal**, **eql**, or **eq** for this function? Why?

3. Show a graphic representation of the following list:

$$(S (NP (DET)(N)) (VP (V) (NP (DET)(N))))$$

4. Write the lists that represent the following **cons** cells:

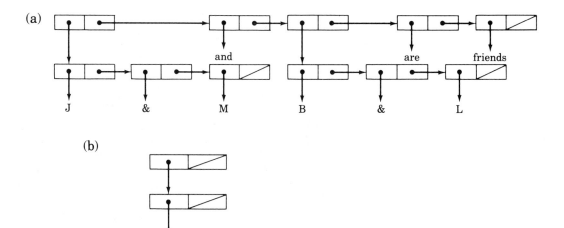

(a)

(b)

4.5 REPRESENTING COMMON DATA OBJECTS IN LISP

Lisp is as versatile as any general-purpose language for programming applications. In this section we will show how some popular data structures may be expressed in Lisp, and therefore how common problems can be solved.

4.5.1 Tables

Tables are one of the most common ways of organizing information. They can be represented in several ways in Lisp. Perhaps the simplest way to write a table is as a list of lists. Each row of the table can be enclosed in parentheses, and then the entire set of rows can be enclosed in parentheses and given a name. Suppose there exists a list of orders placed with a supply company, as shown in Table 4.1. This information can be written in Lisp as:

$$
\text{(setq table4 '((jones 1573 2 330 660)} \\
\text{(adams 1408 3 250 750)} \qquad (4.5) \\
\text{(mitsu 4321 5 100 500)))}
$$

The table has the name TABLE4, and can be edited and, if desired, stored in a file for later updating (editing). One operation that it might be necessary to perform on the table is to print it out in rows. For that the function **print-table,** can be defined.

$$
\text{(defun print-table (tt)} \\
\text{(cond ((null tt) nil)} \qquad (4.6) \\
\text{(t (print (car tt))} \\
\text{(print-table (cdr tt)))))}
$$

(The function **print-table**, of course, will not print the table in a format with aligned columns.)

Recall that the **print** function starts on a new line in each cycle, so that in each row (the **car** of tt) will appear on a new line. We can also sort the table on names or other columns, as desired. For example, using Lispvm, (sortby 'cadddr table4) will arrange the rows in ascending order of the entry on the second to the last column. If new orders come in for this hypothetical business, the table can be updated by loading the old one, editing it to add the new orders, sorting it again, and storing the updated table.

TABLE 4.1. A SAMPLE TABLE

Name	Item #	Quantity	Unit Price	Total
Jones	1573	2	330	660
Adams	1408	3	250	750
Mitsu	4321	5	100	500

Most dialects of Lisp have system functions for treating a list of lists as a table. They refer to such lists of lists as *Association Lists* or ALISTs. Each list in an ALIST is treated at though the first element is a *name,* and the rest of the list is the *value* of the name. So that the **car** is the name and the **cdr** is the value. In our TABLE4, the names are Jones, Adams, and Mitsu, and the values are (1573 2 330 660), (1408 3 250 750), and (4321 5 100 500), respectively. Special functions are provided for retrieving the rows of a table. The function name **assoc,** followed by the 'name' of a row and name of the table, will return the row:

```
(assoc 'jones table4) ==) (JONES 1573 2 330 660)
(assoc 'smith table4) ==) NIL  ;smith is not in table4
```

In Lispvm, the function **get** will return the 'value' of a row:

```
(get table4 adams) ==) (1408 3 250 750)
```

Note that the order of the arguments is not the same in the two functions.

The function **copy-alist**, like **copy-list**, provides a copy of its argument list, but there is a subtle difference between the two. The function **copy-alist** copies the top level of its argument list, as well as all of the **cons** cells (sub-lists) in the argument list. The function **copy-list** copies the top level, but the internal **cons** cells are shared. Consequently, changes made in a copy made by **copy-alist** does not affect the original, but changes made in a copy made by **copy-list** affect the other copy. The following examples and graphic representations illustrate the two procedures.

```
(setq org1 '(new-york (state capital) albany))
(setq copy1 (copy-alist org1))
org1 ==) (NEW-YORK (STATE CAPITAL) ALBANY)
copy1 ==) (NEW-YORK (STATE CAPITAL) ALBANY)
```

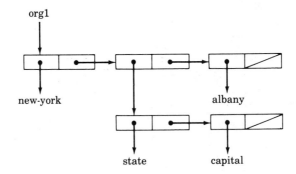

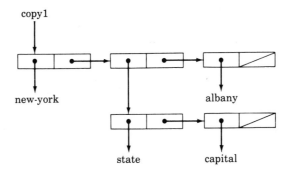

```
(equal org1 copy1) ==> T
(eq org1 copy1) ==> NIL    ;; See Section 4.3
(setf (car copy1) 'usa)
;; SETF is like SETQ; see Section 4.5.3.1
(setf (caadr copy1) 'national)
(setf (last copy1) 'washington)
copy1 ==> (USA (NATIONAL CAPITAL) WASHINGTON)
            ;; We changed the copy
org1 ==> (NEW-YORK (STATE CAPITAL) ALBANY)
            ;; The original has not changed
```

Note that, in the following example, the copy is made by **copy-list**, rather than **copy-alist**:

```
(setq org2 '(a b (c d) e))
(setq copy2 (copy-list org2))
org2 ==> (A B (C D) E)
copy2 ==> (A B (C D) E)
```

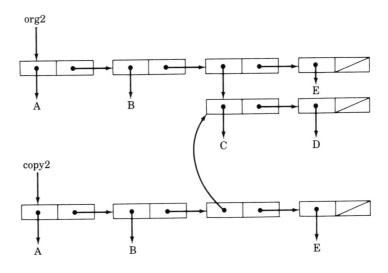

Now, as the above diagram shows, changes in the top level of the copy (copy2) will not affect the original (org2), but changes in the embedded **cons** cells will affect the original.

```
(setf (car copy2) 'x)
(setf (caaddr copy2) 'y)  ;depending on implementation, this line
                          ;may have to be written as
                          ;(setf (car(caddr copy2)) 'y)

org2 ==> (A B (Y D) E)
copy2 ==> (X B (Y D) E)
```

4.5.2 Pair Lists

In Lisp, data is often stored as dotted pairs in an ALIST, and there are several system functions for constructing and retrieving data from such lists. One function that we already know is **setq**. Let us use that to start a phone list:

```
(setq phones '(( jones . 1234444)
               ( adams . 1235555)                    (4.7)
               (mitsu . 1236666) ))
```

Now we can input a name and get the phone number or, conversely, input a phone number and get the name associated with it:

```
(assoc 'jones phones) ==> (JONES . 1234444)
(rassoc 1234444 phones) ==> (JONES . 1234444)
```

The function **rassoc** is a system function in Common Lisp which, given the **cdr** of a pair, returns its **car**, or rather returns the pair. Among the functions in Common Lisp for augmenting pair-lists are **acons** and **pairlis**.

```
(acons 'harman 1237777 phones) ==>
((HARMAN . 1237777) (JONES . 1234444) (ADAMS . 1235555)     (4.8)
     (MITSU . 1236666))
```

```
(pairlis '(meyer messla brindisi)
         '(1238888 1239999 1230000) phones) ==>
((MEYER . 1238888) (MESSLA . 1239999)
 (BRINDISI . 1230000) (HARMAN . 1237777)                     (4.9)
 (JONES . 1234444) (ADAMS . 1235555) (MITSU . 1236666))
```

The **pairlis** function can also be used for starting new pair-lists:

```
(setq newlist (pairlis '(a b c a b a d)
                       '(1 2 3 4 5 6 7) )) ==>             (4.10)
```

```
((A . 1)(B . 2)(C . 3)(A . 4)(B . 5)(A . 6)(D . 7))

(assoc 'a newlist) ==) (A . 1)
(rassoc 2 newlist) ==) (B . 2)
```

Note that, in the pair-list generated in Example (4.10), **assoc** and **rassoc** return the first pairs that match their arguments.

4.5.3 Property Lists

Associated with each symbol in Lisp is a *property list* (PLIST); that is, a list of certain features that form the 'property' of that symbol. The PLISTS of symbols in the system are used by the Lisp system. When the user introduces a symbol, a PLIST is assigned to it, and is set to NIL until a value is defined for it. PLISTS have wide applications, and are an important component of Lisp. There are some significant differences in the treatment of PLISTS between Common Lisp and other dialects. In order to avoid confusion, the discussion in this subsection will be divided into two subsections. In 4.5.3.1, PLISTS in Common Lisp will be described, and in 4.5.3.2 some details of PLISTS will be given for Lispvm. The user who has access to one can ignore the other.

4.5.3.1 Property Lists in Common Lisp

This subsection will begin with the introduction of some new system functions. The form **setf** is like **setq** and **set**, but it is a macro with a wider scope. Like **setq**, it can assign values to variables or place data in positions.

```
(setf x 5)
(setf y '(a b c d))                                    (4.11)
(setf  a 1 b 2 c 3 d 4)
```

The setf macro can also perform the functions of **rplaca** and **rplacd** which, as we have seen, replace the **car** and **cdr** of a list. Thus, given Y as defined in Example (4.11):

```
y ==) (A B C D)
(setf (car y) 2) ==) (2 B C D)                          (4.12)
(setf (cdr y) 3) ==) (2 . 3)
y ==) (2 . 3)
```

These examples show that **setf** in Common Lisp makes these other functions redundant, but they are kept in the language for compatibility and wide usage in other dialects. However, **put** or **putprop** (see subsection 4.5.3.2), which can also be replaced by **setf**, are dropped from many Common Lisp implementations. The above examples also show that **setf** is a destructive function (see Section 2.10). Further discussions for **setf** are given in Section 5.12.

Another system function in Common Lisp is **getf**. The function **get** is a standard function in Lisp. It takes two arguments: a symbol and a property name. For example, if JOHN has been assigned the property name SEX, with the value MALE (see below), then (get 'john 'sex) would return MALE. On the other hand, (get 'john 'age) will return NIL if age is not a property of JOHN, or if its value is NIL. The system function **getf** is similar to **get**, but it operates on the property list rather than on a symbol, so that its general syntax is:

```
(getf ⟨plist⟩ ⟨item⟩)
```

Examples of the use of **getf** are:

```
(setq values '(x 1 y 2 z 3))
(getf values 'y) ==> 2                                    (4.13)
(getf values 'w) ==> NIL
```

In the last line in Example (4.13), the output is NIL, because "w" was not in the list VALUES. However, this result is ambiguous, because if "w" was there with a value NIL, it would still return NIL. To avoid this ambiguity, you can provide for a different output in the function call. For example, the last line in (4.13) could have been written as (getf values 'w 'not-found). Now if "w" were in the list, its value would be returned. But if it were not there, NOT-FOUND would be returned.

With regard to the properties of **setq** and **setf**, note further that both of these forms assign values to variables, but internally, the assigned data is in the dotted pairs format, so that the second member of each pair is the value of the first. Examples:

```
(setq x '(a b c d e f)) ==> (A B C D E F)
    (getf x 'a) ==> B
    (getf x 'b) ==> NIL
    (getf x 'c) ==> D
    (getf x 'd) ==> NIL
    (getf x 'e) ==> F
    (getf x 'f) ==> NIL
```

The above example also shows that if the argument of **getf** is a value in the variable/value pair, the function will return NIL.

Let us now return to the topic of property lists (PLISTS) in Common Lisp. Note that (setf values (x 1 y 2 z 3)) returns a list called VALUES, whose members, X, Y, and Z, have the values 1, 2, and 3, respectively. Often, however, we want to assign many values as the 'property' of a single item. To do this, a combination of **setf** and **get** can be used. Let us define properties for Maxwell:

```
(setf (get 'maxwell 'sex) 'male)
MALE                                                      (4.14)
```

```
(setf (get 'maxwell 'age) 35)
35
(setf (get 'maxwell 'job) 'plumber)
PLUMBER
```

We can now display Maxwell's PLIST by inputting:

```
(symbol-plist 'maxwell)
(JOB PLUMBER AGE 35 SEX MALE)
```

and the individual properties can be retrieved by inputting:

```
(get 'maxwell 'age) ==) 35
```

Note that (getf 'maxwell 'age) will return an error message, because MAXWELL, unlike VALUES in Example (4.13), is not a list, and **getf** requires a list as its first argument.

In Subsection 3.8.2, Example (3.16), a restricted function for negating progressive sentences in English was defined. It was restricted in that it was assumed that a form of the verb "to be" (is, was, am, were, etc.) occurs in the second position of the input sentence and we inserted the work "not" after that. Now this can be generalized by allowing a form of the verb "to be" to occur anywhere in the sentence. First, property lists for "be" verbs will be defined and placed in a dictionary:

```
(setf (get 'was 'pos) 'verb)
(setf (get 'was 'type) 'be)
(setf (get 'was 'num) 'sing)
(setf (get 'was 'tense) 'past)                              (4.15)
(setq dict (cons 'was dict))   ;;assuming that DICT has
                               ;;previously been defined,
                               ;;otherwise (setq dict '(was))
```

We can perform a similar process for other "be" verbs so that, at the end, our dictionary (DICT) will contain, among others, IS, WAS, AM, WERE, . . . , each of which has a property list consisting of part-of-speech (pos), type, number (num), and tense. It should be pointed out that, while **setf** can replace **setq** in its usage, the reverse is not true. For example, in the definitions of properties in Example (4.15), we cannot replace **setf** with **setq**.

For the purposes of the present exercise, we will assume that a dictionary (called DICT) has been defined, which includes the following words: is, was, am, are. These words must at least have the property of TYPE *be* defined for them.

```
dict ==) (IS WAS AM ARE)
(get 'is 'type) ==) BE                                       (4.16)
etc.
```

The function **neg** can now be written, as in Example (4.17).

```
(defun neg (d sentence)
  (cond ((null sentence) nil)
        ((and (member (car sentence) d)
              (not (equal (cadr sentence) 'not))          (4.17)
              (equal (get (car sentence) 'type) 'be))
             (cons (car sentence)
                   (cons 'not (neg d (cdr sentence)))))
        (t (cons (car sentence)(neg d (cdr sentence))))))
```

Note that the function **neg** checks for a word that occurs in the dictionary (parameter d in Example (4.17)), has the TYPE *be,* and is not followed by the word *not* (so that the output will not have double negatives). It will then insert *not* after the word with these properties. Examples:

```
(neg dict '(late last night i was listening to music))
==> (LATE LAST NIGHT I WAS NOT LISTENING TO MUSIC)          (4.18)
(neg dict '(john is a friend of mine))
==> (JOHN IS NOT A FRIEND OF MINE)
```

If you wish, a function can be written to read a sentence and feed it into the **neg** function:

```
(defun neg-reader ()
  (terpri)
  (princ "Please type a sentence in parentheses")          (4.19)
  (terpri)
  (setq sent (read))
  (neg dict sent))
```

Figure 4.17 represents a session using the above functions.

Several examples in Figure 4.17 show that the sentences need not be in the progressive mode, but then the sentences have to be judiciously chosen, otherwise there would problem with the sentences, such as the following:

```
How is this book written?
I have been to the movies.
```

We have seen in the above examples that **setf** can be used to put values in places (such as property lists), and **get** can be used to access places for such data. It follows that **get** can be used with other functions such as **push, pop** (Subsection 4.5.7), **incf, decf,** and so forth for augmenting or taking away elements from a property list.

```
(neg-reader)
Please type a sentence in parentheses
(i am here and you are in town)
(I AM NOT HERE AND YOU ARE NOT IN TOWN)

(neg-reader)
Please type a sentence in parentheses
(we are going to the movies tonight)
(WE ARE NOT GOING TO THE MOVIES TONIGHT)

(neg-reader)
Please type a sentence in parentheses
(i am and you are there and she is somewhere. we are lost)
(I AM NOT AND YOUR ARE NOT THERE AND SHE IS NOT SOMEWHERE. WE ARE
NOT LOST)

(neg-reader)
Please type a sentence in parentheses
  ;;The following sentence is already negated;
  ;;it will not change.
(john is not a friend of mine)
(JOHN IS NOT A FRIEND OF MINE)

(neg-reader)
Please type a sentence in parentheses
(i was here and he was not to be seen)
(I WAS NOT HERE AND HE WAS NOT TO BE SEEN)
  ;;Let us add a word to the dictionary:
    (setf (get 'were 'type) 'be)
    (setq dict (cons 'were dict))

(neg-reader)
Please type a sentence in parentheses
(you were driving too fast on the road)
(YOU WERE NOT DRIVING TOO FAST ON THE ROAD)

(neg-reader)
Please type a sentence in parentheses
  ;;The following sentence has no be verb in it.
  (i have many friends)
  (I HAVE MANY FRIENDS)
```

Figure 4.17. A session with the negation program.

```
(setf (get 'maxwell 'favorite-shows) 'cats)
CATS
(push 'les-miserables (get 'maxwell 'favorite-shows))
LES-MISERABLES
(push 'perfect-crime (get 'maxwell 'favorite-shows))
PERFECT-CRIME
(get 'maxwell 'favorite-shows)
   ==) (PERFECT-CRIME LES-MISERABLES . CATS)
```

Now the entire PLIST of Maxwell is:

```
(symbol-plist 'maxwell) ==)
(FAVORITE-SHOWS (PERFECT-CRIME LES-MISERABLES . CATS) JOB
   PLUMBER AGE 35 SEX MALE)
```

A property and its value can be removed from the list with the function **remprop**:

```
(remprop 'maxwell 'favorite-shows) ==) T
(symbol-plist 'maxwell) ==)
      (JOB PLUMBER AGE 35 SEX MALE)
```

Another function for displaying selected parts of a property-list is **get-properties**. This function returns the contents of a PLIST from a given point in the list.

```
(setq x '(a 1 b 2 c 3 d 4))
(A 1 B 2 C 3 D 4)
(get-properties x '(c))
C
3
(C 3 D 4)
```

Note that, in the above example, **get-properties** returned three outputs. The property name (C), the property value (3), and the rest of the list beginning with the property named in the argument. More examples:

```
(get-properties x '(b))
B
2
(B 2 C 3 D 4)
(get-properties x '(d))
D
4
(D 4)
(get-properties x '(e))
```

```
NIL
NIL
NIL
```

Note that the first argument of **get-properties** must be a list (PLIST). It cannot, therefore, be used directly with the name Maxwell, but it can be used with the property-list of Maxwell, for example:

```
(setq maxwell (symbol-plist 'maxwell))
 ==) (JOB PLUMBER AGE 35 SEX MALE)
(get-properties maxwell '(age))
AGE
35
(AGE 35 SEX MALE)
```

In the next section, we will discuss similar procedures in Lispvm for constructing a dictionary for a translation project. The functions discussed for Lispvm and other similar dialects are comparable to those in Common Lisp, but they may have a different syntax and terminology.

4.5.3.2 Property Lists in Lispvm

To demonstrate property lists for Lispvm, we need to go back to the "translation" exercise at the beginning of Chapter 3, and develop a procedure for constructing a dictionary of words with certain features as their properties.

Suppose that we are building a Spanish-English dictionary and wish to record, for each word, properties like gender, species, number, part of speech, etc. Part of our dictionary may look like Table 4.2.

Our dictionary can be set up as a simple list of the words, and store all of the other information in the property lists that go with the words in the dictionary. This is done with the command:

```
(put (item) (prop-name) (prop-value))
```

Items in the dictionary in Table 4.2 can be entered by the following series of PUT functions:

```
(put mujer eng woman)
(put mujer gender fem)
(put mujer species human)          (4.20)
(put mujer number sing)
(put mujer part-of-speech noun)
(setq mujer (proplist mujer))
```

TABLE 4.2 SAMPLE SPANISH-ENGLISH DICTIONARY

Spanish	English	Gender	Species	Number	Part of Speech
mujer	woman	fem	human	sing	noun
playa	beach	fem	inanim	sing	noun
rojo	red	masc	inanim	sing	adj

The last line in Example (4.20) assigns the property list of MUJER as the property of MUJER. The property list for the identifier (item) MUJER could then be retrieved with the function (proplist mujer) and would look like this:

```
((ENGLISH . WOMAN) (GENDER . FEM) (SPECIES . HUMAN)      (4.21)
 (NUMBER . SING) (PART-OF-SPEECH . NOUN)).
```

As you can see, a property list is a list of dotted pairs of the form (property . value). Individual property values can be recalled with the **get** command. It might look unnecessarily tedious to enter information in this way, but this ability to retrieve property values easily is often worth the extra effort. For example, if you had to find a word in a dictionary that was a noun with feminine gender, you could include the following expressions in a function for a recursive search in the dictionary.

```
(and (equal (get (eval (car dictionary)) pos) noun)
     (equal (get (eval (car dictionary)) gen) fem))
```

This will return TRUE if the item at the **car** of dictionary has the part-of-speech (POS) NOUN and also its genger (GEN) is feminine (FEM). Note the difference in **get** functions between Common Lisp and Lispvm. In the former, **get** takes a symbol for an argument, whereas in the latter **get** can take a form.

```
(get ⟨symbol⟩ ⟨property⟩)   [Common Lisp]
(get ⟨form⟩ ...)            [Lispvm]
(get ⟨plist⟩ ⟨prop-name⟩)  [Lispvm]
(getf ⟨plist⟩ ⟨prop-name⟩) [Common Lisp]
```

For a slightly more complete example, let us suppose that we need a program to identify whether a word or pair of words is a noun-phrase (NP). An NP, for our purposes, is a proper name (PPN), a pronoun (PN), or a noun (N) preceded by a determiner (DET). We will again assume a dictionary (DICT) that has words with their property lists stored in it.

```
(defun nptest (dict)
  (print '(Type a word or two in parentheses))
  (setq s (read))
  (cond ((null s) nil)
        ((or
          (and (member (car s) dict)
               (or (equal (get (eval (car s)) pos) pn)
                   (equal (get (eval (car s)) pos) ppn)))
          (and (member (car s) dict)
               (member (cadr S) dict)
                  (equal (get (eval (car s)) pos) det)
                  (equal (get (eval (cadr s)) pos) n))) 'np)
        (t (print '(try again))
           (nptest (dict)))))
```
(4.22)

Incidentally, the dotted pair form of the entry in a property list conserves memory, because it requires one less cell to store a dotted pair than to store a list of two elements. For a large dictionary, this might make a significant difference.

In the following exercise, you can review how to define and update properties for the *block world,* and how to display the property list or individual properties. As usual, the inputs are in lower case and the Lisp responses are in capitals. Comments are added as needed.

```
(put block size large)
(put block shape cube)
(put block color red)
(proplist block) ==)        ;;property list so far
((SIZE . LARGE) (SHAPE . CUBE) (COLOR . RED))
(setq block (proplist block))  ;;the list assigned
(put block place on-table)
(put block height tall)
(setq block (proplist block))      ;;the list updated
(proplist block) ==)            ;;updated list
((PLACE . ON-TABLE) (HEIGHT . TALL) (SIZE . LARGE)
 (SHAPE . CUBE) (COLOR . RED))
(get block shape) ==) CUBE      ;;individual query
(assoc size block) ==) LARGE    ;;note the order in
                                ;;the last two expressions
```
(4.23)

4.5.4 Characters and Strings

A character is a data object recognized by Lisp as a distinct entity. In the same way that atom 'a is distinguished from list (a), symbol 'a is distinguished from CHAR a. Lisp dialects have varying numbers of system functions and macros that deal with characters. Most Lisp dialects recognize 256 characters. These include the letters a through z and A through Z, digits 0 through 9, and punctuation and other characters, including a space character, a line break character (or new-line), backspace (or rubout), and so forth. Internally, characters are often represented in ASCII (American Standard Code for Information Interchange). The print values of these codes are often given in decimal numbers, so that a = 97, b = 98, A = 65, tab = 9, space = 32, 0 = 48, 5 = 53, and so on.

4.5.4.1 Characters and Strings in Common Lisp

In Common Lisp, characters are represented in the format #\⟨character⟩ and return either characters or ASCII decimal codes, depending on the implementation:

```
#\a ==> 97
#\1 ==> 49
#\linefeed ==> 10
```

Because of the diversity of characters and character representations, there is a consensus in the Common Lisp community that all Common Lisp dialects will have a common core set of 96 characters. These characters, known as the *standard-character set,* consist of space (#\space), new-line (#\newline), and the 94 printing characters that are found on standard computer keyboards. The idea is that if only the standard characters are used in writing Common Lisp programs, they can be read by any Common Lisp system. Unfortunately, this is not always true because there are also some discrepancies in the naming and implementation of the same functions in different dialects.

In the following examples, functions will be given for making and manipulating characters in Common Lisp. The reader is warned that, for the reasons indicated above, the outputs for some of our examples may not be identical in all dialects

```
(character "a") ==> #\a  or 97
(character "A") ==> #\A
(character 'a) ==> #\A  or 65
(character 97) ==> #\a
(character 65) ==> #\A
(character 53) ==> #\5
(setq x #\a) ==> #\a or 97;   x ==> #\a or 97          (4.24)
(char-code x) ==> 97
(code-char x) ==> #\a
(char-upcase #\a) ==> #\A  or 65
(char-downcase #\A) ==> #\a  or 97
```

The following predicate and comparison functions operate on characters:

```
(alpha-char-p #\a) ==> T
(alpha-char-p 'a) ==> NIL    ;'a is not a character          (4.25)
                             ;it is a symbol
```

```
(alpha-char-p "a") ==> NIL    ; "a" is a string
(upper-case-p #\A) ==> T
(alpha-char-p #\3) ==> NIL
(digit-char-p #\3) ==> T
(standard-char-p #\space) ==> T
(standard-char-p #\@) ==> T
(standard-char-p #\rubout) ==> NIL
(setq x #\a) ==> #\a
(setq y #\3) ==> #\3
(both-case-p x) ==> T        ;a is alphanumeric
(both-case-p y) ==> NIL      ;3 is not alphanumeric
(char= x y) ==> NIL          ;not equal
(char= x x) ==> T
(char/= x y) ==> T           ; x not equal to y
(char-equal x x) ==> T
(char-equal y 3) ==> NIL        ;here 3 is not char 3
(char-equal y #\3) ==> T
[There is also char<, char<=, char>, Char>=]
(char-lessp x y) ==> NIL    ;according to the
                            ;ASCII order
(char-lessp y x) ==> T
(char= #\a #\A) ==> NIL
(char-equal #\a #\A) ==> T
```

A *string* is a one-dimensional array or vector whose elements are characters enclosed in double quote marks. The following expressions are examples of strings:

```
"a"
"abcdefgh"
"This is a string"
"123"
"this is mixed string of letters a b c and
         numbers 1 2 3"
```

Lisp has a number of system functions for processing strings, but, as usual, they are not always identical in different dialects of Lisp. Because strings are a subtype of vectors and arrays, some of the functions for vectors and arrays operate also on strings. (vectors and arrays will be discussed in Chapter 5). Positions of elements in a string are counted from zero, so that in "This is a string" the first T is in position zero, h is in position 1, and the first blank after s is in position 4 (blanks count as elements in strings; cf. *space* under characters, earlier).

In Common Lisp, **string** and **make-string** are functions that return strings:

```
(string 'abcde) ==> "ABCDE"
(string 'a) ==> "A"
(string #\a) ==> "a"
(string #\A) ==> "A"
(string #\3) ==> "3"
```

(4.26)

The function **make-string** returns a string with the length and the initial characters specified in the function call:

```
(make-string 10 :initial-element #\x)
==) "xxxxxxxxxx"    ;; a string of 10 x's
(make-string 5 :initial-element #\ )                    (4.27)
==) "     "    ;; a string of 5 blanks
(make-string 5 :initial-element #\space
==) "     "
```

The following system functions operate on strings (recall that string positions count from zero):

```
(setq x "abcdefg") ==) "abcdefg"
(char x 0) ==) #\a     ;The first character in x
(char x 3) ==) #\d     ;The fourth character in x
(length x) ==) 7
(string-search "d" x) ==) 3    ;d in third position from zero.
(string-upcase "this is a string") ==) "THIS IS A STRING"
(string-downcase "THIS I LIKE") ==) "this i like"
(string-capitalize "thIS i likE") ==) "This I Like"
(reverse x) ==) "gfedcba"
(subseq x 2 4) ==) "cd"   ;substring between positions 2-4
(subseq x 2) ==) "cdefg"
(aref n o) ==) #\a or 97 (see Section 5.6)
(remove #\b x) ==) "acdefg"
(string-append "water" "fall") ==) "waterfall"
(eql "abc" "abc") ==) NIL
(eq "abc" "abc") ==) NIL
(equal "abc" "abc") ==) T
(string= "abc" "abc") ==) T
(string= "123" "123") ==) T                               (4.28)
(string< "abc" "adc") ==) 1    ;The first position is less
(string< "abcdefgh" "abcdekgh") ==) 5
(string-lessp "abcd" "acbd") ==) 1
(string-lessp "acbd" "abcd") ==) NIL
[There are similar functions for /= (not-equal), ),
  )=, and (=]
(setf k (char "abc" 1)) ==) #\b     k ==) #\b
    (setf choo '(a b c d)) ==) (A B C D)
    (setf (car choo) (char "xyz" 0)) ==) #\x
    choo ==) (#\x B C D)
(string-trim "ab" "abcdab") ==) "cd"   ;ab trimed on both sides
(string-left-trim "ab" "abcdab") ==) "cdab"
(string-right-trim "ab" "abcdab") ==) "abcd"
(string-trim " "   " wasted space    ") ==) "wasted space"
```

```
(setf phrase "this is a phrase this")
(string-right-trim "this" phrase)==)"this is a phrase"
 phrase ==) "this is a phrase this"
(setf phrase (string-right-trim "this" phrase))
 phrase ==) "this is a phrase"
```

4.5.4.2 Characters and Strings in Lispvm

In Lispvm, **charp** returns the character tested if it is one of the 256 characters recognized by the system. There is also a function called **char2num**, which will return a number between zero and 255, if the character falls in that range. Otherwise, it will return NIL. Note that this number is an internal position, not an ASCII code.

```
(charp a) ==) A  ;; recall that atoms need not
                 ;; be quoted in Lispvm
(charp 'a) ==) A
(charp @) ==) @
(char2num a) ==) 193
(char2num b) ==) 194
```

Lispvm, like many of the other "uncommon" Lisp dialects, has similar functions to Common Lisp for string manipulation, although they may have different names and implementations. Examples of some of the salient functions in Lispvm will be given here.

The function **concat** takes two or more character strings as arguments, and returns a single character string formed by the concatenation of the arguments. An example is shown below.

```
(concat "hello " "there") ==) "hello there"
```

It is also possible for one or more of the arguments to be stored identifiers; that is, a valid Lisp name. In this case, a string called the *print name* of the identifier or symbol is concatenated to the other strings. An example of this is shown here:

```
(concat "hello " john) ==) "hello JOHN"
```

Note that, in each of the above examples, a blank was provided as a character in one of the strings to separate the words in the resulting string. This is necessary if we want to have a space between the words; otherwise no space will be provided by the system. An example of this is:

```
(concat "auto" "matic") ==) "automatic"
```

The function **capacity** takes a character string as its argument and returns the maximum possible size of the string:

```
(setq word "automatic")
(capacity word) ==> 9
```

The function **size** is similar to **capacity**. It returns the current length or the number of characters in a character string:

```
(size word) ==> 9
```

However, these functions do not always return exactly the same result. When applied to vectors, **capacity** returns the bit or character capacity of the vector, which may be larger than the current number of elements in it, while **size**, like **length**, returns the actual number of elements.

The function **elt** takes as its arguments a character string and an integer, "n." It returns the nth element of the string. An error is signalled if "n" is negative or exceeds the current length of the string. An example of **elt** is shown below.

```
(elt "automatic" 4) ==> |m
```

Recall that the first character is in position zero.

The function **substring** takes as its arguments a character string and two integers. The first indicates the starting position of the desired substring, and the second gives its length:

```
(substring "hello, how are you?" 7 3) ==> "how"
```

Note that the output is a string, and therefore delimited by double quote marks. On the other hand, the function **elt** does not return a string, but rather a single character, which is preceded by | to distinguish it from a possible identifier with the same name (cf. character marker #\ in Common Lisp).

The function **strpos** takes two character strings, an integer "n," and nil for its arguments. It searches the second string for a substring identical to the first argument. It begins the search in position "n" of the second argument. The function returns the position where the substring occurs, if it does; otherwise it will return NIL. Examples:

```
(strpos "to" "automatic" 0 nil) ==> 2
(strpos "ho" "automatic" 0 nil) ==> NIL          (4.29)
(strpos "mat" "automatic" 2 nil) ==> 4
(strpos "to" "automatic" 4 nil) ==> NIL
```

The above functions are examples of those provided in Lispvm for searching strings; there are others. There are also several functions that change the elements or update a string. In the following discussion, we will assume that you have defined:

```
(setq phrase " 'Tis the merry month of May.")
```

The function **downcase** acts on a string by changing any upper case letters in the string to lower case:

```
(downcase phrase) ==) " 'tis the merry month of may.)
```

The function **upcase** changes lower case letters to upper case. By applying **downcase** in the above example, we actually changed the value of the original string. Now if we apply **upcase**, we get:

```
(upcase phrase) ==) " 'TIS THE MERRY MONTH OF MAY."
```

The function **setelt** takes a character string, an integer "n," and a character. It replaces the *n*th element of the string with the character in the argument:

```
(setelt phrase 10 b) ==) B    ;; the string started
                              ;; with a blank space in position zero.
```

and the phrase now is " 'TIS THE BERRY MONTH OF MAY." The M in position 10 of the original string has been changed to a B. These functions can, of course, call each other like any other function. Thus, to change the B in the phrase back to an M, we can type:

```
(setelt phrase (strpos "8" phrase 0 nil) M)
```

and the phrase will change again to " 'TIS THE MERRY MONTH OF MAY."

As a last example of string updating functions, let us consider **rplacstr**. This function takes as arguments a character string, an integer indicating a starting position, an integer indicating length, and a replacement string. It returns an updated string:

```
(replacstr phrase (strpos "MERRY" phrase 0 nil) 5 "RAINY")
= " 'TIS THE RAINY MONTH OF MAY."
```

4.5.5 Exercises

1. Construct an inventory table for a store. Each product in the store should be represented by at least a unique number and name, a quantity in stock, and a critical number that indicates orders for new supplies must be placed when the quantity of the product reduces to that number. Write a function or functions for searching for items in the table, checking current quantities, and placing orders for new supplies when necessary.

2. Write a function for inserting a name in a telephone directory at its proper alphabetic sequence. For example, if the following names are listed:

```
Gartener, Elias      444-5656
Gasman, Judith       656-3232
Gatkann, Peter       777-8877
```

and you want to enter Gassmann, Fred, it should go between Gasman and Gat-kann.

3. Construct a dictionary that will contain words with mutually exclusive parts-of-speech: determiners, proper-nouns, nouns, etc. Write a program that reads the individual words of an input sentence and outputs them, together with their parts-of-speech. If a word is not in the dictionary, an appropriate message should be printed. Use the **format** function for all outputs.

4. Write a function that will compare two lists and print the number of elements that occur in both lists. For example, comparing (a b c f g h) and (k g a t n p) should return 2, since a and g occur in both lists.

5. Write a function **emphasize** that will take a sentence as input. If any word in the sentence is an adjective, the function should add the word 'very' before the adjective. Thus, if the input is "The hungry bears ate the sweet honey," the function should return "The very hungry bears ate the very sweet honey." (Due to Nina Wachholder)

6. Construct a course list for an academic department, where the course name is the identifier, and its number, classroom, and professor are its property. Write a program for the retrieval of course information, and also for its updating.

7. Assume that the telephone directory in Exercise 2 was updated randomly by adding names at the end of listing. Write a program to sort the directory, but first change to uppercase all the names, and remove any excess blanks around the names.

8. Write a function that takes a character and a string for arguments and counts the number of occurrences of the character in the string; e.g., [a, "ala-bama"] $\Rightarrow$ 4

9. Write a function that takes a positive integer "n" and a character as arguments, and returns a string of "n" characters.

4.5.6 Sets

The easiest way to handle sets in Lisp is to write them as lists, using parentheses where you would ordinarily use set brackets. We have already encountered examples of set functions, as applied to lists in Section 2.7. We will give some further examples in this subsection, with some additional details. However, before dealing with examples, we need to mention a few additional operations in Common Lisp.

The pound sign, #, has been used on several occasions, particularly when we talked about characters. Let us be a bit more specific now. # is a macro character. It is an indicator that what follows it has a special meaning or role. Examples:

$\#\backslash$:   What follows can be a character or name
        of a character (print-name): $\#\backslash$a = character a.
$\#'$:   What follows is a function name:
        $\#'$equal = function EQUAL.
$\#$b $\#$o $\#$x   :   Radix 2, 8, 16 numbers:
        $\#$b1001 = 9, $\#$x79 = 121.

#(:   What follows is a vector:
#(a b c d) = a vector of 4 elements.

Common Lisp has a large number of *keywords,* which are preceded by a colon. Examples are: :test, :key, :initial-element. These and others can be used in function calls or function constructions (see further in text).

Returning to sets, let us review some of the commonly used set functions. Even with Common Lisp, these functions are implementation-dependent, and the examples that are given do not behave exactly the same in all dialects; but at this point the user should be able to test them for the particular dialect that is being used.

The function **union** takes two set or list arguments, and returns a set of elements unique to the two sets. The function **intersection** returns the elements that are in both sets. The function **set-difference** (**setdifference** in Lispvm) returns a list of the elements in list one that are not in list two. The order of elements in the resulting sets is implementation-dependent, and may vary in different dialects.

```
(union '(a b c d) '(e f g a b))
          ==) (E F G A B C D)                         (4.30)
(intersection '((a b) c) '(a b c)) ==) (C)
(set-difference '(a b c d) '(e f g a b)) ==) (C D)
```

In Example (4.30), Common Lisp uses the **eql** function to determine the equality of elements in the top-level of the two argument sets; but you can use :test and :key keywords to direct the use of other equality functions, or use other functions for a different search in the lists or sets:

```
(setq set1 '(a b c d e f))
(setq set2 '((a b) (c d) (e f)))
(setq set3 '((a b) e f))
(setq str1 '("b" "c" "a" "d"))
(setq Str2 '("c" "a"))
(intersection set2 set3) ==) NIL                      (4.31)
(intersection set2 set3 :test #'equal) ==) (A B)
 ;Recall that (eql '(a b) '(a b)) ==) NIL, but
 ;(equal '(a b) '(a b)) ==) T
(intersection str1 str2 :test #'string-equal)
          ==) ("c" "a")
```

Recall that the **member** function takes an item and a list (or set) as arguments and, if item occurs in the list, returns the sublist beginning with the item. In Common Lisp, there are also **member-if** and **member-if-not**, which test whether an item in the list satisfies (or does not satisfy) a predicate function, and returns a sublist beginning with the item:

```
(member 'c set1) ==> (C D E F)
(member '(a b) set2) ==> NIL
(member '(a b) set2 :test #'equal)
     ==> ((A B) (C D) (E F))
(member 'c set2 :key #'caadr)      ;c matches with the
     ==> ((C D) (E F))   ;car of car of cdr of set2
(member-if #'atom set1) ==> (A B C D E F)  ;elements
                              ;of set1 are atoms

(member-if #'listp set1) ==> NIL
(member-if #'listp set2) ==> ((A B) (C D) (E F))
(setq set4 '(a b c (e f) (g h)))
(member-if #'listp set4)     ;The portion which is
   ==> ((E F) (G H))   ;true for the predicate LISTP
                          ;begins with (e f).
(member-if-not #'listp set4)   ;LISTP fails with the
   ==> (A B C (E F) (G H))   ;first element 'a.
(member-if-not #'atom set1) ==> NIL
(member-if #'(lambda (x) (not (atom x))) set4)
     ==> ((E F) (G H))     ;This example shows that
                   ;you could have a whole lambda expression
              ;as the argument of #.  The above function
              ;call searches list set4 for the first
              ;occurrence of an entity that is not
              ;an atom.
(setq digits '(2 3 4 5 6 1 0 2 3 -5 -6))
(member-if #'(lambda (x) (> x 5)) digits)
     ==> (6 1 0 2 3 -5 -6)   ;Returns a sublist
              ;beginning with the first digit that
              ; is greater than 5.
(member-if-not #'plusp digits) ==> (-5 -6)
;[in some implementations 0 is not plusp]
```

(4.32)

The function **subsetp** is a predicate function. It takes two sets, and returns T if the first set occurs as a subset of the second set:

```
(subsetp '(a b) set2) ==> T
(subsetp '(a c) set2) ==> NIL
```

(4.33)

Recall that the function **adjoin** adds an element at the beginning of a list, if the item is not already in the list. The function **adjoin** tests for membership only at the top-level of the list:

```
(adjoin 'a set1) ==> (A B C D E F)  ;a already there.
(adjoin 'k set1) ==> (K A B C D E F)
```

```
(adjoin 'b set2) ==> (B (A B) (C D) (E F))
(adjoin '(a b) set2) ==> ((A B) (A B) (C D) (E F))
          ;Recall (eql '(a b) '(a b)) ==> NIL
(adjoin '(a b) set2 :test #'equal)
   ==> ((A B) (C D) (E F))    ;(equal '(a b) '(a b))==>T
```

4.5.7 Trees

Another way of representing data structures is by tree construction. In fact, many of the structures we have discussed so far can be represented by trees. A familiar representation is a 'family tree,' tracing one's own genealogy or that of a historical figure. However, here we will be considering trees in a restricted and formal sense. A tree is defined as a collection of nodes and branches, where each node has only one entry point (that is, only one branch can enter a node), but any number of exit branches. Thus, each node can have only one parent (*mother*), but any number of *daughters*. There is one 'distinguished' node, called the *root node,* which does not have any branch entering it. The nodes that have no branches coming out of them are called *leaves*. Nodes connected to a single mother node are called *sisters*. A tree is normally represented with the root node on the top, with branches going downward to the hierarchy of nodes, and ending in leaves. As the direction of the branches is 'understood' as stated, the direction is not marked with arrows in a tree. In the presentation of trees, we will use upper-case letters to write the *names* of the root and intermediate nodes, and lower-case letters to write the names of the leaves.

Entries in a telephone directory can be represented as in Figure 4.18:

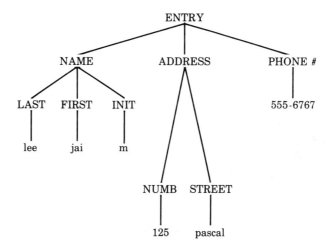

Figure 4.18. Tree representation of an entry in a phone book.

Arithmetic expressions, like a + b*c, can be drawn as shown in Figure 4.19.

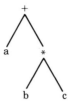

Figure 4.19. An arithmetic tree.

Sentences like "The old train left the station" can be represented as

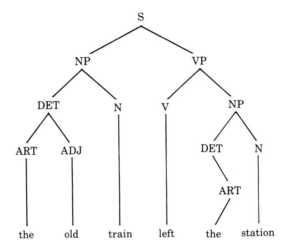

Figure 4.20. A linguistic phrase structure tree.

The tree in Figure 4.20 is called a *binary* tree. Another name for a leaf is a *terminal node,* and the nodes immediately dominating terminals are called *pre-terminals*. In a binary tree, each node has at most two daughters.

Note, incidentally, that the nodes in the tree in Figure 4.20 are *subtrees* of the root. There are other variations in tree terminology in the literature. A slightly more precise definition of a tree and subtree, and some of the variant terminology, are given in the following definition:

```
A tree, T, is a nonempty finite set of
elements called nodes such that:
1) T contains a distinguished node R, called
      the root of T and
```

2) the remaining nodes of T form an ordered   (4.34)
   collection of zero or more disjoint trees
   T1, T2, ... , Tm. The trees T1 ... Tm are called
   the subtrees of R, and the roots of T1 ... Tm are
   called successors of R.

Other terms found in the literature include parent, ancestor, children, left child, right child, sibling, frontier (for leaf), and so on.

In any discipline involving sequential decision making, trees may be used to describe the branching of alternatives as the consequences of each decision, leading to new decisions and new consequences, which in turn lead to new decisions, and so forth. Game trees are but one popular example. Organizational charts, tables of contents, and inventories of goods are other bodies of data that can be appropriately represented as trees. The usefulness of the tree structure has led to entire chapters of books devoted to algorithms for moving through trees, finding things in them, and other operations. We will investigate a few of these applications.

The definition of a tree given in Example (4.34) is an example of a recursive definition—a definition in which the term being defined is defined in terms of smaller objects like itself. Many of the functions that operate on trees are recursive in the same sense, in that the functions call themselves on subtrees of the original tree. Before writing functions to operate on trees, however, we need to decide on a simple representation of a tree in Lisp. Consider the tree in Figure 4.21:

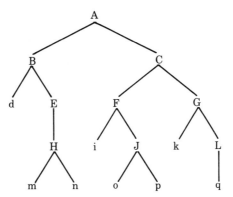

Figure 4.21. A tree representing the structure of (d m n i o p k q).

One way to write this tree as a list is to represent each subtree as a list containing its root followed by its subtrees. So the tree in Figure 4.21 would be in the format shown in Figure 4.22, called *labeled bracketing,* where 'labels' are names of the nodes (upper-case symbols) other than terminals.

$$\begin{array}{c} \text{(A (B (d) (E (H (m) (n))))} \\ \text{(C (F (i) (J (o) (p)))} \\ \text{(G (k) (L (q)))))} \end{array}$$

Figure 4.22. Labeled bracketing representation of the structure of (d m n i o p k q).

Note that the leaves are single elements of their lists because they have no subtrees. An interesting exercise is to write a function to take a tree expressed as such a list and extract from it a list of its leaves. Let's call the tree in Figure 4.21 MAGNOLIA, define it by (setq magnolia '(a . . . . . etc)), and then define the function **foliage** for extracting the leaves.

```
(defun foliage (tree)
       (cond ((null tree) nil)
             ((atom (car tree)) (foliage (cdr tree)))
             ((null (cdar tree))(append (car tree)        (4.35)
                                   (foliage (cdr tree))))
          (t (append (foliage (car tree))
                     (foliage (cdr tree)))))))
```

If we then input (foliage magnolia), (D M N I O P K Q) is returned.

The function asks about the first element of each subtree. If that first element is an atom, then it is a root with subtrees of its own (in particular, it is not a leaf), and the function goes on to find the leaves of the subtree. If the first element is a subtree with only one element, for instance, a list containing exactly one atom, then it is a leaf and is tacked onto the list of leaves of the other subtrees that are yet to be found. If neither of these is the case, then the first element must have subtrees also, and the list of their leaves will be appended to the lists of leaves of the other subtrees (cdr tree). The order in which these questions are asked is significant. We do not want to ask of an atom whether its **car** has a null **cdr**, because only lists have **cdr**s. So the question (atom (car tree)) is asked first. If the answer is yes, then the next question *will not be asked* about that list. We can run through the operation of the function on a small tree—not a binary tree in this case, since the function is not restricted to binary trees. Consider the tree in Figure 4.23

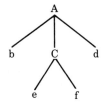

Figure 4.23. Tree representing (A (b) (C (e) (f)) (d)).

Let us call this tree BUSH, and define it in Lisp as:

$$(\text{setq bush '(a (b) (c (e) (f)) (d)))} \tag{4.36}$$

Now if the **foliage** function is called by inputting (foliage bush), the following steps will be processed (you can call the **trace** or **step** function to observe the process).

At the beginning, (null bush) is not true, so the next condition is evaluated, and (atom (car bush)) is true (it is a), so the function **foliage** is called with (cdr bush) as its argument, which is now ((b) (c (e) (f)) (d)). This is not null, nor is its **car** an atom, so the function goes on to look at the **cdr** of its **car** (that is, the **cdr** of (b)). That *is* null, and so the **car** of BUSH, (b), will be appended to a further call of the function **foliage** with the new **cdr** of BUSH, ((c (e) (f)) (d)). Neither of the first three conditions is true for this list, so the t clause will apply, and the function **foliage** is called with the **car** of BUSH, which is now (c (e)(f)) to be appended to the call of **foliage** with the **cdr** of BUSH, which is now ((d)). Continuing in this manner with repeated function calls, we get to the final process of (append '(b) (append '(e f) '(d))) ⇒ (B E F D), which is the list of the leaves of BUSH.

Other important operations on trees include traversal and search. Traversal is a mechanical way of examining every node in a tree, and there are three popular and well-known procedures for doing this. They are referred to as *preorder, inorder,* and *postorder* traversal, because when applied to trees that represent arithmetic expressions like the one above, they yield the prefix, infix, or postfix forms, respectively, of the expressions. For example, given the tree in Figure 4.24:

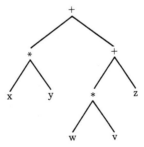

Figure 4.24. The structure of (x * y) + ((w * v) + z).

which represents x*y + w*v + z, a postorder traversal results in xy*wv*z+ +. This is also sometimes referred to as a depth-first traversal. Its formal definition is, not surprisingly, recursive:

(1) Traverse in postorder the subtrees of the tree.

(2) Visit the root of the tree.

A function that will perform this traversal, call it **postord**, can be denned as:

```
(defun postord (tree)
    (cond ((null tree) nil)
          ((atom (car tree))
                        (append (postord (cdr tree))          (4.37)
                                (list (car tree))))
          (t (append (postord (car tree))
                     (postord (cdr tree)) )))))
```

As the function in Example (4.37) moves through the list that represents the tree, if the next element is an atom, then it has subtrees that must be traversed before the root is "visited." Otherwise, the next item in the list is, itself, an entire subtree, which must be traversed along with any other subtrees that follow.

To test the **postord** function, we will assign the structure of the arithmetic expression underlying the tree in Figure 4.24 to a variable called MATH-TREE, in accordance with the convention for *labeled bracketing*:

```
(setq math-tree '(+ (* (x)(y)) (+ (* (w)(v)) (z)) ))
```

The function **postord** can then be called with MATH-TREE as its argument to obtain the postfix (or reversed-Polish—see Exercise 3 in Subsection 4.5.8) notation of the expression:

```
(postord math-tree ==) (X Y * W V * Z + +)
```

Further examples of tree manipulations are included as exercises in the next subsection.

4.5.8 Exercises

1. Consider the following function on trees and trace its behavior on MAGNOLIA, defined in Figure 4.22. What is the value of (take-a-walk-in magnolia)?

```
(defun take-a-walk-in (tree)
    (cond ((null tree) nil)
          ((atom tree)(list tree))
          (t (append (take-a-walk-in (car tree))
                     (take-a-walk-in (cdr tree)))))))
```

2. Consider the tree LILAC, shown below. Represent it in list form and apply the function **foliage** to it, tracing the behavior of the function.

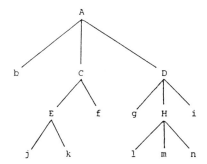

3. Preorder or prefix is also referred to as Polish notation, after the Polish logician J. Lukasiewicz, who invented the prefix notation for logic. Recall that expressions in Lisp are also in prefix notation. Write the function **preord**, which takes a normal arithmetic expression in infix notation and converts it to Polish notation. For example, the expression x*y + w*v + z should be returned as + * X Y + * W V Z.

4. Consider the following organization chart for a corporation. Represent the tree as a list and write a function to obtain a list of those people who supervise no one.

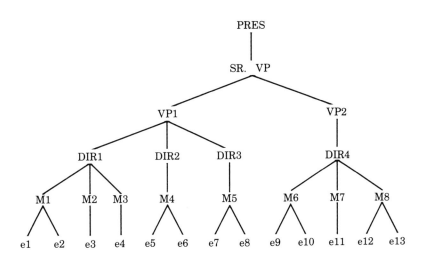

5. Augment the tree of Exercise 4 by including each person's salary, and compute the average salary of the "low men on the totem pole."

6. Construct a tree to represent the chapter and section organization of this book. Write a program that can take a chapter number as an argument, and return a list of sections under that chapter.

4.5.9 Stacks

A stack is a list of objects that has additions and deletions made to it at only one end. That end is referred to as the *top* of the stack even if it appears to be the bottom end. Because deletions are made from the same point in the list where additions were last made, stacks are said to have a "last in, first out" (lifo) pattern of growth and attrition. Many real-life situations behave in this way. One example is the firing of personnel in many companies on the basis of least seniority—so the last in is the first out. In some cafeterias, clean plates are kept in a stack with a spring on the bottom that keeps the level of the top of the stack constant. Plates are added to the stack and taken from the stack always from the top and so, here too, the last in is the first out. Another feature of a stack is evident from this example: the only element of the stack that *is* accessible is the top element. An element can be accessed only if all of those above it are removed, one by one. Although these examples may seem silly, stacks have very important applications in all aspects of computer science. The processes of adding an element to a stack and removing the top element from a stack are called *pushing* and *popping,* respectively. Stacks are easy to implement in Lisp (and are, in fact, part of the core of every Lisp system). Any list can be treated as a stack if we only insert and delete elements from one end. Suppose that we decide to write our stacks as lists with the left end corresponding to the "top." Then, to "push" an element *x* onto a stack *s,* we can use the Lisp function **push**. This function takes as its arguments an item that is to be added to a stack, and a stack. It returns the updated stack with the item added. Thus, if S = (A B C) and we use:

$$(\text{push 'x s})$$

then S = (X A B C) will be returned. Note that the value of "S" has been changed permanently (a global change). We can accomplish the same result by writing (setq s (cons 'x s)). However, to write a function that achieves this in a general way (for example, assigning a global value within another function) requires certain facilities which have not been discussed so far.

The function **pop** takes one argument—a stack—and pops the "top" element from it. Here are some examples of **push** and **pop** functions:

```
(setq stack1 '(a b c))
(setq stack2 '(a (f g) h k))
(push 'a stack1) ==> (A A B C)
stack1 ==> (A A B C)
(pop stack1) ==> A
stack1 ==> (A B C)
(pop stack2) ==> A
(pop stack2) ==> (F G)
stack2 ==> (H K)
(pop stack2) ==> H
```
(4.38)

```
(pop stack2) ==) K
stack2 ==) NIL
(pop stack2) ==) NIL
(push 'a stack2) ==) (A)
(push '(f g) stack2) ==) ((F G) A)
```

Common Lisp has another function, called **pushnew**, which is a macro and adds an element to the top of the stack only if the element is not already in the stack.

```
(setq stack3 '(a (f g) h k))
(pushnew 'a stack3) ==) (A (F G) H K)
(pushnew '(f g) stack3 :test #'equal)                    (4.39)
    ==) (A (F G) H K)
(pushnew '(f g) stack3) ==) ((F G) A (F G) H K)
```

The predicate function **endp** returns T if a stack (list) is empty, otherwise it returns NIL. Function **list-length** returns the number of elements at the top level of a list: (list-length '(a (f g) h k)) $\Rightarrow$ 4.

4.5.10 Queues

A queue is a set of objects to which additions are made at one end and deletions from the opposite end. The most common example is the waiting line at the bank or grocery store. We join the line at the "back" and are taken off the line, or "served," from the front. Queues can also be easily imitated in Lisp.

```
(defun queue (s w)
  (cond ((null s) (push w s))
        (t (setq s (reverse (cons w (reverse s)))))))

(setq x '(a b c d))                                       (4.40)
(setq x (queue x 'e)) ==) (A B C D E)
x ==) (A B C D E)
(pop x) ==) (B C D E)
x ==) (B C D E)
```

Note that, in Lispvm, **addtolist** is a destructive function and adds an element at the end of a list, so that it can be used for the simulation of a queue:

```
(setq x '(a b c d))
(addtolist x e) ==) (A B C D E)
x ==) (A B C D E)                                         (4.41)
(pop x) ==) (B C D E)
x ==) (B C D E)
```

4.6 SUGGESTIONS FOR PROJECTS

Projects are larger exercises that may require from a few hours for completion to a lifetime of research and development. Normally, a serious project is a program or a system of programs consisting of many functions, databases, and so forth. We are not going to propose any 'lifetime' projects here! It is recommended that you start thinking and planning for one or more of these projects, but for final implementation you may want to study Chapter 5 first, especially if you are using Common Lisp.

Project 1. We will discuss and do the first project for you and leave the rest for you to do. This is an exercise that is often given in an introductory course in computer science for writing in whatever programming language is taught in that introductory course. It is called the eight queens problem, or puzzle. Recall that a queen can move in any direction on a chess board, vertically, horizontally, and diagonally, and it threatens or "checks" any other chessmen that are on its paths. The problem is to place eight queens on a single chess board such that none of them threaten any other. To solve this problem in Lisp, we will adopt a program from a number of exercises in Yuasa and Hagiya (1987) and Yuasa (1988). As you will see, there is more than one solution for the eight queens problem. Figure 4.25 presents one solution:

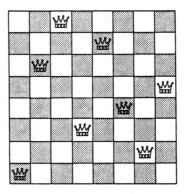

Figure 4.25. One solution to the eight queens problem.

First, we will define the function **queen** with the parameter "n" for the number of queens to be placed. This function will call the function **queens**, which does most of the work. Note that **queens** has six parameters, so that when it is called by **queen**, apart from "n," five other dummy arguments are passed, which initialize the values of the **queens** parameters. The only other function is **print-queens**, which is called by **queens** and displays on the monitor the replica of a chess board with queens placed in safe positions.

```
(defun queen (n)
   (queens n 0 0 nil nil nil))

(defun queens (n i j column left right)
   (cond ((equal i n) (terpri)
      (print-queens n column) nil)
         ((equal j n) nil)
         ((or (member j column)
              (member (+ i j) left)
              (member (- i j) right))
          (queens n i (1+ j) column left right))
         ((queens n (1+ i) 0 (cons j column)
                             (cons (+ i j) left)
                             (cons (- i j) right)))
         ((queens n i (1+ j) column left right))))

(defun print-queens (n x)
   (break "Press Ctrl-P to print more;
           else press Ctrl-C to stop")
   (do ((y x (cdr y)))
       ((null y)) (terpri)
       (do ((i 0 (1+ i)))
           ((equal i (car y))) (princ ". "))
          (princ "Q ")
       (do ((i 0 (1+ i)))
           ((equal i (- n (car y) 1)))
          (princ ". ")))))
```

(4.42)

The **break** form in **print-queens** causes the computer to pause for input (see Section 3.10). The keychord *Ctrl-P,* in the dialect that we are using (GCLisp), is equivalent to inputting the function (continue). If *Ctrl-P* is pressed, a replica of a chess board, with "n" queens placed, will appear on the monitor followed by the break message again. Every time you (continue), a new solution will appear, until they are exhausted; then the solutions will be repeated or NIL will appear. Finally, pressing *Ctrl-C* in this dialect gets out of the break and back to the top-level, where the processing stops. Here are some examples:

```
(queen 8)
Press Ctrl-P to print; else press Ctrl-C to stop
1) [continue]
```

```
. . Q . . . . .
. . . . Q . . .
. Q . . . . . .
. . . . . . . Q
. . . . . Q . .
. . . Q . . . .
. . . . . . Q .
Q . . . . . . .
```

(4.43)

```
Press Ctrl-P to print; else press Ctrl-C to stop

1) [continue]

. . . . Q . . .
. Q . . . . . .
. . . Q . . . .
. . . . . . Q .
. . Q . . . . .
. . . . . . . Q
. . . . . Q . .
Q . . . . . . .


Press Ctrl-P to print; else press Ctrl-C to stop
1)
Top-Level
```

In the above example, we see two of the solutions to the problem. Note that the way the functions are written, this program can be run for any number of queens. If "n" is 4, a four by four board is produced, with four queens placed. If "n" is ten, a ten by ten board with ten queens is produced:

```
(queen 4)
Press Ctrl-P to print; else press Ctrl-C to stop
1) [continue]
. . Q .
Q . . .
. . . Q
. Q . .

Press Ctrl-P to print; else press Ctrl-C to stop      (4.44)

1)

Top-Level
```

```
(queen 10)

Press Ctrl-P to print; else press Ctrl-C to stop

1> [continue]

. . . . . . . Q . .
. . . . Q . . . . .
. Q . . . . . . . .
. . . Q . . . . . .
. . . . . . . . . Q
. . . . . . Q . . .
. . . . . . . . Q .
. . . . . Q . . . .
. . Q . . . . . . .
Q . . . . . . . . .
```

Project 2. This project is another exercise in a celebrated problem known as the Missionaries and Cannibals. There are three missionaries and three cannibals on the left bank of a river. They want to cross over to the right bank with a boat that can carry a maximum of two people at each crossing. In the process of back and forth crossing, if the cannibals outnumber the missionaries on either bank of the river, the missionaries will be eaten. What is a safe strategy (for the missionaries) for the six to cross the river?

For a computer program to solve this problem, you must formalize it to some precize formulation. Let us use M for missionary, C for cannibal, and B for boat. The description of the initial state is then:

$$Left\text{-}Bank = [M\ M\ M\ C\ C\ C\ B]$$
$$Right\text{-}Bank = [\ ]\ or\ NIL$$

The goal state is:

$$Left\text{-}Bank = [\ ]$$
$$Right\text{-}Bank = [M\ M\ M\ C\ C\ C\ B]$$

You have to fill, in between, the various transition states. This can be represented in a tree structure, where the root represents the initial state and some path in tree climbing will lead to the goal state.

What are the possible moves at each state? At the initial state, five moves are possible: [C], [M], [M C], [M M], and [C C]; so that the construction of the tree may begin as in Figure 4.26:

Figure 4.26. The initial branching of the tree for Problem 2.

At first observation, it may seem that the tree will grow exponentially. But this is not the case in practice, because at each new node, the branching possibility does not remain five. For example, when there are, say, three C's left on the left bank, only two moves are possible: [C] and [C C]. Furthermore, in that particular situation, it does not make sense for one C to go over because then he has to come back to bring the boat and nothing will be achieved, so that the only logical move is [C C]. Now suppose that the tree looks something like Figure 4.27:

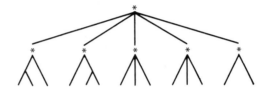

Figure 4.27. A more expanded tree of Figure 4.26.

We can do a depth-first search of the tree, that is, go down one branch, say the left-most, to the end. If there is no success, back up to a previous branching node and go down that path. But the missionaries cannot afford this luxury, because if they follow one of the wrong paths, they won't be around to try the alternative paths! The solution must be planned, and paths determined, before any moves are made. You can solve the problem manually by taking three chips of one color and three chips of another color and juggle them around until you find the right moves. But it will not do for you to write a program to print the sequence of moves that you have discovered. The computer program must solve the problem in a general way. Here are some of the procedures (stated in a slightly more precise form) that must be kept in mind in designing your program:

1. Cannibalism occurs on either bank of the river, with or without the boat:
   If the number of cannibals > the number of missionaries
   Then if the number of missionaries /= 0
   Then the cannibals eat the missionaries
2. Undesireable looping occurs:
   If the current state = a previous state
   Then backup for an alternative path

3. Invalid move:

> *If* the number of C/M < the number required by move
> *Then* abandon move

To avoid *cannibalism,* make a list of all illegal states (ILS) on the left bank, that is, all possible combinations of numbers of missionaries, cannibals, and boat on the left bank that will lead to an *eat* state. Before making any move, make sure that the move does not involve an illegal state in the ILS list. You can make the list manually, but you should write a program to 'discover' the illegal states and compile the list. Incidentally, it might be more convenient for adding to and subtracting from, if you represent the states in triplets, such as (3 3 1) for [M M M C C C B], (0 2 0) for [C C], etc.

Looping can occur if the program enters a state that it has entered in one of the previous moves. This can lead to a circular search, and must be checked against.

An example of an *invalid move* is the case where a particular move calls for a move-list (1 1 1) from the right bank, but the state of the bank is (0 2 1), then the move does not apply. The move function can have all possible moves (maximum of 5) for an argument, but apply the one that is applicable in each action.

Finally, the program must have **format** expressions or other printing expressions to print the sequence of moves for solving the problem, for example:

```
LB: [M M M C C C B]    :::    RB: []
        Move [C C B]   :::
        LB: [M M M C]  :::    RB: [C C B]
                       :::    Move [C B]
    LB: [M M M C C B]  :::    RB: [C]
        etc.
```

Reference: Bundy (1978).

Project 3. The *rules* in Example (4.45), below, are for a *phrase structure* grammar for simple sentences in English, in which the following abbreviations are used: S (sentence), NP (noun phrase), VP (verb phrase), AUX (auxiliary), C (complimentizer), PRO (pronoun), P (preposition), N (noun), V (verb), ADJ (adjective), DET (determiner), ADV (adverb), and PP (prepositional phrase).

$$
\begin{aligned}
S &\longrightarrow NP\ AUX\ VP \\
S &\longrightarrow C\ NP\ VP \\
NP &\longrightarrow DET\ ADJ\ N \\
NP &\longrightarrow PRO \\
VP &\longrightarrow V\ NP\ PP \\
VP &\longrightarrow V\ NP\ NP \\
VP &\longrightarrow V\ S \\
VP &\longrightarrow V\ ADV
\end{aligned}
\qquad (4.45)
$$

Let us call the grammar in Example (4.45) G, and the language described by this grammar, L. The rules in G are called *rewrite rules*. The first rule, for instance, can be interpreted as saying that a sentence, according to G, is a noun phrase (NP), followed by an auxiliary (AUX), followed by a verb phrase (VP); for example, [the old teacher] [will] [leave the school] (with each phrase bracketed separately; needless to say, there may be internal bracketing in each phrase). Some of the components in the rules may be optional. You can have sentences such as

```
The old teacher will leave the parocial school
The teacher left
I left
Leave!
etc.
```

It is left to you to account for these in your implementation (see the references at the end of this project description). It should also be pointed out that G in Example (4.45) is proposed only for the purposes of this project, and has no relevance to current linguistic theories.

G can 'generate' the sentences listed above, as well as other sentences, such as: I said that I was wrong, John gave the book to Mary, John gave Mary the book, the cat jumped on the table, and so forth. However, it will also 'generate' such bizarre sentences as: The tree jumped on the balloon, the mountain chased the helicopter, etc.

A. Construct a dictionary of common English words, with a property list for each word giving the parts of speech, number, tense, human/nonhuman, animate/ inanimate, and any other features that are necessary to avoid the generation of ill-formed sentences. For example, nouns and adjectives could be marked for those beginning with vowel or consonant, for taking the determiner *a* versus *an;* verbs could be marked for transitivity, and many other such details.

B. Write a program to generate a given number of sentences by randomly selecting nouns, verbs, determiners, adjectives, and so forth, and constructing sentences in accordance with the rules of G. However, the sentences should be well-formed—no bizarre sentences. This can be done by checking on the properties of the words, to make sure that they are appropriate for combination into phrases. In order for the sentences to be different, you must randomly select the appropriate words from the dictionary. Most Lisp dialects have a system function called **random**, which returns a pseudo-random number. Each time you call **random**, a new number will appear. This number, call it *n,* can be suitably modified to fall within the range of the dictionary. It can then be used to get the *n*th word in the dictionary. Common Lisp has a function called **random**, which can return an integer between zero and the number that is the argument of the function. If you have a dictionary of 2000 words, every time you input (random 2000), a new number between zero and 2000 will be returned. If you wish, you can make separate lists for nouns, verbs, adjectives, and so on, and randomly select different parts of speech from different lists.

C. Write a second program, which can take a sentence as input, and return the structural description of the sentence in accordance with the grammar G. For example, if the sentence is: "I will read the letter," your program should output:

$$(S\ (NP(PRO(i)))\ (AUX(will))\ (VP\ (V(read))$$
$$(NP(DET(the))(N(letter)))\ )\ )$$

or it can return the output in the form of a tree structure:

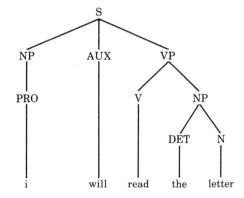

The program that analyzes sentences in this manner is called a *parser*. Parsers have important roles in computational linguistics, artificial intelligence, and compiler construction. The study of parsers can be a life-long project.

References: Aho and Ullman (1972), Moyne (1985).

Project 4. We have given some simplistic examples of *block world* in the text, but sophisticated models can and have been constructed, and building such models can be challenging and fun. For example, consider Figure 4.28:

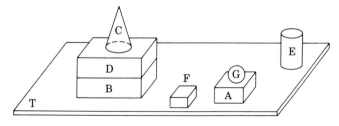

Figure 4.28. Block world example.

If you instruct a robot (computer program) to place the block A on the top of block B, it must first clear the top of A, then move C and D from the top of B, before moving A to B. Furthermore, it must find a space on the table T for the removed objects. If you ask the robot to put the cylinder E in box F, the robot must see if the box is big enough, has room in it, empty it, etc. If you ask the robot to place the globe G on the top of the cone C, it must know that it cannot be done, and so forth.

You can include features in the property-lists of blocks that can be tested for each action. For example, a feature of a cone is that it cannot support another object. The features of the size and shapes of blocks can be tested for compatibility.

In addition, you must provide functions for grasping blocks, moving blocks, and placing blocks on available or 'goal' spaces.

References: Charniak and McDermott (1985), Winograd (1972), Winston (1984).

5

Extensions

___

5.1 INTRODUCTION

So far we have covered the main system functions and facilities of Lisp language. In this chapter, some of the extensions and additional capabilities of the language will be described particularly as they apply to Common Lisp. The chapter also contains some reviews of material discussed in the previous chapters.

5.2 A REVIEW OF BASIC ELEMENTS AND DATA TYPES

Although Lisp is mainly designed for manipulating lists, we have already seen that modern Lisp systems have rich and efficient procedures for numerical and mathematical computations. Numbers can be represented as positive and negative integers, and as floating-point numbers. The largest (smallest) number is dependent on implementation. In the full implementation of Common Lisp, there are system-defined *constants* that can give the maximum (minimum) numbers for a given system. For example, the constant MOST-POSITIVE-FIXNUM will give the value of the largest integer available.

Numbers are normally represented in base 10, decimal numbers, but, with the use of the pound sign (#), and radix marker (r), they can be represented in other bases. For example, #2r1101 represents radix-2 number 1101, or decimal 13; #16r7d represents radix-16 number 7d, or decimal 125. We have already seen that the most common radices have special notations in Common Lisp: #b, #o, and #x for binary, octal, and hexadecimal numbers, respectively.

Common Lisp can also handle complex numbers. #c is the marker for a complex number. Complex numbers are made up of a real part and an imaginary part. #c(4 5) is a complex number, with 4 and 5 as real and imaginary parts, respectively. Arithmetic operations can be performed on complex numbers:

```
(+ #c(3 5) #c(2 4) ) ==> #c(5 9)
```

There are also system functions for extracting the parts of a complex number:

```
(realpart  #c(-2.3 5)) ==> -2.3
(imagpart  #c(-2.3 5)) ==> 5.0
```

'Imaginary' operation on a number, such as the square-root of a negative real number, will produce a complex number:

```
(sqrt -2.0) ==> #c(0.0 1.4142...)
```

Note that complex numbers may not be implemented for a particular dialect of Common Lisp, but you can easily write your own functions to create and do many of the operations (see Exercise 1 in Section 5.5).

Again, subject to implementation, ratios may be represented in Common Lisp by two integers, a numerator and a denominator, which are also the names of functions for extracting these values. Thus, 1/2 is a ratio data type in which:

```
(numerator 1/2) ==> 1
(denominator 1/2) ==> 2
```

Speaking of data types, apart from the number types mentioned above, there are symbols, lists, functions, characters, strings, arrays, sequences, keywords, atoms, and so forth. There is a function in Common Lisp, **type-of**, which can verify the type of a data item:

```
(type-of 7) ==> FIXNUM            ;7 is an integer (fix number)
(type-of 7.5) ==> SINGLE-FLOAT
(setq x 5) ==> 5
(type-of x) ==> FIXNUM
(type-of #\a) ==> STANDARD-CHAR   ;Standard characters
                                  ;on the keyboard.
(type-of '(a b c)) ==> CONS       ;a chain of cons cells=list
(type-of 3/2) ==> RATIO
```

There is also a predicate function, **typep**, which can be used as shown in the following examples:

```
(setq y 15) ==> 15
(typep y 'number) ==> T  ;value of y is a number type
```

```
(typep 'a 'number) ==> NIL
(typep 'a 'symbol) ==> T
(typep '(a b c) 'list) ==> T
(typep "This message" 'string) ==> T
```

The predicate function **subtypep** takes two arguments and determines whether the first argument is a subtype of the second argument:

```
(subtypep 'integer 'number) ==> T T
(subtypep 'float 'number) ==> T T
(subtypep (type-of '(a b c)) 'list) ==> T T
```

Note that **subtypep** returns two values. The second value determines if the two arguments can be related. If that is T, then the first value states whether the first argument is a subtype of the second argument:

```
(subtypep 'list 'number) ==> NIL T  ;LIST and NUMBER can
                                    ;be compared, but LIST is not a
                                    ;subtype of number.
(subtypep 'number 'symbol) ==> NIL T
(subtypep 'integer 'number) ==> T  T
(subtypep 'number  'integer) ==> NIL  T
```

You can write your own functions for type and subtype:

```
(setq animals '(lion dog elephant cat tiger))
  (defun my-type-of (x)
    (if (member x animals) 'animal nil))
  ==> MY-TYPE-OF
  (my-type-of 'cat) ==> ANIMAL
  (my-type-of 'wolf) ==> NIL
```
(5.1)

```
(defun my-subtypep (x y)
  (if (member x y) t nil))
==> MY-SUBTYPEP
(my-subtypep 'elephant 'animals) ==> T
(my-subtypep 'animals 'elephant) ==> NIL
(my-subtypep 'bees 'animals) ==> NIL
```
(5.2)

Arrays are collections of data elements arranged in a Cartesian coordinate space. An array can be thought of as a grid with slots, where each slot can hold an object and is indexed by a series of positive integers. The indices determine the position of the objects. An array can have any number of dimensions. A two-dimensional array, called a *matrix,* is given in Figure 5.1.

$$
\begin{array}{c|cccc}
 & 0 & 1 & 2 & 3 \\
\hline
0 & 1 & 2 & 3 & 4 \\
1 & 5 & 6 & 7 & 8 \\
2 & 0 & 0 & 0 & 0 \\
\end{array}
$$

Figure 5.1. Example of a two-dimensional array.

Number 7 in this array is represented as 7_{12}, indicating that it is in row 1, column 2 of the array. In Lisp, we can represent an array as a list of lists, for example:

```
#2A( (1 2 3 4) (5 6 7 8) (0 0 0 0) )
```

This is a two-dimensional array of 3 by 4 (three rows, four columns).

In this book, we will deal only with a one-dimensional array, called a *vector*, which will be discussed further in Section 5.6.

One data type can often (but not always) be converted to another. We have already seen such conversions as:

```
(string 'abc) ==) "ABC"
(float 5) ==) 5.0
(list 'a) ==) (A)
```

A system function in Common Lisp, **coerce**, provides for various conversations, as in the following examples:

```
(coerce 3/2 'float) ==) 1.5    ;ratio to float
(coerce '(a b c) 'vector) ==) #(a b c)  ;list to vector
(coerce "a" 'character) ==) #\a    ;string to character
```

5.3 BINDING AND UNBINDING

A variable is a name that can be associated with a value. The process of associating a value with a variable or a name is called *binding,* and a variable that is associated with a value is called a *bound variable.* Assignment is the process of assigning a value to a name. Intuitively, we think of assignment as a slot with a name into which we place data. The name is then the 'address' of the data. It was noted in Chapter 4 that the address may contain a pointer to the data, which may be stored in another place in the memory. The system functions **setq** and **setf** are the principle assignment functions in Lisp.

```
(setq x 5) ==) 5
```

Gives "x" the value of 5. From then on, unless a new value is reassigned to "x," every time you use "x" or input "x," it will evaluate to 5: $x \Rightarrow 5$.

Now consider the following function:

```
(defun foo (x)
  (cond ((zerop x) nil)
        (t (print x)
           (foo (- x 1))))))               (5.3)
==> FOO
```

Assuming that "x" has been assigned the value 5, as above, let us call **foo**:

```
(foo x) ==>  5
             4
             3                              (5.4)
             2
             1
             NIL
```

Within the function call in Example (5.4), the value of "x" changes from 5 to 4, 3, 2, 1, and finally to 0, which ends the process. But now, if you input "x," you will still get 5 as its value. Within the function **foo** the "x" has been *bound* to 4, 3, 2, 1, and 0, but its assigned value has not changed. On the other hand, if we call **foo** with another value, the parameter of **foo** (x) is bound to the new value. But this is the *local value,* and the assigned value (also called the *global value*) remains unchanged:

```
(foo 3) ==>  3
             2
             1
             NIL
x ==> 5
```

When a function is defined, the whole body of the function is assigned as the value of its name. There is a way of writing functions in some dialects of Lisp that gives an overt representation of this process. For example, in Lispvm, the function in Example (5.3) can be written as follows:

```
(setq foo '(lambda (x)
  (cond ((zerop x) nil)
        ('t (print x)
            (foo (- x 1))))))              (5.5)
```

To repeat, in the above example, "x" has the *global* value 5, but takes *local* values within the **foo** function. Consider, however, the following example:

```
(defun foo2 ( )
   (setq x 'a))
==) FOO2                                              (5.6)
(foo2) ==) A          ;call foo2 returns A
 x ==) A    ;global value of x has changed to A
```

Note that, in Example (5.6), "x" is not in the lambda list of **foo**2. (In computer programming jargon, this is called an "undeclared" variable.) If we had written (defun foo2 (x) (setq x 'a)), "x" would have been defined as local, and its global value of 5 would not have changed.

Example (5.6), which assigns a global value within a function, can cause problems if it is embedded in another function, or is called by another function, because it can create a conflict of values for the same variable. The function **let** in Common Lisp avoids this problem. The function **let** assigns a value to an undeclared variable without making it global:

```
(defun foo3 ( )
 (let ((x 'a)) (list x) ))
==) FOO3                                              (5.7)
(foo3) ==) A
 x ==) 5              ;global value of x preserved
```

The function **let** can be in the form of a complex expression, which may include other functions. The general syntax of the special form **let** is:

```
(let ( (⟨variable⟩  ⟨value⟩)

              . . .
        (⟨variable⟩  ⟨value⟩) )
      (⟨expression⟩)                                  (5.8)

              . . .
      (⟨expression⟩)   )
```

The following examples demonstrate some of the characteristics of **let**.

```
(let ((a 3))       ;let binds a to 3
(list (* a 4)(+ a a)))   ;the scope of variable "a"     (5.9)
   ==) (12 6)    ;extends into the body of let.
```

```
(let ((a 3) (b 5))
   (defun foo (x y)      ;a function defined within
       (cond ((= x y) x)        ;the body of let.          (5.10)
             (t (+ x y))))
   (foo a b))     ;function call inside let.
==) 8    ;a is not equal to b, hence a+b=8 is given.
```

```
(let ((a 3)) (let ((b (* a a))) (list a b)))            (5.11)
   ==) (3 9)
```

```
(let ((name 'lee)) (print name))
   ==> LEE
       LEE
```

(5.12)

```
(let ((name 'lee)) (print name) nil)
   ==> LEE
       NIL
```

```
(defun big-number (n)
   (let ((m (* n n n))) (expt m m)))
==> BIG-NUMBER
(big-number 2) ==> 16777216
(big-number 5) ==> ERROR: Integer overflow
 ;The number was too big for the author's pc!
```

(5.13)

```
However, consider this:
(big-number 5.0) ==> 1.262931158075170+262
 ;in float ("scientific notation")
```

Exercise: Try to analyze the following expression, given with its output (adopted from Yuasa (1988) pp. 20–21):

```
(let ((a 3)) (list a (let ((a (* a a))) (+ a a))
   a (let ((a (+ a a))) (* a a)) a))
      ==> (3 18 3 36 3)
```

In the following examples, compare **setq** with **let**. The function **setq** binds (assigns) global values, whereas **let** binds local values.

```
(setq x 1 y 2 z 3) ==> 3
x ==> 1    y ==> 2    z ==> 3
(let ((a 1)(b 2)(c 3))) ==> NIL
a ==> ERROR: Unbounded variable: A
(let ((a 1)(b 2)(c 3)) (list a b c)) ==> (1 2 3)
a ==> ERROR: Unbounded variable: A
```

(5.14)

A property of **let** is that it binds its parameters simultaneously, so that in (let ((a 3) (b 5))), a and b are bound at the same time. This property of **let** can cause a problem if, in a series of bindings, you try to use the value of the first binding in the second one. For example, in

$$(\text{let } ((a\ 3)\ (b\ (*\ a\ a))))$$

"a" and "b" are bound simultaneously, but in trying to bind "b" with the value of (* a a), an error message is returned because "a" is unbound. In Common Lisp there is a variant of **let**, with the notation **let***, which binds serially, so that in

```
(let * ((a 3) (b (* a a))))
```

"a" is first bound to 3, and then, when it comes to the binding of "b," "a" has a value and "b" is bound to $3 \times 3 = 9$. Examples:

```
(let ((a 3) (b (* a a))) (* a b b))
  ==> ERROR: Unbound variable A                    (5.15)
(let* ((a 3) (b (* a a))) (* a b b))
  ==> 243        ; 3x9x9=243
```

A similar process of 'parallel processing' occurs with the function **psetq**. The following example illustrates this process:

```
(setq x 10)
x ==> 10
(setq x 2 y (* x x))
x ==> 2   y ==> 4                                  (5.16)
(psetq x 2 y (* x x))
x ==> 2   y ==> 100
```

In the first **setq** form in Example (5.16), "x" is assigned the value 10. In the second, **setq** "x" is bound to 2, and then "y" is bound to $2 \times 2 = 4$. In the **psetq** form, however, "x" and "y" are bound simultaneously, so that when "y" is being bound, the value of "x" is still 10 and y is bound to $10 \times 10 = 100$ (assuming that the second **setq** in Example (5.16) has not been executed).

In Common Lisp, the function **symbol-value** returns the value of its argument if the argument is a bound variable with a *global* value:

```
(setq x 5)
(let ((y 3)))
(symbol-value 'x) ==> 5
(symbol-value 'y) ==> ERROR: Unbound variable
                   ;The value of y is not global.
```

Study the following examples for further elaboration:

```
(setq x 5 y 10)
(let ((x 3)) (symbol-value 'x)) ==> 5
    ;symbol-value returns the global value of x

(let ((x y)) (list x)) ==> 10    ;local vale of x
(defun strange (y)                                 (5.17)
  (let ((y 3)) (list (* y y) (symbol-value 'y))))
  ==> STRANGE
(strange 5) ==> (9 10)  ;The global value of y=10
(strange 0) ==> (9 10)
```

```
(defun explain (x)
    (* (symbol-value 'x) x))
    ==> EXPLAIN
    (explain 6) ==> 30

(setq x 5)
(let ((x 3)) (list (symbol-value 'x)x)) ==> (5 3)
```

In the example, function **explain**, the symbol-value of 'x is the global value 5 set by the **setq** at the top of Example (5.17). The second "x" is the parameter of the function and is bound to 6 by the function call (explain 6), so that the function evaluates to $5 \times 6 = 30$.

Finally, there is a function for unbinding a bound variable. It is called **makunbound**, and it is useful for releasing unwanted variables to save memory:

```
(setf x '(one two three))
  x ==> (ONE TWO THREE)
(makunbound 'x)
  x ==> ERROR: Unbound variable X
```

There is also a function, **fmakunbound**, for unbinding function names:

```
(defun square (n)
    (* n n))
(square 3) ==> 9
(fmakunbound 'square)
(square 3) ==> ERROR: Undefined function SQUARE
```

We have already seen the predicate function **boundp**, which returns true if its argument is a bound variable:

```
(setf x 'a)
(boundp 'x) ==> T
(boundp 'y) ==> NIL
(boundp x) ==> NIL   ;Note the lack of quote '
```

5.4 EXPANSIONS IN LAMBDA EXPRESSIONS

Recall that the list of parameters of a function is called a *lambda list,* and in Section 2.11 we saw that *lambda expressions* can be constructed as nameless functions. So far, the parameter forms given for functions and lambda expressions have been restrictive, in that if the function had, say, three parameters, the call to this function had to have exactly three arguments. Common Lisp provides certain flexibilities that relax the above restriction. In the parameter lists of functions and lambda expressions, there can be certain optional elements that may or may not be entered in the call to the function. In this section, we will discuss *&optional, &rest, &aux,* and *&key, lambda-list keywords* for variables, which can be used in a lambda list to provide flexibility. We will first give examples of the use of each keyword separately and then show how they can be used in combination.

The *&optional* variables are optional variables that can be given with or without initial values; examples:

```
(defun exam-1 (a b &optional c d)
    (list a b c d)) ==> EXAM-1
(exam-1 1 2) ==> (1 2 NIL NIL)
(exam-1 2 3 4) ==> (2 3 4 NIL)
(exam-1 2 3 4 5) ==> (2 3 4 5)
```
(5.18)

In the first call, (exam-1 1 2), a is bound to 1, "b" is bound to 2, and "c" and "d" are bound to NIL. In the last call, (exam-1 2 3 4 5), "a," "b," "c," and "d" are bound to 2, 3, 4, and 5, respectively.

```
(defun exam-2 (a b &optional (c 5) (d 6))
    (+ a b c d)) ==> EXAM-2
(exam-2 3 4) ==> 18    ;3+4+5+6 = 18
(exam-2 3 4 0 0) ==> 7  ;arguments override the
                        ;initial value of parameters.
(exam-2 3 4 10 10) ==> 27
```
(5.19)

```
(defun exam-3 (a b &optional (c 5 c-flag) d)
       (list a b c c-flag d)) ==> EXAM-3
(exam-3 1 2 5 7) ==> (1 2 5 T 7)
(exam-3 1 2 3 4) ==> (1 2 3 T 4)
(exam-3 1 2 3) ==> (1 2 3 T NIL)
(exam-3 1 2 10 2) ==> (1 2 10 T 2)
(exam-3 1 2) ==> (1 2 5 NIL NIL)
```
(5.20)

The variable **c-flag** in the parameter list of **exam-3** is a boolean variable (returns T or NIL), which is NIL if "c" uses its default value. Otherwise, if "c" takes a value given by the argument of the call, even if the given value is the same as the default value, the value of **c-flag** is T. The general syntax of **c-flag** is (alpha beta-flag), where *alpha* and *beta* are any variables. The variables *alpha* and *beta* may or may not be the same variables, and suffix *-flag* is optional. The first line in Example (5.20) could have been written as (defun exam-3 (a b &optional (c 5 d) e), where "d" would have acted as the flag for "c" (see further on and Exercise 8 in Section 5.5 for additional examples).

The *&rest* variables allow for any number of arguments in the function call, and collect them into one list for output processing:

```
(defun exam-4 (a &rest b)
   (list a b)) ==> EXAM-4
(exam-4 5) ==> (5 NIL)
(exam-4 'x 'y) ==> (X (Y))
(exam-4 1 2 3 4 5 6) ==> (1 (2 3 4 5 6))
   ;a is bound to 1 and b is bound to (2 3 4 5 6)
(exam-4 (list 1 2 3 4 5)) ==> ((1 2 3 4 5) NIL)
   ;In this call "a" is bound to (1 2 3 4 5) and
   "b" is bound to NIL.
(exam-4 (apply '+ (list 1 2 3 4 5))) ==> (15 NIL)
```
(5.21)

In the last line of Example (5.21), the system function **apply** applies addition to the **list** of numbers. Thus, **exam-4** can be used, among other things, to add numbers in any arbitrary list of numbers. This can be further simplified as in the following example:

```
(defun exam-4a (&rest x) (apply '+ x))
(exam-4a 2 3 4 5) ==> 14
```

The function apply is a mapping function (see Section 2.11) that applies a function to a list of arguments.

```
(defun exam-5 (a b &rest c)
   (list a b c)) ==> EXAM-5
(exam-5 5 6) ==> (5 6 NIL)
(exam-5 'a 'b 'c 'd 'e 'f) ==> (A B (C D E F))
```
(5.22)

```
(defun exam-6 (&rest a)
 (list a)) ==> EXAM-6
(exam-6) ==> (NIL)
(exam-6 'x) ==> ((X))
(exam-6 'x 'y 'z)==> ((X Y Z))
(exam-6 (apply 'car (list (list 'x 'y 'z)))) ==> ((X))
```
(5.23)

Compare the last call of **exam-6** with:

```
(apply 'car (list (list 'x 'y '3))) ==> X
```

The *&aux* variables are auxiliary variables that cannot receive their values from function calls. Their values are local and must be given inside the lambda list:

```
(defun exam-7 (a b &aux (c 5) (d 6))
   (+ a b c d)) ==> EXAM-7
(exam-7 2 3) ==> 16    ;2+3+5+6=16
```
(5.24)

```
(defun exam-8 (a b &aux (c 'z))
   (list a b c)) ==> EXAM-8                          (5.25)
(exam-8 'x 'y) ==> (X Y Z)
```

Note that the same result as in Example (5.25) can be obtained by using the function **let** for local binding:

```
(defun exam-9 (a b)
   (let ((c 'z)) (list a b c))) ==> EXAM-9
(exam-9 'x 'y) ==> (X Y Z)
```

(5.26)

```
(defun exam-9a (a b)
   (let ((c 10)) (* a b c)))
==> EXAM-9A
(exam-9a 2 3) ==> 60              ;2x3x10=60
```

Before using *&key,* let us make the definition of the term *keyword* a bit more precise. So far, the term has often been used in its general sense, of a word that is recognized by Lisp as part of its vocabulary, for example, names of the system functions. However, most of the words in the vocabulary of Lisp are not reserved words, and can be redefined by the user. Lispvm has only one reserved word, NIL, and other dialects have only a handful of reserved words. In this sense, function names are not keywords, but Common Lisp has a number of other *keywords.* For example, the optional variable indicators that we have discussed in this section are known as *lambda-list keywords.* Other system keywords or keywords defined by the user usually have a colon (:) in front of them (see Section 5.11).

The *&KEY* variables within a lambda list specify keywords used in a function or lambda expression:

```
((lambda (a &key d)
   (list a d)) 2 :d 3) ==> (2 (:D 3))              (5.27)
;The output is a list with members 2 and a
;keyword D with value 3.
```

We will now give some examples of the uses of lambda-list keywords in combinations:

```
((lambda (a b &optional c &rest d)
   (list a b c d)) 1 2 3 4)                         (5.28)
      ==> (1 2 3 (4))
```

```
((lambda (a b &optional (c 4) d &rest e &aux (f 7))
   (list a b c d e f)) 2 3)                         (5.29)
      ==> (2 3 4 NIL NIL 7)
```

In the output of the lambda expression in Example (5.29), "a" is bound to 2; "b" is bound to 3; the optional "c" is bound by its initial value to 4; "d" and "e" are NIL; and "f" is bound to 7, its initial value under *&AUX*.

$$
\begin{aligned}
&((\text{lambda } (a\ b\ \&\text{optional } c\ d\ \&\text{rest } e\ \&\text{aux } (f\ 5)) \\
&\quad (\text{list } a\ b\ c\ d\ e\ f))\ 1\ 2\ 3\ 4\ 5\ 6) \\
&\quad ==\rangle\ (1\ 2\ 3\ 4\ (5\ 6)\ 5)
\end{aligned} \tag{5.30}
$$

In Example (5.30), "a" is bound to 1; "b" is bound to 2; "c" is bound to 3; "d" is bound to 4; 5 and 6 are bound to "e" as list (5 6); and "f" is bound to its initial value of 5.

$$
\begin{aligned}
&((\text{lambda } (a\ \&\text{optional } b\ \&\text{rest } c\ \&\text{key } (d\ 5)) \\
&\quad (\text{list } a\ b\ c\ d))\ 1\ 2\ 3\ :d) \\
&\quad ==\rangle\ (1\ 2\ 3\ (:D\ 5))
\end{aligned} \tag{5.31}
$$

$$
\begin{aligned}
&(\text{defun exam-10 } (a\ b\ \&\text{optional } (c\ 3\ c\text{-flag}) \\
&\quad d\ \&\text{rest } e\ \&\text{aux } (f\ 6)\ (g\ 10)) \\
&\quad (\text{list } a\ b\ c\ c\text{-flag } d\ e\ f\ g)) \\
&\text{EXAM-10} \\
&(\text{exam-10 } 1\ 2)\ ==\rangle\ (1\ 2\ 3\ \text{NIL NIL NIL } 6\ 10)
\end{aligned} \tag{5.32}
$$

"a" is bound to 1; "b" is bound to 2; "c" is bound to its initial value, 3; *c-flag* is set to NIL because "c" is bound to its initial value; "d" and "e" are NIL; and "f" and "g" are bound to their initial values, 6 and 10, respectively.

```
(exam-10 1 2 4) ==) (1 2 4 T NIL NIL 6 10)
```

In this call of **exam-10**, "c" is bound to 4 and *c-flag* is set to T, because "c" is not bound to its initial value.

```
(exam-10 1 2 3 4 5 6 7 8 9)
   ==) (1 2 3 T 4 (5 6 7 8 9) 6 10)
```

In this call, "c" is bound to 3 supplied by the argument of the call; although this value is the same as the initial value of "c", it is a 'supplied' value and therefore *c-flag* is set to T. The list (5 6 7 8 9) is bound to "e", and "f" and "g" again get their initial values.

```
(exam-10 1 2 nil 4) ==) (1 2 NIL T 4 NIL 6 10)
(exam-10 'i 'j 'k 'l 'm 'n 'o 'p 'q)
   ==) (I J K T L (M N O P Q) 6 10)
```

Note again the T for *c-flag* in the above output.

Subject to implementation, there is also *&allow-other-keys,* which, similar to *&rest,* allows keywords that are not specified in the lambda list to be used.

5.5 EXERCISES

1. Write a function to extract the real and imaginary parts of a complex number.

2. Write a function to extract the numerator and denominator of the ratio x/y, where "x" and "y" are arbitrary numbers.

3. Verify what types the following data items are: 55, 5.75, "a", 'a, #\a, (x y z), 1/2.

4. Write a predicate function, **my-typep**, which verifies the type of its argument; e.g., (my-typep 5 'number) ⇒ T, (my-typep 'a 'number) ⇒ NIL.

5. What is the value of x after the following procedures have been executed?

```
(setq x '(a b c d)) ==> (A B C D)
(defun foo ( )
  (prog (x)
  tag1 (cond ((null x) (return 'empty))
             (t (setq x (cdr x)) (go tag1)))))
  ==> FOO
(foo) ==> EMPTY
```

6. The following is an attempt to write a function to compute the square of any number "n". Does it work? Why?

```
(defun square (n)
  (let ((x n) (y (* x x)))
    (format nil "The square of ~s is ~s" n y)))
```

7. (psetq x 5 y (* x 2)) ⇒ ERROR. Why?

8. What are the values of the following expressions:

```
((lambda (a b &optional (c (* a b)) d &rest e)
   (list a b c d e)) 1 2)

((lambda (a &optional (b (* a a)) d) &rest e)
   (list a b d e)) 1 2 3 4 5 6)

((lambda (a &optional (b (+ a a)) c) d)
   (list a b c d)) 2 3 4)

(defun new-exam (a b &optional c (d (+ a b)) e) f
  &rest g) (list a b c d e f g))
NEW-EXAM
(new-exam 5) ==> ?
(new-exam 5 6) ==> ?
(new-exam 5 6 3) ==> ?
(new-exam 5 6 3 7) ==> ?
```

```
(new-exam 5 6 3 7 8 9 10 12 'a 'b) ==) ?
(apply 'car (list (new-exam 1 2 3 4 5 6))) ==) ?
(apply 'print(list(new-exam 1 2 3 4 5 6 7 8))nil) ==)?
```

5.6 ARRAYS

In Common Lisp, there is a system function **make-array** (**make-vec** in Lispvm, for creating vectors) for creating arrays. For example, (make-array '(2 3)) will create a 2 by 3 two-dimensional array. Since a vector is a subtype of an array, namely a one-dimensional array, array functions will apply to vectors. There are also subtypes of vectors: bit-vector (a vector whose elements are only zeros and ones), string-vector, integer-vector, and so forth. In general, a vector can have any number of elements of any of the data types recognized by the language. Elements or objects in a vector can be accessed by indices, starting with zero for the first element. Recall that a vector is identified with a pound sign; for example, #(a b c) is a vector of three elements, where "a" is in position zero (indexed by zero) and "c" is in position two.

The form (make-array 5) creates a vector of length 5 (0 through 4), but it is empty. We can write vectors with objects in them in several ways:

```
#(1 2 3 a b c)
(vector 1 2 3) ==) #(1 2 3)
```

There are, however, also *keywords* that can be used with **make-array** for various specifications of vectors. The following examples will illustrate these:

```
(make-array 10 :initial-element #\a)
 ;This will create a vector of ten "a" characters.
(make-array 5 :initial-contents '(a b c d e))
 ;This will be the vector #(A B C D E).
```

In the above examples, the actual outputs from the forms will be specifications that vary according to implementation: It may be something like #<VECTOR T 10 904F:38C6>, according to one implementation, but we need not be concerned with that. The vector is there and can be accessed, as will presently be seen. We can also give a name to a vector by assignment:

```
(setf vec (make-array 3 :initial-contents '(a 2 b)))
```

The elements of an array can be accessed by the function **aref**. The general format of **aref** is:

```
(aref ⟨array-name⟩ ⟨index⟩)
```

Thus, using VEC, we can get the following results:

```
(aref vec 0) ==) A
(aref vec 1) ==) 2
(aref vec 2) ==) B
(aref vec 3) ==) ERROR ;out of bound of vec.
```

Note also the following:

```
(length vec) ==) 3
(vectorp vec) ==) T    ;another predicate function
(vectorp 'a) ==) NIL
(arrayp vec) ==) T
(type-of vec) ==) (VECTOR T 3)
```

Let us now define a vector with some initial values and use a combination of **setf** and **aref** to change the values

```
(setq fibonacci (make-array 8 :initial-element 1))
    (setf (aref fibonacci 2) 2)
    (setf (aref fibonacci 3) 3)
    (setf (aref fibonacci 4) 5)
    (setf (aref fibonacci 5) 8)
    (setf (aref fibonacci 6) 13)
    (setf (aref fibonacci 7) 21)
```
(5.33)

In Example (5.33), the first line creates a vector called FIBONACCI of size 8 with a 1 placed in each position (indexed 0 to 7). Then the forms following the first line change the 1 in positions 2 to 2, in position 3 to 3, in position 4 to 5, and so on to the end, so that the vector would be #(1 1 2 3 5 8 13 21). The Fibonacci sequence or Fibonacci number series was discovered by the great Italian mathematician, Leonardo of Pisa (also known as Fibonacci), in the Middle Ages (eleventh–twelfth centuries), and has certain interesting and significant properties, which are not our concern here. Each number in the sequence after the first two ones is made up of the sum of the previous two numbers. The sequence, of course, extends infinitely.

Let us now write a function to generate Fibonacci sequences of any arbitrary length n:

```
(defun fibonacci (n &aux (fib (make-array n
                      :initial-element 1)))
    (prog ((i 2))
    tag1 (cond ((= i n) (return fib))
           (t(setf (aref fib i) (+ (aref fib (- i 2))
                           (aref fib (- i 1)))))
             (setf i (1+ i))
             (go tag1)))))
```
(5.34)

If the **fibonacci** function is called by, say, (fibonacci 5), a vector expression may result which, depending on implementation, may be #<VECTOR T 5 904F:AEE4>. You won't see the Fibonacci numbers, and you cannot reveal them by using **aref** because **fib** in Example (5.34) gets local values, but outside of the function **fibonacci**, it is unbounded (it can, of course be called with (setq vec (fibonacci 5))). In order to see the numbers, we will make a few changes in the **fibonacci** function to print a list of the numbers as well as creating the vector. The vector in this case is redundant, but we have it for exercise!

```
(defun fibonacci2 (n &aux (fib (make-array n
                            :initial-element 1)))
    (prog ((i 2) (L '(1 1)))
tag1 (cond ((= i n) (return (list L fib)))
          (t (setf (aref fib i) (+ (aref fib (- i 2))
                                   (aref fib (- i 1)))))
             (setq L (reverse (cons (aref fib i)          (5.35)
                                   (reverse L))))
             (setf i (1+ i))
             (go tag1)))))
FIBONACCI2
(fibonacci2 10) ==>
((1 1 2 3 5 8 13 21 34 55)  #(VECTOR T 10 904F:A579))
```

For another example, we will write a function for the product of a real number times a vector. The real number is called a *scalar*. Product of a scalar "k" times vector (a b c) is a vector, and is defined as k(a b c) = (ka kb kc).

```
(defun scalar (k vec n &aux (m (make-array n)))
    (let ((c 0))
      (dotimes (i n c)                                    (5.36)
         (setq c (* (aref vec i) k))
         (setf (aref m i) c))))
```

The **scalar** function in Example (5.36) contains the system function **dotimes**, which we have not seen before. The function **dotimes** is a useful iteration construct in Common Lisp, which repeats specified operations, counting from zero to an integer "n", not including "n". Its general syntax is:

```
(dotimes (<variable> <counter> <result>)
      <expression-1> ... <expression-n> )
```

Examples:

```
(let ((L nil))
   (dotimes (i 10 L)                                      (5.37)
      (setq L (cons (* i i) L))))
==> (81 64 49 36 25 16 9 4 1 0)
```

In the above **dotimes** iteration, the variable "i" takes values from 0 to 9, and in each cycle, "i" is multiplied by itself and is **cons**ed in the list L.

In the next example, we will compute the sum of integers from 0 to n-1:

```
(defun sum (n)
  (let ((m 0))
    (dotimes (i n m)                        (5.38)
      (setq m (+ i m)))))
(sum 101) ==) 5050   ;sum of integers from 1 to 100
```

Now let us call the **scalar** function in Example (5.36):

```
(scalar 5 #(1 2 3) 3) ==) 15
```

The arguments are 5 (value of the scalar), vector #(1 2 3), and the size of the vector, 3. The output 15 is the value of the last element of the output vector ($3 \times 5 = 15$). To see all of the results, we can insert a print expression in the function.

```
(defun scalar2 (k vec &aux (m (make-array (length vec))))
  (let ((c 0))
    (dotimes (i (length vec) c)
      (setq c (* (aref vec i) k))
      (setf (aref m i) c)
(print (aref m i)))) nil)
```
(5.39)

```
(scalar2 5 #(2 3 4 5 6))
    10
    15
    20
    25
    30
    NIL
```

The output vector, then, is #(10 15 20 25 30).

We have seen procedures for adding objects to or changing objects in a vector. There are, however, system functions for removing objects from, or adding objects to, a vector (similar to the operations on stacks discussed in subsection 4.5.9). The function **vector-pop** removes the first element of a vector and returns it as output. The function **vector-push** adds an element to the end of a vector. The function **vector-push-extend** adds an element to the end of a vector, and if the vector is full, its size is extended. There is also a *keyword, :fill-pointer,* which can be at any point in a vector, to allow insertions and removals at that point, rather than at the beginning of the vector. When *:fill-pointer* is set, **vector-push** will change the value of *fill-pointer.*

$$(\text{setq } v \ (\text{make-array } 5 \ :\text{initial-contents } '(2 \ a \ 3 \ b \ 4) \qquad (5.40)$$
$$:\text{fill-pointer } 3))$$

In Example (5.40), "v" is assigned the vector #(2 A 3 B 4) with *fill-pointer* pointing at position 3, that is, at B. Although the overall size or 'capacity' of this vector is 5, the length available for push and pop is from the position of the pointer; that is, the access is from the place of the pointer to the beginning of the vector. However, the pointer can move and the available length will change accordingly. Examples:

```
(array-length v) ==> 5          ;number of elements
(length v) ==> 3                ;length from the pointer
(array-active-length v) ==> 3   ;from the pointer
(fill-pointer v) ==> 3          ;position of the pointer
(vector-push 'x v) ==> 3        ;position of "x"
(fill-pointer v) ==> 4          ;new position of the pointer
(vector-pop v) ==> X            ;"X" returned from the front of
                                 the pointer
(fill-pointer v) ==> 3          ;pointer moves forward
```

Note that, as the pointer moves, the position for push and pop, as well as the value returned by the **length** function, will change, but the size of the vector remains constant. The vector, "V", was defined above with size 5. Positions are indexed from 0 to 4. Irrespective of the position of the pointer, all elements in the vector are accessible through the use of the **aref** function. If you try to insert an element beyond the limits of the vector, it will fail. For example, if the pointer is set at position 4 (end) of vector "V", then:

$$(\text{vector-push } 'y \ v) \ ==> \text{NIL}$$

Some of the functions and keywords discussed here are implementation-dependent. In the example in Figure 5.2, we will illustrate the movements of the pointer for an implementation in which **vector-pop** is nondestructive, that is, the pointer moves forward over the 'popped' element, but the element is not removed from the vector. On the other hand, **vector-push** is destructive, in that the pushed element replaces the element under the pointer.

If you run the sequence of forms in Figure 5.2, you will not be able to see the contents of the vector as the changes shown in the picture. But you can use the following function to look at the array after any move.

```
(defun show-vector (v)
   (let ((l nil))
      (dotimes (i (length v) l)
         (setq l (cons (aref v i) l)))             (5.41)
      (setq l (reverse l))))
==> SHOW-VECTOR
(show-vector vec) ==> (A B C X Y Z G H I J)
```

```
(setf vec (make-array 10
        :inital-contents '(a b c d e f g h i j)
        :fill-pointer 5) )
```

```
                                    0  1 2 3 4 5 6 7 8 9
vec                                 A B C D E F G H I J
(fill-pointer vec) ⇒ 5 ──────────────────────┤
(length vec) ⇒ 5


(vector-pop vec) ⇒ E                A B C D E F G H I J
(fill-pointer vec) ⇒ 4 ───────────────────┤


(vector-pop vec) ⇒ D                A B C D E F G H I J
(fill-pointer vec) ⇒ 3 ─────────────────┤


(vector-push 'x vec) ⇒ 3            A B C X E F G H I J
(fill-pinter vec) ⇒ 4 ──────────────────┤


(vector-push 'Y vec) ⇒ 4            A B C X Y F G H I J
(fill-pointer vec) ⇒ 5 ─────────────────┤


(vector-push 'z vec) ⇒ 5            A B C X Y Z G H I J
(fill-pointer vec) ⇒ 6 ──────────────────────┤


(vector-pop vec) ⇒ Z                A B C X Y Z G H I J
(fill-pointer vec) ⇒ 5 ─────────────────┤

(array-active-length vec) ⇒ 5
(array-length vec) ⇒ 10)
(aref vec (fill-pointer vec)) ⇒ Y
```

Figure 5.2. Example of the movement of fill-pointer.

In Example (5.41), the function is called after all of the forms in Figure 5.2 have been executed. The output is that of the last display of VEC in Figure 5.2.

Note, incidentally, that the function **show-vector** can be used to display the contents of some of the vectors described previously. The following example is an illustration (see Example (5.34)).

```
(defun fibonacci3 (n &aux (fib (make-array n:initial-element 1)))
   (prog ((i 2))
      tag1 (cond ((= i n) (return (show-vector fib)))
                 (t (setf (aref fib i)(+ (aref fib (- i 2))
                         (aref fib (- i 1))))
                 (setf i (1+ i))
                 (go tag1)))))

(fibonacci3 8) ==> (1 1 2 3 5 8 13 21)
```

The functions **vector-pop** and **vector-push** do not work with vectors that do not have *fill-pointer*. A vector that does not have *fill-pointer* and can contain any type of data type is called a *simple* vector:

```
(setf sv (make-array 5 :initial-contents '(a b 3 4 5)))
  (simple-vector-p sv) ==> T
  (svref sv 3) ==> 4
```

The function **simple-vector-p** is a predicate function, and **svref** is a variant of **aref** for accessing simple vectors.

The function **copy-array-contents** takes two vector arguments and copies the contents of the first vector argument into the second:

```
(setq vec1 (make array 5 :initial-contents
          '(a b c d e) ))
    ==> #(VECTOR T 5 88B6:43C4)
    (setq vec2 (make array 5 :initial-element nil))
    ==> #(VECTOR T 5 88B6:4803)
  (copy-array-contents vec1 vec2)
    ==> T
        (show-vector vec2)
    ==> (A B C D E)
```

String vectors can be created with the **make-string** function (see subsection 4.5.4).

A *sequence* is an arrangement of data types, such as in a list or a vector. Vectors and lists can be grouped together to form a sequence. For example, ((1 2 3) #(a b c)) is a sequence (or sequences). There are a number of functions that apply to lists, as well as to vectors and sequences. The following are some examples, (subject to implementation):

```
(length '(a b c d)) ==> 4
(length #(a b c d)) ==> 4
(reverse '(a b c d)) ==> (D C B A)
(reverse #(a b c d)) ==> #(D C B A)
(remove 'a '(a b a b a c)) ==> (B B C)
(remove 'a #(a b a b a c)) ==> #(B B C)
```

Recall that **remove** is the nondestructive version of **delete**. The latter also applies as above.

The function **concatenate** (see also **nconc**) can create a sequence and also change data types.

```
(concatenate 'list #(a b c d) '(1 2 3))
  ==> (A B C D 1 2 3)
(concatenate 'vector #(a b c d) '(1 2 3))
  ==> #(A B C D 1 2 3)
```

```
(setq list1 '(a b c))
(setq list2 (copy-list list1))
     list1 ==> (A B C)
     list2 ==> (A B C)
```

The function **copy-seq** does the same as **copy-list**, but for sequences:

```
(setq x '(1 2 3) y #(a b c))
(setq x1 (copy-seq x))
x1 ==> (1 2 3)
(setq y1 (copy-seq y))
y1 ==> #(A B C)
```

The function **subseq** returns a specified subsequence of a sequence:

```
(setq L '(a b c d e f))
(setq v #(a b c d e f))
(subseq L 0) ==> (A B C D E F)
(subseq L 3) ==> (D E F)
(subseq L 5) ==> (F)
(subseq L 2 4) ==> (C D)
(subseq L 0 3) ==> (A B C)
(subseq v 0 3) ==> #(A B C)
     etc.
```

5.7 VARIANTS OF FUNCTIONS AND FORMS

A full implementation of Common Lisp would have over 700 system functions, macro expressions, and other forms. Many of these are variants of the same process, with different or identical processing approaches. For example, (car '(a b c d)) and (first '(a b c d)) are variants of a procedure for extracting the first element of a list. The difference is mostly terminological, but the underlying process is the same. On the other hand, both (+ x 1) and (incf x) increment the value of "x" by 1, but their underlying process and side effects are quite different. (+ x 1) is a simple function and the value of "x" changes *locally,* whereas **incf** is a macro that expands to assignment, and the value of "x" changes *globally.* Consider the following sequence of forms:

```
(setq x 5) ==> 5
x ==> 5            ;global value of x
(+ x 1) ==> 6
x ==> 5            ;global value has not changed
(incf x) ==> 6
x ==> 6            ;the new global value of x
```

You can expose the underlying difference between + and **INCF** by using the system function **macroexpand**. This function displays the set of codes that make up a macro. Recall that the macro name is an abbreviation for a sequence of forms, a program, which is generated and inserted into your program at the time of compilation or execution.

```
(macroexpand (incf x))
   ==) (setf x (1+ x))
```

5.7.1 Sequential and Parallel Processing

We have seen various forms used for iteration and for carrying out operations on sequences of data. Included among these have been the macro expressions **do**, **dotimes**, **prog**, **progn**, and the mapping functions first discussed in Section 2.11. In this subsection, we will present some variants of these. We use the term 'parallel processing' not in the strict sense of its use in computer science, but in the sense of simultaneous binding of variables, as we have already seen in Section 5.3 in connection with the difference between **let** and **let***. In Example (1.28), Section 1.9, we defined the following function to compute the value of a number "m" to the power of "n":

```
(defun power (m n)
   (do ((prod 1) (counter n (1- counter)))
       ((zerop counter) (return prod))
       (setq prod (* m prod))))                          (1.28)
==) POWER
(power 5 3) ==) 125
```

In this example, the **do** expression repeats the execution of the forms in its scope until a condition is satisfied (i.e., the counter becomes zero), when the execution ends and the value computed is returned. The **do** macro, using **let**, binds its *variables,* prod and counter, to 1 and *n* simultaneously, but the value of its *step-form,* (1- counter) is bound *after* each cycle of execution. There is a variant of **do**, **do***, which uses **let*** and does sequential binding, including the binding of the step-form *before* the first cycle. Therefore, we cannot replace **do*** for **do** in Example (1.28), because we would not get the right number of multiplications for the **power** function. However, we can use **do*** if we change the sequence of executions, as in Example (5.42).

```
(defun power (m n)
   (do* ((prod 1 (* m prod))
         (counter n (1- counter)))
        ((zerop counter) prod)))                         (5.42)
==) POWER
(power 5 3) ==) 125
```

Another useful variant of **do** is **dolist**. It performs an operation on a list sequentially from left to right until the list is exhausted, then it terminates:

```
(defun list-sum (list)
   (let ((sum 0))
      (dolist (i list sum)                        (5.43)
         (setq sum (+ i sum)))))
==) LIST-SUM
(list-sum '(2 3 4)) ==) 9
```

The following example simulates the system function **reverse**:

```
(defun my-reverse (list)
   (let ((y nil))                                 (5.43a)
      (dolist (x list y)
         (setq y (cons x y)))))
MY-REVERSE
         (my-reverse '(a b c d e))
(E D C B A)
```

Note the similarity between **dolist** and **dotimes**.

The function **loop** is a macro form that repeats the evaluation of a series of forms in its body until a condition followed by a **return** or **throw** causes the end. In the following example we use **loop** to define a function for undoing lists.

```
(defun undo-list (list)
(loop
    (print (car list))
    (setq list (cdr list))
    (if (endp list) (return 'done))))
==) UNDO-LIST
(undo-list '(a b c d e))
A                                                  (5.44)
B
C
D
E
DONE
```

There is a system function, **values-list**, which does the same as the **undo-list** function:

```
(values-list '(a b c d e))
A
B
C
```

```
                              D
                              E
```

The following variant of the function **undo-list** will print the output on a horizontal line:

```
(defun undo-list2 (list)
   (loop
        (format t "~a " (car list))
        (setq list (cdr list))
        (if (endp list) (return nil))))
   (undo-list2 '(a b c d e)) ==) A B C D E
```

The **endp** form in Example (5.44) is a predicate function that returns T if its argument is NIL, so that in the above example, when the list becomes empty the word DONE is returned. We have seen the use of **return** before; the form **throw**, mentioned earlier, will be discussed later in this chapter.

Some dialects of Lisp (e.g., Lispvm) and some implementations of Common Lisp do not have the **loop** function, discussed above, and users of these system often use *loop* as tags in **prog** constructions with **go**. Such users, when switching to Common Lisp, should be warned that **loop** may be a macro and could not be used as a label or tag.

There are several variants of the **prog** macro: **prog**, **prog***, **progn**, **prog1**, **prog2**, and **progv**. The function **prog**, as we have seen, can head an unnamed block, which may include variables with initial values, expressions, labels, **return**s, and **go** forms, which transfer control to labels. The function **progn** executes the forms within its body in the order given, but returns only the value of the last form evaluated. The difference between **prog** and **prog*** is again the question of parallel versus sequential binding. In their expansions, **prog** uses **let**, whereas **prog*** uses **let***. While **progn** returns the last result evaluated, **prog1** and **prog2** return the first and second results evaluated respectively, and discard other results. Some examples follow:

```
(progn (setf x 2) (setf y (1+ x)) (setf z (1+ y)))==) 4
(prog1 (setf x 2) (setf y (1+ x)) (setf z (1+ y)))==) 2
(prog2 (setf x 2) (setf y (1+ x)) (setf z (1+ y)))==) 3
(progn (setf x 2) (setf y (1+ x)) (setf z (1+ y))
        (list x y z)) ==) (2 3 4)
(prog1 (setf x 2) (setf y (1+ x)) (setf z (1+ y))
        (list x y z)) ==) 2  ;Note that 2 is not a list
(prog2 (setf x 2) (setf y (1+ x)) (setf z (1+ y))
        (list x y z)) ==) 3
```

Compare the above with the **values** function in the following example:

```
(values (+ 5 6) (* 2 3) (- 6 3) ) ==) 11 6  3
```

We also have **progv**, which can locally bind a global variable, execute a number of expressions, and return a value without changing the global value of the variable:

```
(setq x 5) ==) 5
(progv '(x) '(3) (- x 1)) ==) 2
   x ==) 5
```

The function **progv** can have a list of variables, a list of initial values, and any number of expressions that can operate on those variables. If any of the variables are global, their global values will not change outside the body of **progv**, even if they are assigned (with **setq, setf**) values within the body.

```
(progv '(x) '(3) (setq x (1- x))) ==) 2
 x ==) 5

(progv '(x y z) '(2 3 4) (setf x 7)
   (setf y (1+ x)) (setf z (1+ y)))
      ==) 9  ;value of the last expression returned
 x ==) 5    ;global value of "x" unchanged

  (progv '(x y z) '(2 3 4) x (setf y (+ 2 x))
         (setf z (+ 2 y)) (list x y z))
         ==) (2 4 6)
  x ==) 5     ;global value of x
  y ==) ERROR: unbound variable: y
              ;"y" has no global value
```

Note that, in the last example, "x" has the initial value (2) set by PROGV, but the values for "y" and "z" are derived values.

A conditional expression that evaluates a series of forms from left to right is **when**. It applies a test case and if the test is satisfied evaluates the forms in its body and returns the value of the last form evaluated:

```
(setq n 5)
(when (numberp n) (setg m (1+ n)) (setg p (1+ m))
      (setg q (1+ p))) ==) 8
```

An opposite of the above process is obtained by the function **unless**, which returns the last value if the test is nil (not satisfied):

```
(unless (symbolp n) (setq m (1+ n)) (setq p (1+ m))
        (setq q (1+ p))) ==) 8
```

The **when** function behaves the same as the combination of **if** and **progn** given in the following example:

```
(if (numberp n) (progn (setq m (1+ n)) (setq p (1+ m))
    (setq q (1+ p)) )) ==> 8
```

There is also a **case** macro, which is like the conditional expression **cond**. It only evaluates one of the forms in its body that satisfies the condition:

```
(defun number (x)
        (case x (1 'one) (2 'two)
                (3 'three) (4 'four)
                otherwise ('too-large!)))
    ==> NUMBER
    (number 2) ==> TWO
    (number 6) ==> TOO-LARGE!
```

For another example, consider the following:

```
(defun part-of-speech (x)
    (case x ('book 'noun) ('good 'adjective)
            ('read 'verb) (otherwise 'dont-know)))
    ==> PART-OF-SPEECH
(part-of-speech 'book) ==> NOUN                                    (5.45)
(part-of-speech 'good) ==> ADJECTIVE
(part-of-speech 'bananas) ==> DONT-KNOW
```

In Section 1.9, we gave an example of a **prog** macro with **go**, and we have given other examples of the use of **go** on several other occasions. The **go** and **goto** forms have been common in other programming languages, and **go** had much more relevance in the earlier versions of Lisp. We have given several examples to show its use, but we recommend that its use be avoided as far as possible. The **go** constructs are inefficient, and in large programs make reading and following the logic of the program difficult. With the introduction of the powerful variants of the **do** macros, the use of **go** can be avoided.

5.7.2 Variants of Function Definitions

The most common way of defining a function is to use **defun**. We have also seen the use of lambda expressions for defining executable unnamed functions. In this section, we will consider local functions, functions for calling other functions, and multiple-valued functions.

The function **flet** is a special form, which can be used to define a function that is recognized locally, within the scope of **flet**. The local function defined in this manner has no meaning outside of the body of **flet**, or may have different meaning than what is defined within **flet**.

```
(defun square (n) (* n n))
==> SQUARE
(flet ((square (n) (+ n n)))                         (5.46)
(square 5))
==> 10
(square 5) ==> 25
```

The last call in Example (5.46) is for the square function defined by **defun**, and (square 5) evaluates to 25. The square function defined within **flet** doubles the argument, but it is only recognized within the scope of **flet**. This facility allows the definition of local functions with any name without any danger of destroying previously defined functions. In the following example, we will redefine the system function **list** to assume that its parameters are numbers, and add them up rather than listing them. We will redefine **list** as a local function, so that it will not interfere with the system function with the same name.

```
(flet ((list (&rest x)
         (apply '+ x)))
       (list 2 3 4 5))                               (5.47)
  ==> 14
(list 2 3 4 5) ==> (2 3 4 5)
```

We will shortly say more about the function **apply**.

Note, however, that if another function is called within the scope of **flet**, even if it has the same name as the local function defined by **flet**, the call will refer to the global, and not the local, function by that name:

```
(flet ((list (&rest x) (apply '+ x))
       (foo (x) (list x)))
      (foo 2 3 4 5))                                 (5.48)
 ==> (2 3 4 5)
```

There is another form for defining local functions that has a wider scope than **flet**. It is called **labels**. Within **labels**, function calls can refer to the same locally defined function:

```
(labels ((list (&rest x) (apply '+ x))
         (foo (x) (list x)))
        (foo 2 3 4 5))                               (5.49)
 ==> 14
```

The reader should be warned that **flet** and **labels** are not widely implemented in versions of Common Lisp. But, as stated before, you can find out for yourself. If you use **flet** and, provided that you have not made other mistakes, you get a message to the effect that **flet** is an undefined function name, you will know that it is not implemented for your system!

The functions **funcall** and **apply** are system functions that call other functions. We have already seen some uses of **apply**. The first argument of **apply** is interpreted as a function name, and the rest of the arguments, normally a list, are arguments of that function name. In Section 2.6, we noted that some Lisp dialects (e.g., Lispvm and Franz Lisp) have arithmetic operators represented both as symbols: +, *, etc. and as spelled-out names: **plus**, **times**, etc. In Common Lisp, we have only the symbols. We showed that you can write a function:

```
(defun plus (x y) (+ x y))
```

But this will allow only the addition of two numbers. Now, with the use of Lambda-list keywords and **apply**, we can define **plus**, etc. for any number of operands:

```
(defun plus (&rest x)
  (apply '+ x))
==) PLUS
(plus 2 3 4 5) ==) 14
```
(5.50)

Similarly, **apply** can be used to redefine almost any of the system functions, except special forms and macros. (We do not recommend this exercise!)

The function **funcall** is like **apply**, in that its first argument is interpreted as a function name, and other arguments as the arguments of the name. However, **funcall** is not a mapping function and does not 'penetrate' a list in the above sense. In Example (5.50), **apply** cannot be replaced by **funcall**; but the following can be done:

```
(setq plus '+)
(funcall plus 2 3 4) ==) 9
```
(5.51)

The function **funcall** can be generalized by giving a variable as its first argument, and then calling it by binding a function name to this variable.

```
(defun square (x) (* x x))
  ==) SQUARE
(defun double (x) (* x 2))
  ==) DOUBLE
(defun foo (f n) (funcall f n))
  ==) FOO
(foo 'square 5) ==) 25
(foo 'double 5) ==) 10
```
(5.52)

In the following example, a function will be given for converting number course grades to letter grades, and another function for computing the average of course grades received in a semester. We then write a generalized choice function using

funcall, which will call one or the other of the above functions, depending on data submitted for its argument.

```
(defun grade-conversion (x)
  (cond (((< x 65 ) 'f)
        (((<= x 75) 'c)
        (((<= x 80) 'b-)
        (((<= x 85) 'b)
        (((<= x 90) 'b+)
        ((> x 90) 'a)
        (t 'wrong-data)))
  ==> GRADE-CONVERSION

(defun average (L)                                          (5.53)
  (setq y (/ (apply '+ L) (length L))))
  ==> AVERAGE

(defun choice (a)
  (if (listp a) (funcall 'average a)
                (funcall 'grade-conversion a)))
  ==> CHOICE

(choice '(90 89 76 68 100)) ==> 84.6
(choice 85) ==> B
```

The argument of **funcall** can also be a lambda expression or, depending on implementation, other forms such as conditional expression.

```
(funcall '(lambda (a &rest b) (list a b)) 2 3 4 5)
    ==> (2 (3 4 5))
```

Another function for naming functions is **function**. The abbreviation for that is #', which we have seen:

```
(member '(a b) '(a (a b) (c d)) :test #'equal)
    ==> ((a b) (c d))
(member 'b '(a (a b) (c d)) :test #'equal
        :key #'cadr) ==> ((a b) (c d))
```

In the above examples, #'equal and #'cadr can be written as (function equal) and (function cadr).

A function defined by **defun** normally returns one value and terminates. Most of the system functions also return one value. But there are some exceptions; for example, we have seen that **floor** and **ceiling** return two values:

```
(floor 13 5) ==) 2 3      ;13/5=2, remainder 3
(ceiling 13 5) ==) 3 -2  ;13/5=2.6, rounded up
                          ;to 3 and -2
```

The standard multivalued functions in Common Lisp are **values** and **values-list**, which we have also seen. Here are some further examples:

```
(values 'a 'b 'c) ==) A B C
(values-list '(a b c)) ==) A B C
(setq x 5 y 6) ==) 6
(values (if () x y) 'yes 'no) (if () y x) 'yes 'no))
    ==) NO   YES
(values (* x x) (* x 2) (+ x 1) (- x 3))
    ==) 25   10   6   2
```

Some other multivalued functions/macros are listed in the following paragraphs.

The function **multiple-value-setq** is a form of assignment function. It takes a list of variables and a number of expressions for arguments. The values of the arguments are assigned as the values of the variables in the list. If there are more variables than values produced, the remaining variables receive NIL values. If there are more values than variables, the excess values are ignored.

```
(multiple-value-setq (a b c d) (values-list '(3 4 5 6)))
==) 3
```

The value of the first variable is returned, but all of the variables have values, and the values are set (global). We can see that by inputting:

```
(values a b c d) ==) 3 4 5 6
Also a ==) 3, b ==) 4, etc.
```

Recall that **prog1** executives a number of forms and returns the value of the first form. If the first form has more than one value, **prog1** returns only the first one of these multivalues. The **multiple-value-prog1** special form returns all of the values of the first form. Compare the following:

```
(prog1 (floor 13 5)) ==) 2
(multiple-value-prog1 (floor 13 5)) ==) 2   3
```

The function **multiple-value-bind** is similar to **multiple-value-setq**, except that in the former the binding is local (not set). The difference between the two is the same as the difference between **setq** and **let**. Thus, **multiple-value-bind** is a more general form of **let**.

```
(multiple-value-bind (a b c d f)
    (values-list '(95 90 85 75 60))
    (list a b c d f))
    ==> (95 90 85 75 60)
 a ==> ERROR: unbound variable: A    ;a has no global binding

(multiple-value-bind (x) (floor 13 5) (list x))==>(2)
(multiple-value-bind (x y) (floor 13 5) (list x y))==>(2 3)
(multiple-value-bind (x y z) (floor 13 5) (list x y z))
    ==> (2 3 NIL)
```

The function **multiple-value-list** takes a form as its argument and after evaluating the form returns all of the values in a list.

```
(multi-value-list (floor 13 5)) ==> (2 3)
```

Note that **multiple-value-list** and **values-list** differ in that the former constructs a list of outputs, while the latter reduces a list to a string of its elements.

5.8 EXERCISES

1. The sum of two vectors is defined by the formula

$$(a\ b\ c) + (d\ e\ f) = (a{+}d\ b{+}e\ c{+}f)$$

Write a function to compute the sum of any two vectors and produce the resulting vector.

2. The *inner* product of two vectors is defined by the formula

$$(a\ b\ c)\ .\ (d\ e\ f) = (a.d + b.e + c.f)$$

where dots denote multiplication. Write a function to produce the inner product of any two vectors.

3. Given a vector "v," consisting of a set of odd and even numbers, write a function that will create two vectors, one containing all of the odd numbers and the other all of the even numbers in "v."

4. Write a function to concatenate any given two strings into one.

5. In the following sequence of expressions, place the output values in the boxes and explain.

```
(setq x 5)
(let ((x 2) (y (* x x))) (list x y)) ==> [  ]
(let* ((x 2) (y (* x x))) (list x y)) ==> [  ]
```

6. Is there a simpler way of writing Examples (1.28) or (5.42)?

7. A bank has three interest rates (10 percent, 12 percent, and 18 percent) for loans to class A, class B, and class C customers, respectively. Assume that the total interest is computed for the period of loan and added to the principal. Then this sum is divided into the number of months of the loan period to determine the monthly payment dues. Write one function with variable function calls to compute the monthly payment for any amount of loan for any period and any of the three classes of customers.

5.9 PACKAGES, BLOCKS, AND STRUCTURES

When you define a function with **defun**, you create a block of codes headed by the name of the function as its identifier. When you create a file or files of data, you may create modules and packages. When you create a collection of data, that is not quite the same as an array, you may create a structure. In this section, we will discuss these three types of data organization.

5.9.1 Blocks

There are different procedures in Lisp for creating blocks. A block can be of any size, and may or may not have a name and may contain other blocks. The macros **prog** and **do** head un-named blocks; functions are named blocks. In Common Lisp, there is a special form function called **block**, which can contain any number of expressions and returns the evaluation of the last expression:

```
(setq x 5)
(block k x (setq y (1+ x)) (setq z (1+ y))) ==> 7
```

However, you can use a **return** function to catch an intermediate result. If a block has a name (in the above example, "k" is the name of the block), you can use **return-from** <name> with a value. The return forms must be within the scope of **block**.

```
(block k x (setq y (1+ x)) (setq z (1+ y))
    (return-from k y)) ==> 6
(block x (if (numberp x) x (return-from x 'end)))
  ==> 5
(block x (if (numberp 'x) x (return-from x 'end)))
  ==> END
```

Note that, in the last two examples, "x" is the name of the blocks, but there is also a variable "x."

For another example, consider the following:

```
(defun tell (x)
  (block find
    (print x)
    (if (numberp x) (return-from find (* x x))
        (format nil "~s is not a number" x))))      (5.54)
==> TELL
(tell 5) ==> 5
              25
(tell 'what) ==> WHAT
                 "WHAT is not a number"
```

Blocks can be nested:

```
(block my-name
  (print 'max)
    (block your-name
      (print 'sally)                    (5.55)
(return-from my-name)
    (print 'wendy) 'end))
==> MAX  SALLY  NIL
```

Note that the output does not go beyond the return point. A variant of **block** and **return** is **catch** and **throw**. The special form **catch** creates a block the same as **block**, but **throw** need not be within the body of **catch**. In fact, **catch** and **throw** can be in different functions. The syntax of **catch** is:

```
(catch '⟨name⟩ ⟨expression⟩ ... ⟨expression⟩
       (throw '⟨name⟩ ⟨value⟩) )
```

The name must be quoted in both places. The following examples demonstrate some aspects of **catch** and **throw**.

```
(catch 'tag (print 'max) (throw 'tag))
    ==> MAX NIL
(catch 'taq1 (setq n 5) (setq m (1+ n)) (setq p (1+ m))
    (setq q (1+ p)) (throw 'taq1 m)) ==> 6          (5.56)
    ;; Compare the above with:
(progn (setq n 5) (setq m (1+ n)) (setq p (1+ m))
    (setq q (1+ p))) ==> 8

(defun strike-1 ( ) (catch 'ball
    (setf n 1) (strike-2))) ==> STRIKE-1
(defun strike-2 ( ) (catch 'ball
    (setf n (1+ n)) (strike-3))) ==> STRIKE-2
(defun strike-3 ( ) (catch 'ball                    (5.57)
    (setf n (1+ n)) (out))) ==> STRIKE-3
(defun out ( ) (throw 'ball
```

```
          (format nil "~s strikes, OUT!" n))) ==> OUT
          (strike-1) ==> "3 strikes, OUT!"
```

Another block-marking form is **tagbody**, which can contain tags (labels) and **go** forms for the jumping of control from one expression to another.

```
(tagbody (if (numberp x) (go tag1) (go tag2))
         tag1 (print 'x-is-a-number) (go tag3)          (5.58)
         tag2 (print 'x-is-not-a-number)
         tag3 nil)

(tagbody
   (setq x 5)
 1 (setq x (1+ x))
   (print x)
   (if (> x 10) (go 2) (go 1))
 2 (print (* x x)))
   ==> 6
       7                                                 (5.59)
       8
       9
       10
       11
       121
       NIL
```

We have seen that forms such as **progn** and **block** can contain a number of expressions, but they return the value of the last expression. There is a special form in Common Lisp, **unwind-protect**, which can be used in a way to show more than one result:

```
(defun test1 (x)
   (unwind-protect
      (setq x (* x 2))
      (setq x (* x x))
      (print x)))
==> TEST1
(test1 5) ==> 100
             10                                          (5.60)

(let ((x 5))
   (unwind-protect
      (progn (setf x (* x 2)) (* x x))
      (print x))) ==> 10
                      100
```

Compare the above with the following:

```
(defun test2 (x)
    (setq x (* x 2)) (setq x (* x x))
        (print x) nil)
==> TEST2
(test2 5) ==> 100
                NIL
```
(5.61)

5.9.2 Packages

When a symbol is used in Lisp, two objects are created: a name for a data type and the actual data or the value ('meaning') of the name. The name can have variations; for example, it could have been written in caps, in lower case, or in mixed cases. The Lisp system converts all of the variations into a fixed underlying representation (in most systems, in caps). This is called the *print name* of the symbol, which is a character string data type. There are system functions for showing the print name and value of a symbol.

```
(symbol-name 'abc) ==> "ABC"
(symbol-name 'aBc) ==> "ABC"
(symbol-name nil) ==> "NIL"
(setq x 5) ==> 5
(symbol-name 'x) ==> "X"
(symbol-value 'x) ==> 5

(defun find (x)
  (if (numberp x) x x)) ==> FIND
    (find 5) ==> 5
    (find 'abc) ==> ABC
  (symbol-name 'find) ==> "FIND"
  (symbol-value 'find) ==> ERROR: Unbound variable
  (symbol-function 'find) ==>
(LISP :: SCANNED LAMBDA ((X) (IF (NUMBERP X) X X)))
```

The output from **symbol-function** is implementation-dependent. What we have given above is from GCLisp.

Symbols can be enclosed in a pair of straight strokes |: |x|, |abc|. When this is done (and again subject to implementation), the print name can be in mixed case: (symbol-name '|aBc|) → "aBc"; (symbol-name '|abc|) → "abc", and so forth. Symbols bound in strokes can be used as any other symbols; for example, as the names of functions:

```
(defun |square| (x) (* x x)) ==> |square|
(|square| 5) ==> 25
```

Note, incidentally, that '|(2 3 4)| is not a list, but a symbol:

```
(listp '(2 3 4)) ==> T
(listp '|(2 3 4)|) ==> NIL
(symbolp '|(2 3 4)|) ==> T
(consp '|(2 3 4)|) ==> NIL
```

The function **consp** in the above example is a predicate function that returns true (T) if its argument is a **cons** cell (see Chapter 4). Recall that a **cons** cell has two slots for pointers to **car** and **cdr**. A list is an abstract entity that can be empty, but a **cons** cell cannot be empty because, if nothing else, it will have a pointer to NIL. The following examples illustrate this observation:

```
(listp ()) ==> T
(listp nil) ==> T
(consp ()) ==> NIL
(consp nil) ==> NIL
```

Of course, any list except an empty one is also a **cons** structure. Recall also that NIL is the only element in Lisp that is both an atom and a list.

There is also a function, **gensym**, for generating arbitrary symbols:

```
(gensym) ==> #:G-5
(gensym) ==> #:G-6
(gensym "which-") ==> #:|which-7|
(gensym) ==> #:|which-8|
```

All this long diversion about symbols was to lead us to the discussion of packages, to which we now return.

When a user introduces a symbol, it is placed in a *user package,* together with its print name. This becomes a private dictionary for each user. In this way, more than one user can use the same machine, or use networked machines, without a conflict in names. Furthermore, when a large program is created, it can be broken down into modules and packages, and each module can be worked on independently, without concern about conflicting names, because the internal symbols in each portion can be made invisible to the other portions.

Each Common Lisp system has at least four packages:

```
Lisp package
System package
Keyword package
User package
```

A *module* can be created with the **provide** function:

```
(provide <module name>)
```

There is a global variable *modules*, which maintains a list of the modules created. The function **require** can be used to load a module:

```
(require <module name>)
```

and the function **unprovide** removes a module name from the list *modules*. Modules may contain one or more packages, but normally they contain one package. In this book, we will assume a module contains one package, and just talk about packages.

There is a global variable *package*, whose value is the current package. The defult value of *package* is the user package. When the user enters Lisp, this package is activated and all of the symbols used will be registered in this package. The current package can be displayed by inputting:

```
*package* ==) #<PACKAGE USER>
```

The function **list-all-packages** displays all packages in the system, and the packages created by the user (see below). This function does not take an argument.

From any package, other packages can be accessed. So far, all of this has been automatic, and we have not been concerned with the procedures for package creation and manipulation. But there are a number of procedures and functions in the system for the user. You can change the current package with

```
(setq *package* (find-package 'lisp))
==) #<PACKAGE LISP>
LISP:_
```

When the current package is changed to anything other than the **user**, a prompt will appear on the screen with the name of the new package. The function **find-package** is a system function. Lisp is the name of one of the permanent packages in the system, but you can create your own packages with any name, and put the same symbols in different packages without creating conflicts. However, symbols can be made *internal* or *external* in each package. Internal symbols are only recognized within a package, whereas external symbols can be accessed by other packages. In this way, symbols can be *imported* and *exported* between packages.

Another, more commonly used, system function for switching packages and creating new packages is **in-package**, followed by a name. The name must be quoted. Assuming that our normal prompt for being in the user package is an asterisk (*) with a blinking cursor (_), let us change current packages, create some new ones, and observe the prompts for each, as shown in Figure 5.3.

In Figure 5.3, we have created two new packages called MATH and LING. Let us define a pair of different functions with the same name and put one into each of the new packages (those for the MATH package are shown in Figure 5.4).

While we are in the MATH package, let us put some more data in it, shown in Figure 5.5.

```
*__ (in-package 'lisp)
#<PACKAGE LISP>

LISP:__ (in-package 'keyword)
#<PACKAGE KEYWORD>

KEYWORD:__ (in-package 'user)
#<PACKAGE USER>

*__ (in-package 'math)
#<PACKAGE MATH>

MATH:__ (in-package 'ling)
#<PACKAGE LING>

LING:__ (in-package 'user)
#<PACKAGE USER>


*__
```

Figure 5.3. Changing and creating packages.

We have now the following entered in the MATH package: the functions **find**, **my-log**, **my-e-raise**, and **loan**, and the symbols add and computer. These are all so far *internal* symbols in the MATH package, and are not directly available for other packages. In some implementations, symbols cannot be registered in the way that we have done in Figure 5.5; they must be entered by the function **intern** in the format:

```
(intern  "add")
(intern  "computer")
```


```
*__ (in-package 'math)
#<PACKAGE MATH>

MATH:__  (defun find (x)
             (setq x (* x x)))
          FIND

MATH:__  (find 10)
          100

MATH:__
```

Figure 5.4. The MATH package.

```
MATH:___    (defun my-log (n b)
                (setq x (log n b)))
            MY-LOG      ;; This function returns the logarithm of
                        ;; number n in the base b.

MATH:___  ;;
MATH:___    (defun my-e-raise (n)
                (setq x (exp n)))
            (MY-E-RAISE ;; This function raises e to the
                        ;; power of n. e is the base of
                        ;; the natural logarithms.

MATH:___    (defun loan (principal interest years)
                (setq total (* principal (expt
                            (+ 1.0 interest) years))))
            LOAN ;; This function computes the total
                 ;; payment on a loan or mortgage

MATH:___    'add
            ADD      ;; Symbol add is entered in the package

MATH:___    'computer
            COMPUTER

MATH:___
```

Figure 5.5. The MATH package extended.

Let us now create another package, LING, shown in Figure 5.6.

The LING package has the bound variable *nouns,* the function **find**, and the symbols syntax and computer as its internal data. To use the MATH version of **find**, you have to be in the MATH package, and to use the LING version of **find**, you have to be in the LING package. Symbols can, however, be *exported* and used in other packages. For example, while in MATH package, we can use the **export** function to make the add symbol available to the LING and USER packages:

```
MATH:_ (export 'add)
```

Now add becomes an *external* symbol of MATH. The system function, **intern**, can also be used to verify or to get a symbol in a package. The general syntax of **intern** is:

```
(intern <character string> <package name>)
```

The ⟨package name⟩ can be omitted if you are searching for a symbol within a package in which you are using **intern**. If the symbol is not found in the package,

```
MATH:___  (in-package 'ling)
          #<PACKAGE LING>

LING:___  (setq nouns '(books sky pen computers desk))
          (BOOKS SKY PEN COMPUTERS DESK)

LING:___  (defun find (word)
             (if (member word nouns) 'it-is-a-noun '?))
          FIND

LING:___  (find 'sky)
          IT-IS-A-NOUN

LING:___  (find 'stop)
          ?

LING:___  'syntax
          SYNTAX

LING:___  'computer
          COMPUTER

LING:___
```

Figure 5.6. The LING package.

intern will insert the symbol in the package as a new symbol. Furthermore, in addition to returning the name of the symbol, **intern** will return its status as INTERNAL, EXTERNAL, or NIL in the case of new symbol. Examples:

```
(intern "add" 'math)
ADD
:EXTERNAL

(intern "computer" 'math)
COMPUTER
:INTERNAL

(intern "new-sym" 'math)
|new-sym|
NIL
```

Another function for finding a symbol in a package is **find-symbol**. it works in the same way as **intern**, except that, if a symbol is not found, **find-symbol** does not enter it into the package as a new symbol.

```
(find-symbol "computer" 'math)
MATH::|computer|
:INTERNAL

(find-symbol "add" 'math)
MATH::|add|
:EXTERNAL

(find-symbol "nouns" 'math)
NIL
```

To make an external symbol of one package available to another package, you can use the function **import**; for example, while in LING package, if you type (import 'math:add), the symbol add will become visible to LING. If you try to import the symbol computer, you will get a message of conflict. There are two ways that you can resolve the conflict. One way is to remove computer from the host package (LING). This is done by using the function **unintern**:

```
(unintern "computer" 'ling)
```

The name of the package can be left out if you are already in the package. The second way is to *shadow* the name in the package.

Shadowing is concerned with binding. The following example from Steele (1984) illustrates this process:

```
(defun test (x z)
   (let ((z (* x 2))) (print z)) z)
(test 5 6) ==> 10 6                                    (5.62)
```

In the call of TEST, the parameters "x" and "z" are bound to the arguments 5 and 6, respectively. But the inner "z" (the object of **let** in the second line of Example (5.62)) 'shadows' the outer "z" and gets the value of 10 ($5 \times 2 = 10$). (print z) is within the scope of **let**, so 10 is the output of that, but the second "z" on line 2 is not within the scope of **let**, and its value is 6.

There are two shadowing functions in Common Lips, **shadow** and **shadowing-import**. If you try to import the function **find** from the package MATH to the package LING, there would be conflict, because there is another function **find** in LING. However, if you use the function **shadowing-import**, the **find** in LING becomes shadowed and the **find** in MATH becomes available. Study the following sequence of actions in Figure 5.7.

The **shadow** function does the opposite of the above, that is, if an imported symbol is in conflict with a host symbol, then the imported symbol is shadowed and the host symbol remains active. In the example in Figure 5.7, if we use (shadow 'math:find), the **math:find** function will be shadowed, and the original **find** of LING remains active. The packages maintain a list of symbols that have been shadowed, and you can examine this list with the function **package-shad-**

```
LING:___   (find 'book)
           IT-IS-A-NOUN

LING:___   (shadowing-import 'math:find)
           T

LING:___   (find 5)
           25


LING:___
```

Figure 5.7. An example of shadowing-import.

owing-symbols. For example, (package-shadowing-symbols 'ling) will display the list of symbols that have been shadowed in LING. When you use the **shadow** function, if its argument is not already in the package that is, if you use (shadow 'math:add) while in the package LING, and add is not a symbol in LING, it will be added to the LING package.

We should point out that, in all the operations for importing, exporting, and shadowing mentioned above, you need not do one symbol at a time; you can give a list of symbols for a wholesale transaction. For example, in MATH you can write (export '(find my-log my-e-raise loan)). There are also ways of using another package without import/exporting. The function **use-packe** will make an entire package visible to another package. Any conflicts will, of course, have to be resolved. Another way of using a symbol in another package is this:

```
LING:_ (math:find 5) ==> 25
```

In this example, while in the LING package we have called the **math:find** function with an argument. This way, we can use both of the **find** functions in the same package:

```
LING:_ (find 'sky) ==> IT-IS-A-NOUN
LING:_ (math:find 10) ==> 100
```

A package can be renamed by using the function **rename-package**:

```
MATH:_ (rename-package 'math 'new-math)
        NIL
NEW-MATH:_
```

The function **find-all-symbols** will list the occurrence of a symbol in all packages:

```
(find-all-symbols 'find)
 ==> (LING::FIND  MATH::FIND)
```

The function **symbol-package** will display the home package of a symbol:

```
(symbol-package 'loan) ==) #(PACKAGE MATH)
(symbol-package 'car) ==) #(PACKAGE LISP)
```

There are also do-iterative functions for performing operations globally on all symbols in a package. We will give examples of **do-symbols, do-external-symbols**, and **do-all-symbols**. First, let us enter some symbols in the default USER package, shown in Figure 5.8.

The USER package in Figure 5.8 now contains the symbols find, jj, kk, and mm. Symbols jj and kk have been made external.

The three **do-symbols** forms mentioned above have the following syntax:

```
(do-symbols (⟨variable⟩ ⟨package call⟩ ⟨value⟩)
        ⟨expression⟩ ... ⟨expression⟩ )
```

The function **do-symbols** binds each symbol in the package to the <variable> and performs operations specified in the <expressions> on it. The <value> is the final value of the function that you normally set to NIL or some other message such as 'done, 'finish, etc.

```
(do-symbols (s (find-package 'user) nil)              (5.63)
    (if (symbolp s) (print s)))
```

The function in Example (5.63) will print the symbols in the USER package that we placed in Figure 5.8. However, all of the functions in the Lisp package are external and are available to other packages, so that, depending on the implementation, the function in Example (5.63) may also print a long list of all of the symbols in the Lisp package.

```
(do-external-symbols (s (find-package 'user)
        nil)
        (if (symbolp s) (print s)))              (5.64)
        ==)   KK
              JJ
              NIL
```

In Figure 5.8, we exported kk and jj so that they became external symbols of the USER package.

If you use the function **do-all-symbols**, all of the symbols in the entire system will be bound in turn to the <variable>, and you will get a very large output from Example (5.65). Note that, in this case, you do not have to specify a package, because it will affect all packages.

```
(do-all-symbols (s nil) (print s))              (5.65)
```

```
*__   (intern "find")
               |find|
               NIL
*__   (intern "jj")
               |jj|
               NIL
*__   (intern "kk")
               |kk|
               NIL
*__   (intern "mm")
               |mm|
               NIL
*__   (export '(jj kk))
               T

*__
```

Figure 5.8. Entering symbols in the USER package.

5.9.3. Structures

A *structure* is a collection of data that can be organized in a desired way. Recall that, in an array, we accessed a piece of data by using an index number that gave the position of the piece. In a structure, we use the names of the components, or sub-structures, of a structure to access the data in that part.

The macro **defstruct** is used to name a structure and its components or parts. For example, the following defines a house in general:

$$
\begin{aligned}
&\text{(defstruct house} \\
&\quad \text{living-room dining-room} \\
&\quad \text{bath-rooms bed-rooms} \\
&\quad \text{study play-room kitchen} \\
&\quad \text{basement)}
\end{aligned}
\qquad (5.66)
$$

The syntax for **defstruct**, as defined above, is:

```
(defstruct ⟨name⟩ ⟨component⟩ ... ⟨component⟩)
```

You can create an *instance* of a general structure, or a particular structure, by using make-<name>, and then giving values to the keywords representing components:

$$
\begin{aligned}
&\text{(setq my-house (make-house} \\
&\quad \text{:living-room 'one} \\
&\quad \text{:dining-room 'one}
\end{aligned}
\qquad (5.67)
$$

```
:bed-rooms 4
:bath-rooms 3
:study 'one))
```

Now you can make queries about the particular house in Example (5.67):

```
(house-bed-rooms my-house) ==) 3
(house-kitchen my-house) ==) NIL   ;we forgot kitchen!
(house-study my-house) ==) 'one
(house-basement my-house) ==) NIL
```

You can make changes in MY-HOUSE in the following way:

```
(setf (house-kitchen my-house) 'one)
(setf (house-bath-rooms my-house) 4)
```

Also note:

```
(typep my-house 'house) ==) T
(typep 'my-car 'house) ==) NIL
(type-of my-house) ==) HOUSE
```

Make-<name> is called the *constructor*. It can be used as a keyword to change the name of the function for creating an instance of the general structure (see Example (5.67)).

```
(defstruct (house
   (:constructor new-house))   ; instead of make-house
      (rooms)(bath-rooms)(kitchen))
```
(5.68)
```
(setq my-house (new-house :rooms 5 :bath-rooms 2
                 :kitchen 1))
(setq your-house (new-house :rooms 6 :bath-rooms 4
                 :kitchen 1))
```

Value can be given to components in the general structure defined by **defstruct**. If these values are not changed in the definition of an instance of the general structure, they become default values of the particular structure.

5.10 EXERCISES

1. Write an iterative function to compute the sum of numbers in a list, using the **loop** macro.

2. Write a program to compute the expression

$$\text{square root } ((a + b) / (c - d))$$

ten times. Each time prompting you to supply values for a, b, c, and d.

3. Write a function with **progn** containing five expressions to return the results of the evaluation of all of the five expressions, rather than the last one.

4. Consider the following formulas for the expansion of $(a + b)^n$:

$$(a + b)^2 = a^2 + 2ab + b^2$$
$$(a + b)^3 = a^3 + 3a^2b + 3ab^2 + b^3$$
$$(a + b)^4 = a^4 + 4a^3b + 6a^2b^2 + 4ab^3 + b^4$$

The integers 2,3,4,6, ... in the expansion formulas are called the *coefficients* of the terms in the expansion. Recall that, if we arrange the coefficients in the order of the increasing *n*, we form a construction which is known as *Pascal's Triangle*.

$(a + b)^0$					1			
$(a + b)^1$					1	1		
$(a + b)^2$				1	2	1		
$(a + b)^3$			1	3		3	1	
$(a + b)^4$		1	4	6		4	1	
$(a + b)^5$	1	5	10		10	5	1	

Note that each row of the triangle begins and ends with a 1, and that each of the other integers in the row is the sum of two integers in the row above it.

Write a program to generate a Pascal's Triangle for any integer "n" for the expansion of $(a + b)^0 - (a + b)^n$. If you are mathematically oriented, use the general binomial formula in your function.

5. Using **dotimes** write a function to generate a list of integers from 0 to "n".

6. Design a *package* with a list of objects ('secrets') that you want to share with others and those that you want to keep private. Furthermore, make distinctions between objects that you want to share with some others but not all others.

7. define a general structure for toy blocks, including shape, color, and size. Then define some instances of such block worlds with specific details.

8. Assume that a simple English sentence (S) is composed of a noun-phrase (NP) and a verb-phrase (VP). An NP is composed of a determiner (DET) and a noun (N) and a VP is composed of a verb (V) and an NP. The following phrase structure grammar represents this language:

```
S --> NP VP
NP --> DET N
VP --> V NP
```

Write a structure to represent this grammar and functions for randomly selecting determiners, nouns, and verbs from a list containing these words and generating a predetermined number of sentences. (This is a much simpler version of the project recommended in Section 4.6).

5.11 VARIABLES, KEYWORDS, AND SPECIAL VARIABLES

Throughout this chapter, we have introduced some new functions and operations, but our main concern has been to provide extensions and elaborations for some of the functions that we had already seen. We have also tried to redefine, in a somewhat more precise way, some of the terms that we had used loosely. Continuing with this trend, we will try to elaborate on variables, keywords, constants, special forms, and so forth; terms which we have used frequently in the text.

Variables, as we have seen, are names (or addresses) of slots in the computer memory (or in packages) into which data are placed. The data in the slots are called the *values* of the variables. These values change when we change the data in the slots. In Lisp, there are also constants, whose values are given by the system and normally cannot be changed. Among the constants in most implementations of Common Lisp are:

```
       pi ==) 3.141592653589793
      nil ==) NIL
        t ==) T
(setq nil 5) ==) Error
```

When you use a constant, do not put parentheses around it. Also, you do not have to put a quote mark in front of the constant.The function **defconstant** can be used to define new constants.

```
(defconstant one 1) ==) ONE
(defconstant seven 7) ==) SEVEN
(defconstant my-name 'john) ==) MY-NAME
one ==) 1
seven ==) 7
my-name ==) JOHN
```

Such constants created by the user are a way of making global variables (see below), and it is generally understood that their values remain unchanged. However, unlike the fixed system constant, the values of user-made constants can be changed:

```
(defconstant seven 10) ==) SEVEN
(defconstant my-name 'mary) ==) MY-NAME
seven ==) 10
my-name ==) MARY
```

We have also seen that variables can be local or global. Assignment functions and macros, such as **setq**, **psetq**, **setf**, and **set**, assign values to variables that become global. Variables with the same names as globally defined variables can occur in the parameters of functions or within the scope of forms such as **let**, **let***, and **progv**, and can take different values, but outside of the scope of such forms, the values of global variables remain constant.

$$
\begin{array}{ll}
\text{(setq x 5) ==> 5} & \\
\text{(defun cube (x) (* x x x)) ==> CUBE} & \\
\text{(cube 3) ==> 27} & \\
\text{x ==> 5} & \\
\text{(let ((x 3))} & \text{(5.69)} \\
\quad \text{((setq x (cube x))} & \\
\quad \text{(list (symbol-value 'x) x))} & \\
\text{==> (5 27) ;; Recall that SYMBOL-VALUE} & \\
\quad\quad\quad\quad \text{;; always returns global value} &
\end{array}
$$

Global variables are said to have *dynamic binding*. Local variables have *lexical binding*.

In Common Lisp, there are a number of *special* variables given by the system, which are global with dynamic bindings. These are normally identified by having an asterisk at each end of their names. These variables may be used independently, like the constants mentioned above, or used in functions without having to appear in parameter or lambda lists. The number of such system-defined global variables depends on the implementation. We will look at some of the commonly used ones here.

We have already seen **package**. Its value is the name of the current package in use, with the default value being the USER package. The variable **features** contains the features of the system that a particular version of Common Lisp is implemented for. For example, for the implementation of GCLisp for the IBM PC, you may get the following result:

```
*features* ==> (SYS:IBMPC GCLISP)
```

When you log on to Lisp, create a file, or load an existing file, you usually get some messages telling you what the system is doing; for example:

```
Loading ...
```

You can suppress such messages by setting the value of **load-verbose** to NIL:

```
(setq *load-verbose* nil) ==> NIL.
```

Recall that the function **provide** creates a module (see subsection 5.9.2). The special variable **modules** maintains a list of modules created in the course of writing a large program. The list can be displayed by imputting *modules*. When no modules have been created, the value of *modules* is NIL.

The variable *print-base* contains the radix of the number system in use. Its default value is 10 (base 10). It can be changed with the following results:

```
*print-base* ==) 10
12 ==) 12
(setq *print-base* 2) ==) 10    ;; The output is
                                ;; binary 2, not decimal 10
12 ==) 1100
```

If you set the special symbol *print-radix* to "t", the radix will also be printed in the output:

```
(setq *print-radix* t) ==) T
12 ==) #b1100
```

The following sequence of examples demonstrates the universal base conversion facility in Common Lisp. We will start with *print-radix* and *print-base* set in their default values of NIL and 10, respectively.

```
(setq x '(1 2 3 4 10 16 32))
==) (1 2 3 4 10 16 32)    ; base 10
(setq *print-base* 2) ==) 10
x ==) (1 10 11 100 1010 10000 100000)    ; base 2
(setq *print-radix* t) ==) T
x ==) (#b1 #b10 #b11 #b100 #b1010 #b10000 #b100000)          (5.70)
(setq *print-base* 8) ==) #o10  ;dec. 8 = octal 10
x ==) (#o1 #o2 #o3 #o4 #o12 #o20 #o40) ; base 8
(setq *print-base* 16) ==) x10  ;dec. 16 = hex. 10
x ==) (#x1 #x2 #x3 #x4 #xA #x10 #x20) ; base 16
(setq *print-base* 32) ==) 32r10  ;dec. 32 = 32r 10
x ==) (32r1 32r2 32r3 32r4 32rA ... 32r10) ;base 32
```

The variable *read-base* can be set to read numbers in one base and output in another. For example, if we set *read-base* to 2 and *print-base* to 10, numbers will be read in binary and printed in the their equivalents in decimal.

```
(setq *read-base* 2) ==) 2
1100 ==) 12
(setq *read-base* 'x) ==) X  ;; hexadecimal radix
abc ==) 4052793063
```

We should hasten to caution the reader against the use of the last example. When you set the read mode to hexadecimal, the system will attempt to convert every character you input into a number value, including the form for exiting the system!

The variable *print-case*, if implemented, allows you to set the case so that your standard print output may be in upper, lower, or mixed cases.

Special variables can also be made by the user in a number of ways. The function **proclaim** can be used for this purpose:

$$(\text{proclaim '(special *x*)) ==> NIL}$$

More than one special variable can be declared in one function:

$$(\text{proclaim 'special *m* *n* *p*)) ==> NIL}$$

It is customary to use asterisks in the names of user-defined special variables as well, to distinguish them from other global variables that are created with assignment functions (e.g., **setq**).

We said that special variables can be used in functions without having them appear in their lambda lists. Here is an example for printing sentences that have a given word in them.

```
(proclaim '(special *word*))
(setq text '((this is a book.) (do you like it?)
             (the book is mine.) ))

(defun find ( )                                    (5.71)
   (setq *word* (read))
     (find-aux text))  ;;Note that *word* is not
                       ;;being passed to FIND-AUX
(defun find-aux (text)
  (cond ((null text) nil)
        ((member *word* (car text))
          (append (car text)(find-aux (cdr text))))
        (t (find-aux (cdr text))))))
```

```
(find) book
==> (THIS IS A BOOK.  THE BOOK IS MINE.)
```

The macro **defvar** can also be used to declare a special variable. It can also define a value for the variable.

```
(defvar *y*) ==> *Y*
(defvar *y* 5) ==> *y*
*y* ==> 5
(defvar *x* (+ *y* 2)) ==> *X*
*x* ==> 7
```

Note that when a special variable has a value, its value cannot be changed with a new declaration.

```
(defvar *x* 3) ==> *X*
*x* ==> 7
(defvar *x* (+ 2 3)) ==> *X*
*x* ==> 7
```

You can include documentary remarks within the declarion:

```
(defvar *my-name* 'lee "just that you know!")
==> *MY-NAME*
```

The remark can be displayed with the use of **documentation** in the following format:

```
(documentation '*my-name* 'variable)  ;quotes are required
==> "just that you know!"
```

Such remarks can be included in any function definition:

```
(defun square (x)
  "This function returns the square of its argument"
    (if (numberp x) (* x x) 'not-number ))
==> SQUARE                                                    (5.72)
(square 5) ==> 25
(documentation 'square 'function)
==> "This function returns the square of its argument"
```

The macro **defparameter** works like **defvar**:

```
(defparameter *k* (+ *x* 7) "New Special *k*")
==> *K*
```

The predicate function **special-p** returns T if its argument is a declared special variable:

```
(special-p *k*) ==> T
(special-p *j*) ==> NIL
```

There is also a special form **declare**, which can declare local special variables:

```
(defun foo (x)
    (declare (special x))
      (bar (* x x)))
==> FOO                                                       (5.73)
```

```
(defun bar (x)
   (list (symbol-value 'x) x))
==> BAR
```

```
(foo 5) ==> (5 25)
```

In the call for **foo**, "x" is bound to 5, and treated here as global value. Then "x" is declared special, and the function **bar** is called with the argument (* x x). In the **bar** function, the original global value of x (5) and the local value (25) will be displayed.

Common Lisp has a large number of predefined *keywords*. Keywords can also be defined by the user. The term keyword used in Lisp should not be confused with its use in other programming languages. The names of functions in Lisp are not keywords; they are also not *reserved* words. There are very few reserved words in Lisp that cannot be changed by the user. Recall that every Common Lisp system has a KEYWORD package. All symbols registered in this package, and those entered by the user, are external symbols. Keywords are identified by a colon in front of their names: *:test, :key, :internal, :external*, and so forth. As we have seen, keywords are frequently used in the parameters or lambda lists of functions.

There are several ways that the user can define a keyword:

```
keyword:start ==> :START
keyword::end ==> :end
           :new ==> :new
```

:start, :end, and *:new* will be registered as keywords. We could have selected any other symbol to be a keyword.

```
(defun example (a b &key ((:jump start)
(:halt stop))) ...)
```

In this example :jump and :halt are defined as keywords, with initial values *start* and *stop*, respectively.

We have seen the use of system keywords with special variables, for example:

```
(setq *print-case* :downcase)
```

If implemented, this will make all of the output come out in lower case.

5.12 SPECIAL FORMS AND MACROS

We have not been always meticulous in making the distinction between special forms, macros, and functions, and have occasionally (especially in earlier chapters) referred to all varieties with the generic name function. At this point, however, we should make the distinction more precise.

Special forms are a relatively small number of expressions in Common Lisp that deal with control and binding. Normally they cannot be redefined, and new forms cannot be created by the user. A special form can be defined as an expression that begins with one of the special names. The number and status of special names may vary in versions of Common Lisp by implementation, but the following is a list of the most common ones:

```
block          progn
catch          prog1
declare        progv
function       quote
if             setq
let            throw
```

These special forms may have similar counterparts among functions and macros, but there are apparent or subtle differences between them. Compare the difference between **prog** (a macro) and **progn** (a special form). In the following exercise, we will show some differences between **setq** (a special form) and **set** (a function).

We have already noted that **setq** is an assignment form that does not evaluate its first argument, so that it does not have to be quoted;

```
(setq x '(a b c)) ==> (A B C)
```

The function **set** also is an assignment form, but it evaluates its first argument so that, if the first argument is to be a variable to receive a value, it must be quoted:

```
(set 'x '(a b c)) ==> (A B C)
```

There are other differences. The first argument of **setq** must be a symbol, a variable to receive value.

```
(setq (car x) ...) ==> ERROR: A symbol was expected
```

However, because **set** evaluates its first argument, its first argument can be a form:

```
(set (car x) 'm) ==> M
x ==> (A B C)
a ==> M    ;; a (car of m) is bound to m

(defun test ()
  (setq x (read))
  (setq y (read))
    (if (> x y) 'greater 'less))
==> TEST
(test)
```

(5.74)

```
           5          ;; input for READ
          10          ;; input for the second READ
==) LESS        ;; output
  (set (test) (list x y))
                            5
                           10
                  ==) (5 10)
```

Another difference between **set** and **setq** is that **set** always assigns a global value, even if it is inside the scope of a local variable with the same name. Recall the following scenario:

```
(setq x 5) ==) 5
(defun test2 (x)
    (setq x 3)
      (list (symbol-value 'x) x))                    (5.75)
==) TEST2
(test2 10) ==) (5 3)
x ==) 5
```

The global value of "x" is 5. Within the scope of **test2**, "x" is first bound to 10, and then to 3. These are both local values. The last line of the function **test2** displays the global value (5) and the final local value, 3. The global value of "x" remains unchanged. Now compare Example (5.75) with the following:

```
(defun test3 (x)
  (set 'x 2)
  (setq x 3)
    (list (symbol-value 'x) x))                      (5.76)
==) TEST3
(test3 10) ==) (2 3)
x ==) 2
```

In the function **test3**, the global value "x" is 5, as assigned under Example (5.75). Again, the parameter "x" is bound to 10 as the local value. But now, **set** changes the global value of "x" to 2, and **setq** changes the local value to 3, so that the output is (2 3). Note that the global value of "x" has changed to 2.

Macros name a process that can expand or generate codes, which will result in calls to functions or special forms. There are, again, certain differences between macros and functions. For example, both (incf x) and (1+ x) add one to the current value of "x", but there is a significant difference between their side-effects.

```
(setq x 5) ==) 5
(1+ x) ==) 6
x ==) 5
(incf x) ==) 6
x ==) 6
```

1+ is a function, and **incf** is a macro, its underlying structure showing that it assigns the value as a global increment. Recall again that we can see the expansion of **incf** by using the **macroexpand** function:

```
(macroexpand '(incf x))
==> (SETQ X (1+ X))  T
```

For another example, recall that both **setq** and **setf** assign values to variables, and both do not evaluate their first symbol arguments.

```
(setq x '(a b c d)) ==> (A B C D)
(setf y '(a b c d) ==> (A B C D)
```

However, **setq** is a special form, and **setf** is a macro. The macro **setf**, unlike **setq**, can take a form as its first argument and evaluate it. In the following example, **setf** will be used to change an element in a list. This is not possible with **setq**.

```
(setf (car x) 'm) ==> M
x ==> (M B C D)
(set (car x) 5) ==> 5
x ==> (M B C D)
m ==> 5
```

You can also define your own macros. However, before discussing macro definition, let us talk about two other procedures that we will need for our discussion. One is the overdue introduction of the very useful *macro character* **backquote**. We are familiar with the quote mark ('), which is also a macro character standing for the special form **quote**. Macro characters are token representations of certain functions or special forms. When they occur in an expression, their associated functions are called, so that the underlying structure of '(a b), for example, is (quote (a b)).

The macro character **backquote** behaves like **quote** in its simple application:

```
'a ==> A
`a ==> A
'(a b c) ==> (A B C)
`(a b c) ==> (A B C)
```

However, if you place a comma in front of a symbol in a list that is introduced by a backquote, the symbol will be evaluated and its value, if any, will be inserted in the list.

```
(setq x 5)
`(a b ,x c) ==> (A B 5 C)
(setq y '(k l m)) ==> (K L M)
`(a b ,y c) ==> (A B (K L M) C)
```

If you place another macro character, @, after the comma in front of the symbol in the last line of the above example, it will have the following effect:

```
`(a b ,@y c) ==> (A B K L M C)
```

@ has the effect of appending (k l m) to the list (a b c) at the location where "y" occurs (see further on).

The other procedure that we want to mention is the system function **list***. Compare the following results between **list** and **list***:

```
(list 'a 'b '(c d e)) ==> (A B (C D E))
(list* 'a 'b '(c d e)) ==> (A B C D E)
(list 'a 'b) ==> (A B)
(list* 'a 'b) ==> (A . B)
(list 'a 'b 'c) ==> (A B C)
(list* 'a 'b 'c) ==> (A B . C)
(list '(a b c) '(d e f)) ==> ((A B C) (D E F))
(list* '(a b c) '(d e f)) ==> ((A B C) D E F)
(list '(a b c) 'd) ==> ((A B C) D)
(list* '(a b c) 'd) ==> ((A B C) . D)
```

If you examine the above examples carefully, you will see that the procedure in **list*** is that its last argument is **cons**ed with the arguments that come before the last. Thus (list* 'a 'b 'c) is equivalent to (cons 'a (cons 'b 'c)) $\Rightarrow$ (A B . C).

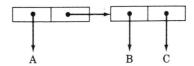

Let us now return to macro definition. We will first use the macro **defmacro** to define a macro, which we will call **repeat**. We want the **repeat** macro to repeat the operations specified in its argument for a given number of times.

$$
\begin{array}{ll}
\text{(defmacro repeat (form n)} & \\
\quad \text{`(do ((count ,n (1- count)))} & \text{(5.77)} \\
\quad\quad \text{((zerop count) nil) form))} & \\
\text{==> REPEAT} &
\end{array}
$$

Note that **defmacro**, like a function definition (**defun**), takes a name and a lambda list of its parameters. The lambda list can include all of the optional and extended variables that functions and lambda expressions can have. The 'body' of **defmacro** contains the codes that will be the object of the function call, which will be generated by the macro (**repeat** in the case of the present example)

```
(repeat (print 'it-works!) 3)
IT-WORKS!
IT-WORKS!
IT-WORKS!
NIL

(repeat (print (gensym)) 5)  ;; Generates
                             ;; arbitrary symbols and
#:G-20                       ;; prints them.
#:G-21
#:G-22
#:G-23
#:G-24
NIL

(repeat (print (cons 'a'(b c d))) 3)
(A B C D)
(A B C D)
(A B C D)
NIL
```

Note that the variable *count* in the underlying structure of **repeat** changes its value from "n" to 0. We can show that in this way:

```
(repeat (print count) 10)
10
9
8
7
6
5
4
3
2
1
NIL
```

Now, for perhaps a more useful application of the macro **repeat**, we can use it in conjunction with the changing values of *count* to print the contents of an array.

```
(setq vec #(a b c d e f g))
==) #(VECTOR T 7 88B6:6F93)
(repeat (print (aref vec count)) 5)
G
F
E
```

```
            D
            C
          NIL
```

For another example, let us write a macro for an **exclusive-or** function. Recall that **exclusive-or** returns true if only one, but not both, of its arguments is true.

```
(defmacro exclusive-or (cond1 cond2)
      `(or (and ,cond1 (not ,cond2))
           (and ,cond2 (not ,cond1))))
==) EXCLUSIVE-OR                                        (5.78)

(exclusive-or (= 5 5) (= 5 4)) ==) T
(exclusive-or (= 5 5) (= 6 6)) ==) NIL
```

Here is a macro for the function **sub1** in Lispvm, written for Common Lisp:

```
(defmacro sub1 (x)
    (let ((m x))
         (list 'setq m (list '1- m))))        (5.79)
==) SUB1
(setq y 5)
(sub1 y) ==) 4
```

We observe from Example (5.79) that the use of the backquote and comma is not obligatory in the definition of macros. Recall that the special form **when** takes a conditional or test expression and a series of forms. If the test is satisfied, the forms are executed from left to right, but only the value of the last form evaluated is displayed. In the following exercise, we will write several versions of a macro for creating our own version of **when**.

```
(setq x 5) ==) 5
(defmacro my-when (condition &rest body)
        (list 'if condition
            (cons 'progn body)))                       (5.80)
==) MY-WHEN

(my-when (numberp x) x (setq y (1+ x)) (setq z (1+ y)))
==) 7
```

The code that is generated by the **defmacro** in the above macro call is the following:

```
(if (numberp x) (progn x (setq y (1+ x)) (setq z (1+ y))))
```

Thus, the variable body is bound to the expressions following **progn**. The *&rest*

operator in the lambda list collects all of the expressions in the body in a list. However, in Example (5.80), the lambda list can also be given as a 'pattern' in dotted list form:

```
(defmacro your-when (condition . body)
        (list 'if condition                           (5.81)
              (cons 'progn body)))
    ==) YOUR-WHEN
```

In the following version of **when**, we will use the backquote/comma variation for definition:

```
(defmacro her-when (condition . body)
        `(if ,condition (progn . ,body)))           (5.82)
    ==) HER-WHEN
```

The implementation of macros and special forms is not universal in all versions of Common Lisp. However, the following predicate functions can be used to determine if a name is a function, macro, or a special form.

```
(functionp '(name))
(macro-function '(name))
(special-form-p '(name))
```

Examples:

```
(functionp 'car) ==) T
(functionp 'abc) ==) NIL
(macro-function 'incf) ==) T
(macro-function 'if) ==) NIL
(special-form-p 'if) ==) T
(special-form-p 'car) ==) NIL
```

5.13 FILE HANDLING IN COMMON LISP

In Chapter 3, we saw that all modern dialects of Lisp have an editing mode in which the user can create and manipulate files. The "edit commands" within the editor are not quite the same as the system functions of Lisp. However, in Common Lisp there are also a number of functions and macros that can be used directly for file handling. In this section, we will describe some of the more common and useful procedures for this purpose.

There are two topics that are directly related to files and file handling: *streams* and *input/output* or I/O. So far, we have assumed that you have been typing on the keyboard of a computer terminal or personal computer; the data input was echoed on the screen of the monitor; and the results of, for example, calling a function, were displayed on the monitor. We will now look at some of the underlying procedures involved in this activity, and show how you can directly print into files for permanent storage and read from them. We will also see the controls that can be imposed on the flow of data.

5.13.1 Streams

Streams can be thought of as buffers or channels for input/output and for interaction with files. In Common Lisp, stream is a data object, and there are a number global variables with *dynamic closure,* predefined with default values for the activity of streams. Among these global variables are the following:

standard-input	The default value is input-stream. The data in input-stream assigned to this variable is read by the Lisp Reader.
standard-output	The Lisp Printer writes data on output-stream that is assigned to this variable.
query-io	The default value of this global variable is an input/output-stream. It is used for asking the user to make decisions about data flow or other procedures. The functions **y-or-n-p** and **yes-or-no-p** (see further on in text) can be used to make such queries.
debug-io	The initial global value of this variable is an input/output-stream. It is used for interaction with debugging procedures in the Lisp system (see Chapter 3 and further on in text).
terminal-io	The default value is an input/output-stream concerned with reading from the keyboard and displaying on the monitor screen.
trace-output	The initial global value is an output-stream that displays the results of a **trace** function (see further on in the text).

So far, all of this has been automatic, and we were not concerned with them, but as a user, you have certain controls over them and can make changes, which we will see in the course of the remainder of this chapter.

The **y-or-n-p** (also **yes-or-no-p**) function mentioned under *query-io* is an interesting and useful function, which permits the user to make a decision between alternative events or procedures. You can use the function to ask a question about appropriate actions to be taken depending on whether the user enters "y" or "n" (or the long forms *yes* or *no*). The difference between the abbreviated (y, n) and full forms (yes, no) is that, in the abbreviated form, when you type "y" or "n," the system immediately executes the procedures, whereas in the long form you have to use the *ENTER* key after typing *yes* or *no*, before any action is taken. The latter procedure allows you an additional step in which to think and ponder about your decision before the final action. We will use only the abbreviated form in the following examples.

```
(defun test (w)
        (y-or-n-p "Do you wish a ~s message?" w)
        (setq token (read))
        (if (equal token 'y)
                (list 'here 'is 'a w 'message)
                        'no-thank-you))
    ==> TEST
```

(5.83)

```
(test 'good) ==> Do you wish a GOOD message? (Y or N)
        y y     ;; You have to type your response twice.
        ==> (HERE IS A GOOD MESSAGE)
(test 'lousy) ==> Do you wish a LOUSY message? (Y or N)
        n n
        ==> NO-THANK-YOU
```

Let us do a slightly more useful exercise. The function **delete-file** deletes a file named in its argument. Suppose we want to give a warning to the user before he/she deletes a file.

```
(defun file-erase (file)
(setq w (read))
        (y-or-n-p "Are you sure you want to
                    erase this file?")
        (if (equal w 'y) (delete-file file)
                        'thank-you))
==> FILE-ERASE
```

(5.84)

Now suppose we have a file called FILE5.LSP.

```
(file-erase "file5.lsp")
==> Are you sure you want to erase this file? (Y or N)
y y
"file5.lsp"    ;; The file is erased

(file-erase "file5.lsp")
==> Are you sure you want to erase this file? (Y or N)
n n
THANK-YOU    ;; File is not erased
```

Apart from the streams associated with the above global variables, you can create new streams by using various system functions. Keep in mind that an *input stream* is a buffer that you read data from, and an *output stream* is a buffer that you write data into. The function **make-string-input-stream** creates a new input stream and places its string argument in it:

```
(setq ins1 (make-string-input-stream
       "This-is-a-new-stream"))
  ==) (DYNAMIC CLOSURE)
(read ins1) ==) THIS-IS-A-NEW-STREAM
```

You can specify a substring of the argument to be included in the new stream:

```
(setq ins2 (make-string-input-stream "abcdefg" 2 4))
==) (DYNAMIC CLOSURE)
(read ins2) ==) CD
```

As always, counting is from zero, so that, in the string abcdefg, "a" is in position 0, and "c" is in position 2.

The function **make-string-output-stream** creates a new output stream. You can use the **print** function to put data into an output stream. You can display data in an output stream through the use of the function **get-output-stream-string**.

```
(setq outs1 (make-string-output-stream))
     ==) (DYNAMIC CLOSURE)
(print "This-is-string-one" outs1)
(print "This-is-string-two" outs1)
(get-output-stream-string outs1)

==) "
THIS-IS-STRING-ONE
THIS-IS-STRING-TWO "
```

Streams, both input and output, can be closed by using the function **close**:

```
(close outs1)
```

When a stream is closed, you cannot write to it or read from it.

A string in a stream can be read character by character. When a character is read, the read pointer moves to the next character so that the next read will read the next character. However, immediately after reading a character, you can 'push' it back by *unreading* it.

```
(setq ins1 (make-string-input-stream "abcdefgh"))
(read-char ins1) ==) #\a
```

Depending on the implementation, the output of **read-char** in the above example may be the ASCII representation of "a", that is, 97.

```
(read-char inst1) ==) #\b
(read-char inst1) ==) #\c
(unread-char #\c inst1) ==) #\c
(read-char inst1) ==) #\c
(read inst1) ==) DEFGH  ;; The rest of the string
(read-char inst1) ==) ERROR: end of file on stream
```

If the string has delimiters in it, such as a space or open parenthesis, the **read** function will read all characters up to the delimiter, but elements within a pair of parentheses (a list) are read as a unit, including the internal spaces.

```
(setq inst4 (make-string-input-stream
"string and list(a b c d) together"))
(read-char inst4) ==) #\"
(read inst4) ==) STRING
(read inst4) ==) AND
(read inst4) ==) LIST
(read inst4) ==) (A B C D)
(read inst4) ==) TOGETHER
```

The function **read-line** reads an entire line, including blanks, up to the line break or newline internal marker. In the above example, after (read inst4) $\Rightarrow$ STRING, the following will read the remainder of the current line:

```
(read-line inst4) ==) AND LIST(A B C D) TOGETHER
```

The **peek-char** function reads a character from the stream without moving the pointer. It is equivalent to a sequence of **read-char**, followed by an **unread-char**.

5.13.2 Input/Output

Most of the I/O procedures have already been discussed in various sections of this book. The use of global variables for number systems *read-base*, *print-base*, *print-radix*; the use of macro characters and the operators #, b, o x, ˜s, ˜a, ˜&, ˜%, etc.; **read**, **print**, **read-char**, **print-char**, etc.; various forms of print functions, **format**, and **terpri**, the **y-or-n-p** functions; and so forth. In this section, we will add a few additional procedures, in no particular order.

There are special read and write functions for strings. The **read-from-string** reads characters from a string and returns two values: the characters read and the index of the next character to be read.

```
(read-from-string "abcdefg")
==) ABCDEFG
        8
```

There are keyword parameters that limit the range of reading:

```
(read-from-string "abcdefg" :start 0 :end 3)
==) ABC
        4    ;; pointer is on the 4th character
```

Don't confuse position with character. In the above example, after reading ABC, the pointer is on the third position of the string counting from zero, but on the fourth character of the string.

Recall that, when a character is read from a stream, the pointer moves to the next character, skipping any blanks. The keyword *preserve-whitespace,* if set to T, does not skip blanks, so that the pointer would be on the next blank.

```
(read-from-string "a  b  c  d" nil 'eof
        :preserve-whitespace t)
==) A
        1   ;; nil and 'eof are values for :start, :end
(read-from-string "a  b  c  d" nil 'eof
        :preserve-whitespace nil)
==) A
        2
```

Preservation of blanks with the movement of the pointer can be more intuitively presented with the use of the function **read-preserving-whitespace**.

```
(setq st (make-string-input-stream "A B C D"))
(read-preserving-whitespace st) ==) A
(read-char st) ==) #\    ;;blank character
(read-char st) ==) #\    ;;stuck on blank!
(read st) ==) B  ;;next char without preserving blank
```

The function **write-char** writes characters onto an output stream.

```
(setq os (make-string-output-stream))
(write-char #\a os) ==) #\a
(write-char #\b os) ==) #\b
(get-output-stream-string os) ==) AB
```

The function **write-to-string** is the opposite of **read-from-string**; it serves to create a string.

```
(write-to-string 'abcd) ==) "ABCD"
```

5.13.3 Files

Files are identified by *filename* and *filetype*. Filetype is normally a three-character token and, depending on the system, may be attached to the filename with a dot. Thus "file5.jam" is a proper file identification for the system used by the author. A file is accessed by the operating system of a computer through the *pathname,* which contains all of the information needed for the access: the location and name of the directory, the name of the file, and so forth. Depending on the installation procedures of the Lisp system in a computer and within an operating system, most of the components of the pathname may have default values, which will be assigned automatically by the system. For example, the pathname for a file created under Golden Common Lisp, installed in an IBM personal computer, looks like this:

```
"C:\\GCLISP\\(filename).LSP"
```

where C is the name of diskdrive in which the Lisp system is installed, GCLISP is the name of the subdirectory that contains the file, and LSP is the default filetype assigned by the system.

If you want to access an existing file, you can use the **open** function, followed by the name of the file. But since communication with the file is through a stream, you can associate a stream with the file in the following manner:

```
(setq outs (open "oldf.lsp" :direction :output))
```

The keywords :direction and :output indicate that the file is opened as an output file, that is, you can write to it:

```
(print "abcdefg ijk (a b c d)" outs)
(close outs)
```

The string "abdefg ijk (a b c d)" is written in the file through the stream *outs,* and by closing the stream, we have closed the file. We can now reopen the file as an input file to read the data in it.

```
(setq ins (open "oldf.lsp" :direction :input))
(read-char ins) ==) #\"
(read-char ins) ==) #\a
(read ins) ==) BCDEFG
(close ins)
```

It is worth repeating that you must close a file when you have finished working with it, otherwise you may destroy or alter its contents unintentionally. The function **close-all-files** will close all open files, and streams associated with them. Whenever in doubt, use that function. If no files are open, it will return NIL and does no harm.

```
(close-all-files) ==> NIL
```

The third option for :direction is the keyword :io, which allows you to read from and write to a file through the same stream.

We assumed that the file oldf.lsp existed in the system, it, therefore, must have a pathname. We can see that by using the function **directory**.

```
(directory "oldf.lsp")
==> (#.(PATHNAME "C:\\GCLISP\\OLDF.LSP"))
```

The function **probe-file** also returns the pathname, if the file exists, and NIL if it doesn't.

```
(probe-file "oldf.lsp")
==> #.(PATHNAME "C:\\GCLISP\\OLDF.LSP")
(probe-file "newf.lsp") ==> NIL
```

The function (directory "*.*") will print the pathnames of all files in your current directory.

The macro **with-open-file** will automatically open, process, and close a file.

```
(with-open-file
    (stm "oldf.lsp" :direction :output)
    (dotimes (i 5) (print "hello" stm)))
==> NIL
```

The variable *stm* in the above function is the name of the stream associated with the file.

Another way of opening a file is to load it, with a **load** function. If you use the keyword :print set to T with the **load** function, the contents of the file will be printed.

```
(load "oldf.lsp" :print t)
"hello"
"hello"
"hello"
"hello"
"hello"
#.(PATHNAME "C:\\GCLISP\\OLDF.LSP")
```

Suppose that file test.lsp contains a function **cube** that computes the cube of its argument. You can load the file and call the function:

```
(load "test.lsp")
(cube 3) ==> 27
```

If you are not sure that a file exists, you can combine the probe test with the load (or any other action).

```
(when (probe-file "test.lsp")(load "test.lsp"))
```

In the example of opening a file with the **open** function, if the file does not exist, a new file will be created.

```
(setq news (open "newf.lsp"
            :direction :output))
(print '(defun cube (x)                    (5.85)
          (* x x x)) news)
(close news)
```

The file newf.lsp was created new, and we placed a function in it. We can now load the file and call the function.

```
(load "newf.lsp")
(cube 5) ==) 125
```

Note, however, that when you load a file in this manner, there is no stream associated with it and you cannot do any read or write operation in it.

When we created a new file in Example (5.85), the system provided it with a pathname:

```
(directory "newf.lsp")
==) (#.(PATHNAME "C:\\GCLISP\\NEWF.LSP"))
```

You can create a pathname with the function **make-pathname**:

```
(make-pathname :directory "c:/john/nick.jam")
==) #.(PATHNAME "C:\\JOHN\\NICK.JAM")
```

When writing a pathname, you can use a single slash ($/$) or a double back-slash ($\backslash\backslash$). The system converts the single slash to a double back-slash, as evident from the output.

After defining the pathname, we can open the file nick.jam, write to it, close it, and so forth. In the author's system implementation, the directory JOHN in the above pathname automatically changes to the standard installation directory GCLISP:

```
(directory "nick.jam")
   ==) (#.(PATHNAME "C:\\GCLISP\\NICK.JAM"))
```

Another way of creating a pathname is to use the function **pathname**.

```
(setq path (pathname "a:/jjcar/file3.kkk"))
==) #.(PATHNAME "A:\\JJCAR\\FILE3.KKK")
```

After that, you can open and use the file as before. Again your system is likely to change nonstandard directories to its default setting. To see the default setting of your system, use the global variable *default-pathname-defaults*. For the author's system, the following is set:

```
*default-pathname-defaults*
    ==) (PATHNAME "C:\\GCLISP\\FOO.LSP")
```

A file can be renamed with the function **rename-file**:

```
(rename-file "file4.lsp" "file5.lsp")
```

The file named file4 has changed its name to file5.

A file can be deleted with the function **delete-file**:

```
(delete-file "file5.lsp")
==) #.(PATHNAME "C:\\GCLISP\\FILE5.LSP")
    NIL
```

The file named file5 has been deleted:

```
(probe-file "file5.lsp") ==) NIL
```

The dubugging macros **trace** and **step** can be used directly with functions in files, as explained in subsections 3.10.1 and 3.10.2 of Chapter 3.

As a final remark and warning before closing this section, we should point out that when you open a new file, its :direction keyword should be set to :output. It does not make sense to set it to :input because there is nothing in the file to read. However, when you open an existing file as an :output file and write data to it, the previously stored data will be destroyed. As long as the file is open, you can continue writing to it without destruction, but once you close the file and reopen it, whatever you write will destroy the old data (depending on the implementation of certain keywords, the destruction of old data may wait until you close the associated stream, but in the end, the old data will be gone. In the KCL implementation (Yuasa, 1986) the keyword sequence :if-exists :append will apparently (p. 222) cause the output to be written at the end of the existing data without destroying the initial content). If you want to add data or update the existing files, the safest way to do it is under the edit mode, as described in Chapter 3.

In Figure 5.9, we present a summary of file opening, with its keyword parameters given in this text.

The :probe option, if implemented, simply opens and closes a file, if it exists.

```
OPEN  <filename>
      :direction
                        :input
                        :output
                        :io
                        :probe
      :element-type
                            :string-char
                            :character
                            :default
                                etc.
```

Figure 5.9. Data structure of the **open** function.

It is another way of verifying the existence of a file. You can achieve the same result with (when (probe-file <filename> (open . . .

The :element-type keyword, if implemented, allows you to specify the data-type of elements in the file. Any of the permissible data-types may be specified.

5.14 EXERCISES

1. There is a system function **make-broadcast-stream** which, if implemented, takes any number of output-stream names as arguments, and outputs anything written to them to other streams. The syntax for the use of this function is

```
(setq <variable> (make-broadcast-stream
            <stream-name>...<stream-name>))
```

Use this function to write and display additional strings to the output-streams in Section 5.13.

2. Construct a number of streams and use the **make-broadcast-stream** function to show their contents.

3. Write a function to read numbers in decimal, and output them in binary, octal, and hexadecimal bases.

4. Recall the **neg** function in Example (4.18), Subsubsection 4.5.3.1. Write a function to read a progressive sentence and ask the question "Do you want the negation of this sentence" (Y or N). If you respond Y, it should apply the **neg** function; if you respond N, return NIL.

5. Write to a file a number of English nouns and their plural forms as dotted pairs. Also place in the file a function that, given a singular noun, will produce its plural form. Finally, open the file and run the function.

6. Write a function that will make a copy of a given file and make the filename of the copy the same as the original, but change the filetype to BAK. For example, if the original file has the name file4.lsp, the backup copy should have the name file4.bak. [Hint: There are functions in Common Lisp that return the filename and filetype of a pathname separately. For example, (pathname-name "file4.lsp") ⇒ FILE4 and (pathname-type "file4.lsp") ⇒ LSP.]

7. Given a stream of characters that make up words separated by blanks, how do you find the number of words in the stream?

5.15. & REST

The title of this section should not deceive the reader into thinking that the section will contain all the rest that there is in Lisp. Indeed, there are a number of not commonly used or more specialized functions and procedures in both Lispvm and Common Lisp, which will be left out in this introductory text. We assure the reader, however, that with the material given in this text, he/she can use the full power of Lisp for any beginning or advanced project. Common Lisp has several implementations, none of which contain all of the proposed facilities for Lisp. We have frequently used the phrase "subject to implementation" in describing some function. An excellent proposal for a comprehensive implementation of Common Lisp is in Steele (1984).

In this section, we will give a few miscellaneous procedures that have not fallen under the topics of other sections, or have been left out.

A very useful function is **dribble**. If you use that with a filename argument, a file will be opened with automatically assigned pathname components, and all interactions with the terminal in a session will be recorded on it. Then, if you use **dribble** again with no argument, the file will be closed and permanently stored until you delete it.

```
     (dribble "session.lsp")  ;;opens file
"All interactive activity will be recorded"
     (dribble)  ;;closes the file and saves
     (probe-file "session.lsp")
     ==> #.(PATHNAME "C:\\GCLISP\\SESSION.LSP")
```

The macro **time** gives the evaluation time of a form:

```
     (defun cube (x) (* x x x)) ==> CUBE
     (time (cube 100))
      ==> Elapsed Time:
         00:00.00  ;; Too fast for the
         1000000    ;; two-place seconds provided!
     (time (cube (cube 10)))
      ==> Elasped Time: 0:00.06
         1000000000
     (defun cube-cube (x)
"incidentally compare with (cube (cube x)) result"
```

```
(* x x x (* x x x)))
==> CUBE-CUBE
(cube-cube 10) ==> 1000000
```

The function **get-decoded-time** gives the time of day in the following (system-dependent) format:

```
(get-decoded-time)
   59    ;;; seconds
   57    ;;; minutes
   15    ;;; hour
   19    ;;; day
   7     ;;; month
   1990  ;;; year
[That is, July 19 15:57.59]
```

The function **sleep** suspends evaluation for the number of seconds given as its argument.

```
(sleep 5)     ;; pause for 5 seconds
```

The function **get-internal-real-time** will give a single integer, which is the current time in hundreths of a second, since the previous midnight (implementation dependent):

```
(get-internal-real-time) ==> 5759987
```

This number represents 15.999963 hours, or about 4 p.m. Eastern Standard Time, when it was executed on the author's machine.

The functions **lisp-implementation-type** and **lisp-implementation-version** give the type and version of the Common Lisp system you are using.

The function **identity** just returns its argument:

```
(identity 25) ==> 25
(identity 'abc) ==> ABC
```

It can be used in the arguments of other functions.

The function **room** gives the memory allocations and amount of free memory in your computer.

The function **describe** prints information about its argument:

```
(describe 'cadr)
==> Its global value is unbound.
      Its function definition is:
         #(COMPILED FUNCTION 32B6:4533).
```

```
Its property list contains:
Property: LISP::SETF-EXPANDER,
     VALUE: ((CADR LIST) CAR (CDR LIST))
```

The function **apropos** takes a string argument and returns descriptions of each symbol in a given package whose print name contains the string. For example, if you write

```
(apropos "prin" (find-package 'lisp))
```

you will get a long list and descriptions of the symbols prin, print, prin1, prinl, princ, etc.

The function **apropos-list** returns just a list of all symbols whose print name contains the string.

A number of standard Lisp functions have extended forms in Common Lisp, which allow for additional tests or conditions for execution. The list of such functions and forms include the following:

assoc	**assoc-if**	**assoc-if-not**
count	**count-if**	**count-if-not**
delete	**delete-if**	**delete-if-not**
find	**find-if**	**find-if-not**
member	**member-if**	**member-if-not**
position	**position-if**	**position-if-not**
rassoc	**rassoc-if**	**rassoc-if-not**
remove	**remove-if**	**remove-if-not**
subst	**subst-if**	**subst-if-not**
substitute	**substitute-if**	**substitute-if-not**

We have already seen, at least in their simple forms, all of these system functions (except **count**, **find**, and **position**, which are currently not implemented for the "small memory" GCLisp). Augmentations with **if** apply if a test results in non-nil. The augmentation with **if-not** applies if the test results in nil. The following examples with **remove** demonstrate this process.

```
(setq x '(1 2 3 1 2 3))
==> (1 2 3 1 2 3)
(remove 2 x)
==> (1 3 1 3)
x ==> (1 2 3 1 2 3)    ;; REMOVE is nondestructive
(remove-if #'oddp x)   ;; Recall that macro character
                  ;; #' is abbreviation for FUNCTION.
==> (2 2)       ;; Odd numbers removed
(remove-if-not #'oddp x)
==> (1 3 1 3)    ;; Even numbers (not odd) removed
```

Subject to implementation, you can have another augmentation for some of the functions. For example, **remove-duplicates** will remove duplicates of a given object.

```
(remove-duplicates 'a '(a b c a a d e a))
==) (A B C D E)
```

In addition, the application of these functions can be further restricted with some of the Common Lisp keywords that we are now familiar with: :count, :end, :from-end, :key, :start, :test, :test-not, and so on.

```
(setq x '(a b c a b d a a g f b c))
==) (A B C A B D A A G F B C)
(remove 'a x)
==) (B C B D G F B C)
(remove 'a x :count 2)
==) (B C B D A A G F B C)
(remove 'a x :count 2 :from-end t)
==) (A B C A B D G F B C)
(remove 'a x :start 2 :end 5)
==) (A B C B D A A G F B C)
(remove 3 '(1 2 1 2 3 4 3 0 5) :test #'))
==) (3 4 3 5) ;; All less-than-3 elements removed
```

Recall that the function **nth** returns the *n*th element in a sequence. The function **find** searches a sequence and returns the first occurrence of the element indicated in its argument.

```
(find 'a  '(1 2 a b (a b) c))
 ==) A
(find-if #'listp '(1 2 a b (a b) c))
 ==) (A B)
(find 'a '((1 3) (c d) (a b)) :key #'car)
 ==) (A B)
(find #\c "abcdef")
 ==) #\c
```

The function **position** is like **find**, but instead of returning the element found in a sequence, it returns the index (position) of that element.

```
(position 'a '(a b c d e a b))
 ==) 0     ;; The first a is in position 0
(position 'a '(a b c d e a b) :start 3)
 ==) 5  ;; The first a starting from index 3
          ;; is in position 5
```

There is also a function **search**, which matches two sequences and returns the index of the beginning of the first sequence in the second, if it occurs.

```
(search '(a b c) '(j f k a b c m n o))
 ==) 3  ;; The sequence a b c occurs in position
        ;; 3 of the second argument
```

The function **mismatch** is the opposite of **search**; it looks for the first element that does not match in the two arguments.

```
(mismatch '(a b c) '(d e f a b c))
 ==) 0  ;; There is a mismatch in the zero
        ;; position
```

The function **count** returns the number of occurrences of an object in a sequence.

```
(setq x '(a b c (a b) a b a))
 ==) (A B C (A B) A B A)
(count 'a x)
 ==) 3  ;; 3 A's at the top level of x
(count-if #'listp x)
 ==) 1   ;; There is one list within x
(count-if-not #'listp x)
 ==) 6  ;; There are 6 elements that are not
        ;; lists in x
```

Appendix A: An Outline of Procedures for Starting in Lisp

In this appendix, we will go through the procedures for "signing on" and "logging off" in two dialects of Lisp that are extensively represented in this book: Common Lisp and Lispvm. The reader who is using another dialect would do well to skim through this appendix, because many of the procedures are the same or similar in all dialects. Details of editing facilities are given in Chapter 3. Let us begin by listing some of the common terminology used in computing. (A more complete glossary is in Appendix B.)

TABLE A-1. SOME COMPUTING TERMS

Account:	Authorization at a computer facility for a person to use the computer (usually the mainframe).
Buffer:	A temporary storage area in computer memory allocated for working.
Command:	Instruction to a computer. In Lisp, this usually refers to editing commands.
Command Mode:	Computer environment for edit commands.
Cursor:	A blinking or steady bright spot that moves ahead of characters when you input to the monitor, pointing to where the next character will be displayed.
Directory / Subdirectory:	Area or areas in a computer's permanent memory allocated for storing programs and data files. Normally, a listing of all such objects is maintained in a directory or "indexed file," which can be displayed on a terminal screen.
Debug:	Procedures for detecting and correcting errors in programs.
Edit:	The process of creating, correcting, storing, and loading programs and data
Edit Mode:	The computer environment for editing.
Enter:	Pressing the *ENTER* key on the keyboard.
Error Loop:	Levels of error in a computer program.
Interactive Mode:	The process of the interactive creation and evaluation or running of programs.
Logoff:	Procedure for ending a computing session.
Logon:	Procedure for beginning a computing session.
Mainframe:	A large central computer that serves an organization, usually through remote connections.
Operating System:	A resident program (software) which, among other things, controls and manages programming languages and application programs.

TABLE A-1. CONTINUED

Prompt:	A character or character string marking the place of input on a monitor screen. The cursor normally appears to the right of the prompt before data entry begins.
Session:	The time between logon and logoff.
Sign Off:	Same as logoff.
Sign On:	Same as logon.

For demonstration purposes for Common Lisp, we will use the version known as Golden Common Lisp (GCLisp) for personal computers, developed by Gold Hill Computers, Inc. This version runs under the DOS operating system. You must install this Lisp in your computer in accordance with the installation instructions that come with the Lisp package.

Let us assume that you have a computer with a hard-disk drive (this is convenient, but not necessary) and that you have installed Lisp in a subdirectory called GCLISP in Drive C. At the DOS prompt, which may be C:\>, if you type cd\gclisp, the control will move to the subdirectory of Lisp and you can use it. At this point, depending on the DOS procedures used (see the DOS manual for information), the prompt may look like this: C:\GCLISP>. To invoke Lisp, again type gclisp. You will be put in the interactive mode of Lisp called the LISTENER. In this mode, you can enter Lisp programs and data that would be evaluated as you input, and the output will be printed on your monitor screen when you finish each completed program or 'expression'. When you invoke Lisp, some messages will appear at the top of the screen, and then the prompt for Lisp, which is an asterisk, *. The cursor, which is a blinking dash (__), will be next to the prompt and moves with the display data. When you finish, you can input (exit), which is a *logoff* instruction for Lisp. In the following example, we will repeat the above sequence of operations and then show a frame representing a computer screen in which we will write a few Lisp expressions or forms and their evaluations. In this, as in all other examples in this book, what you input at the keyboard will be shown in lower-case letters, and the computer responses will be in capitals, except in certain print forms, where the output may be in lower or mixed cases.

```
C:\)_ cd\gclisp
C:\GCLISP)_ gclisp

  (messages...)
 *_ (+ 5 6 3)
 14
 *_ (first '(milk bread butter potatoes))
 MILK
 *_ (defun example (x y z)
          (cond ((= x y z) 'all-equal)
                (t (max x y z))))
   EXAMPLE
 *_ (example 5 5 5)
 ALL-EQUAL
 *_ (example 5 9 3)
 9
 *_ (exit)
 C:\GCLISP)_
```

When you enter Lisp, as demonstrated above, you will be placed at the "top-level" of Lisp, which is level 0. If you make an error, you will get an error message and be placed at levels 1, 2, . . . down into the "error-loop." To get out of this loop, press the *control (Ctrl)* key and the *C* key simultaneously. Here is an example of an error message: In the above session, after you have input the function **example**, input the sequence in the following frame:

```
*_(example 2 3)
ERROR:
Not enough arguments for the function: EXAMPLE
while evaluating: (EXAMPLE 2 3)
1)_ (example 4 7 6 9)
ERROR:
Too many arguments for the function: EXAMPLE
while evaluating: (EXAMPLE 4 7 6 9)
2)_ Ctrl-C
Top-Level
*_
```

To get into Edit Mode, you must exit Lisp, and at the prompt C:\GCLISP> input gmacs. GMACS is the name of the editor of Golden Common Lisp (see Chapter 3 for details of the use of the editor).

For a session in Lispvm, we will assume that you have the same personal computer, but it is now connected through a modem or direct wiring to a mainframe computer that contains the Lisp system. You must have an Account, which allows you to log onto the VM/CMS operating system, and you must be allocated 3 to 4 megabytes of working memory to work in Lispvm. When you log onto VM, the monitor screen will look something like the following frame:

```
(messages ... )




                                                                VM Read
= = = = = = = = = = = = = = = = = = = = = = = = = = = = = = = =
```

Now input lispvm and *ENTER*. The following screen will appear:

```
 NIL




   Lispedit level 0 ----------------------- Default id: NIL
   (messages ... )
   ===)_
   =======================================
```

You will be in Lispedit (that is, the edit mode of Lispvm). This is called the "divided screen." The arrow, ⇒, at the bottom left of the screen points to the "command line." Anything you input in this line will be evaluated, and the results will be printed in the message area (bottom part) of the screen. If you make an error, an error message will appear in the message area. To get out of the error loop, input (fin d) or (unwind d), where d is any positive digit. If you input, say, (unwind 4), you will go back to level 0 (top-level) but will also be taken out of the edit mode, into the "full screen" (see further in text). On the other hand, if you type, say, (fin 3), you will go to level 0 but stay in the edit mode (details of editing in Lispvm are given in Chapter 3).

Before you have studied the editing facilities in Chapter 3, you do not want to be in the edit mode. Therefore, when you are in the divided screen of Lispedit, press *function-key 3 (F3)*; when a message appears in the message area, asking you to confirm the command, press the *ENTER* key. The following "full screen" will then appear:

```
 




   __
   ==================== VM Read
```

You can do all of the exercises in Chapters 1 and 2 in this screen. When you are finished, input (exitlisp) to get out of Lisp, and then input logoff to get out of the VM. To recapitulate, the sequence of instructions (after the logon procedure specified by your account) for getting into and out of Lispvm is the following:

```
⟨log⟩
lispvm
F3
ENTER
⟨Lisp programs and data⟩
(exitlisp)
logoff
```

Appendix B: Glossary

address: The location in the computer memory of an object.

argument: A value for a function parameter given in a function call.

array: A data structure organized along a coordinate system of any number of dimensions. Access to data is through indices pointing to the location of elements.

ASCII: The acronym of the American Standard Code for Information Interchange. A code system for character data transmission.

assignment: The process of assigning global values to variables; for example, with **setq** or **setf** functions.

association list (alist): A list of pairs in Lisp, in which the first element of the pair is a key element and the second is a datum associated with the key.

atom: A Lisp object that is not a list (e.g., symbols and numbers).

backquote: The character ` in Lisp, which has a special significance in constructing lists (see Section 5.12).

binary: The number system in base 2 consisting of 0's and 1's.

binary tree: A tree structure whose nodes can have, at most, two branches exiting from them.

binding: The process of co-indexing or associating data with a variable; for example, in binding values to the parameters of a function or objects of a **let** expression. Unlike assignment procedure, these bindings are temporary (local), and the variables regain their original values outside of the scope of their binding environments.

bit: A unit in a computer representing a pulse or no pulse, a yes or no, a true or false, a 0 or 1. It is also referred to as a binary bit.

bound variable: A variable that has a value associated with it.

break: A temporary suspension of the execution of a program in Lisp. If the break is caused by an error, it may not be temporary.

break level: The level of a Lisp interaction established due to successive breaks.

buffer: A temporary data storage area in computer memory, normally for input/outout and editing purposes.

byte: The standard size of a data storage unit in a computer memory, normally consisting of eight bits, which can represent one character in binary bits.

character: A data type in Lisp that includes the characters on the keyboard and other characters, such as space, new-line, and so on.

compiler: A computer program that translates and reformulates a program written in a programming language into codes that are understandable and executable by a computer.

complex expression: An expression that contains other expressions or programs.

cons: A Lisp data type consisting of two cells, called **car** and **cdr**. The **car** cell points to the first element of a list, and the **cdr** cell points to the rest of the list.

cursor: A blinking mark on a monitor screen pointing to where a character input from the keyboard will be placed.

d-function: A term used in this book to refer to functions defined by the user, as opposed to the system functions.

data type: Lisp objects are divided into data types, such as arrays, characters, numbers, symbols, lists, and so on.

data: Information presented to a computer for evaluation and manipulation.

database: The storage structure in which data is organized and kept.

debug: The process and procedures for finding errors in a program and correcting them.

default: A value or option taken in a process when no specific value or option has been given.

destructive function: A function that permanently changes the value or nature of data that it deals with (*see also* nondestructive function).

dialect: Varieties of versions or implementations of a programming language.

directory: A storage area where filenames are kept for reference (*see also* file).

disk drive: A hardware component of a computer that houses a disk or diskette for reading and writing.

display: A visual presentation of data on a computer screen.

DOS: An operating system for personal computers (*see* operating system).

dotted list: A list whose last **cons** is a dotted pair [i.e., does not end in nil: (a b c . d)] (*see* Chapter 4).

dotted pair: Representation of a **cons** cell [e.g. (a . b)].

dynamic extent: *See* extent.

edit mode: A special environment for editing programs and data (*see* Chapter 3).

edit: The process of constructing, updating, and correcting programs and data.

editor: System programs for editing.

element: An object or member of a list.

enter: The *ENTER* key on the keyboard, used to enter input data. As a command, it indicates: input data, enter, and return to a new line.

error level: Lisp systems have several levels of error. The Lisp Listener starts at Top Level. When an error occurs, controls goes to Level 1. If there is another error, control goes to Level 2, and so on.

error message: Prestored system messages attempting to describe the type of error.

evaluation: The process of executing the interpretation of a Lisp input.

expression: A collective name for atoms and lists: more precisely, symbolic expression or s-expression.

extent: The length of time during which an object can be accessed is the *extent* of that object. *Dynamic extent* means that the object can be accessed from the time that it is established to the time that it is explicitly disconnected or unestablished. Objects that can be referred to as long as they exist have *indefinite extent*.

file: A storage area with a name (*filename*). A filename may be further augmented with a *filetype* or *extension*. Filenames and filetypes are normally constrained by the system under which they are implemented, and they are stored in a *directory*.

filename: *See* file.

filetype: An extension of a filename for further identification.

form: An expression that is for evaluation is called a form. When a form is a list, its first element is usually a function name.

function call: A function is used by naming it and giving arguments for its parameters. This process is called "function call."

function: A Lisp procedure that has a name, a list of parameters, called a lambdalist, and a body. Typically, it takes input arguments, which are bound to its parameters, and produces an output.

function keys: Special keys on a keyboard, normally marked as F1, F2, etc. and used to carry out specified functions.

garbage collection: A procedure in computer software to free and consolidate memory cells that are no longer in use.

global variable: A variable whose universal value remains unchanged, even if it gets a temporary local value within the scope of a form.

hexadecimal: A number system in base 16. The digits in this system are represented by the numerals 0 through 9, and the letters A through F.

I/O: The programs and facilities for the input and output of data in a computer.

indefinite extent: *See* extent.

indefinite scope: *See* scope.

indexed file: A file designed in Lispvm to hold programs and data. The file can be edited under the edit mode, or Lispedit.

input: Data read by a computer. In Lisp, data read by the Lisp Reader.

interpreter: A program that translates and evaluates input data as it is read.

iteration: The process of repetition of a procedure or action. Lisp has several procedures for repetition. Iteration is contrasted with recursion, in which a procedure invokes itself to do the same task with changed data.

key sequence: The process of pressing a sequence of keys on the keyboard to achieve some result.

keyboard: The typewriter-like key-set of a personal computer or a terminal, where input data and instructions are typed in.

keychord: The process of pressing more than one key on the keyboard simultaneously.

lambda-expression: An object of Lisp that is an unnamed function.

lambda list: The list of parameters of a function.

level 0: *See* top level.

lexical scope: *See* scope.

lexical variable: A variable with lexical scope and indefinite extent. Lexical variables are also called static variables.

list processing: The process of manipulating lists. List processing languages have facilities for manipulating lists.

list: A data type in Lisp that is made up of a chain of **cons**es. A list is bounded by a pair of parentheses. An empty list is represented as ( ) or NIL.

listener: A program in Lisp that interactively reads input data, evaluates them, and outputs the result—the read-eval-print loop component.

load: The process of retrieving a file into a working memory or buffer. When a file is loaded in Lisp, the objects in the file can be evaluated.

local variable: A variable whose value is recognized within the scope of its construct. Outside the scope, the variable may have no value, or may assume its global value. (*see also* global variable).

logoff: The process of ending a computing session with a computer.

logon: The process of starting a computing session with a computer.

macro character: A character in Lisp that is associated with a function. When it appears in the input, the associated function is called and evaluated.

macro: A form that evaluates into a function and function call for its evaluation.

mainframe: A large-scale computer, typically located in a central facility for serving the computing needs of an organization.

memory: The storage device in a computer.

monitor: The screen attached to a terminal or personal computer for the visual observation of input and output data.

multiple value: In Lisp, a function that returns more than one value as output.

nil: A reserved Lisp name that stands for an atom, an empty list, or logical false.

nondestructive function: A function whose effect on its argument is local—within the scope of the function. For example, the function **remove** can be used to remove some elements from a list; but outside of the scope of the function, the list remains unchanged. The function **delete**, on the other hand, can remove elements from a list, and the list will remain changed outside the scope of the function. Therefore, **delete** is a destructive function.

number: A Lisp data type.

object: A Lisp entity of any data type. Functions and other data stored in an indexed file (q.v.).

octal: The number system in base 8. The digits in the octal system consist of 0 through 7.

operating system: A major computer program that manages and controls the operation of a computer, and other programs and languages that run on the computer.

output: The result of any computing activity, which may be displayed on a screen, printed by a printer, stored in memory, or discarded.

package: A Common Lisp object and procedure for the management of named spaces in a computer memory.

parameter: A variable in the definition of a function, which is bound by the value given by the argument of a function call.

pathname: The identification data for a file. A pathname provides all of the necessary data for the operating system to locate and access a file.

pointer: The address in a **cons** cell that points to another cell. In a list-structure, data cells need not necessarily be in consecutive locations in the memory. The **cdr** of each cell can have a pointer to the next logical cell in the sequence. The **cdr** of the last cell in the sequence can then contain NIL, marking the end of the sequence.

predicate function: A function that returns true or false as a result of its evaluation. In Lisp, the dichotomy is between NIL (false) and non-NIL (true).

pretty-printing: The process of printing functions on indented lines, for ease of reading.

print name: A string of characters that represent a symbol in a Lisp package and are displayed in outputs. For example, inputs in lower or mixed case letters may appear as capitals in their print names.

prompt: The symbol that appears on a terminal screen indicating that a program is ready to receive data input.

property list: Each Lisp symbol has an associated property list, containing zero or more features. Each feature, in turn, can be divided into two parts: a key or indicator and a value.

queue: A list that can receive data in one end and remove it from the other end (*see also* stack).

read-eval-print: Every input object in Lisp is subjected to the read-eval-print loop or cycle, where the object is read, evaluated, and the result is returned.

reader: The Lisp input language parser. It reads characters, constructs a Lisp object, and returns it.

recursion: The continued repetion of a process applied to its own result.

recursive function: A function that has a recursion property and calls itself to replicate its operation.

return: The process of passing control back to the calling procedure.

s-expression: Symbolic expression (*see* expression).

scope: The scope of a Lisp object is the environment in a program where that object can be referenced or accessed. There are two kinds of scopes: lexical and indefinite. A symbol with lexical scope can only be referenced within the construct that defines it. A symbol with an indefinite scope can be used anywhere. All predefined Lisp symbols fall within the latter category.

screen: The display screen of a terminal or monitor.

sign on: Same as logon.

sign off: Same as logoff.

special variable: A variable with indefinite scope and dynamic extent (q.v.). Special variables are also called dynamic variables, and are typically marked with asterisk boundaries: *x*, *name*. special variables have global values.

special form: A relatively small number of forms in Common Lisp that are primarily concerned with control and binding. Such forms are usually not redefinable by a user.

stack: Stacks are data structures in the form of lists, where elements can only be placed (pushed) on one end (top) and taken off (popped) from the same end.

step: The process of stepping through a program to observe its flow, detect errors, and correct them.

stream: A Lisp object that acts as a buffer for interface with an I/O device.

symbol manipulation: The act of processing symbols.

symbol: A symbol is used to name a function or a variable. A symbol can also name itself by evaluating to itself. Each symbol is provided with a property list (q.v.), which can be empty.

terminal: The interface device for communication with a computer.

top level: All Lisp interactive processes start at the Top Level of Lisp, which is also called Level 0. Control can move to levels 1, 2, and so on, due to breaks or error encounters.

trace: A debugging procedure for detecting errors in a program.

type: Lisp has many types of data, called *data types*. Type is a category of Lisp object, and there are functions for identifying these types.

unbound variable: A variable that has not been assigned a value or bound to a value.

variable: A data object that represents a value. A variable is named by a symbol, and is assigned a global value by, for example, an assignment function, or a local value binding by, for example, by the special form **let**.

vector: A one-dimensional array. Access to arrays is through indices pointing to the locations of elements.

white space: The blank space between words, for example.

workspace: The space in a computer memory where one runs programs and manipulates data.

Appendix C: Solutions to Selected Exercises

In the following solutions to exercises, if a solution is marked with CL, it is for Common Lisp; if it is marked with LVM, it is for Lispvm; if it has no marking, the solution applies to both dialects. This study will show that, in most cases, it is easy to convert a program in one dialect to run under another.

SECTION 1.4

1. (+ 75 (* 12 10)) ==> 195
   (- (* 25 (- (+ 6 2) 3)) 5) ==> 120
   (- (+ 253 252) (- 6 3)) ==> 502

2. (divide (* 5 4) 6) Value = (3 2)   [LVM]

   Implies that there are three apples for each child and a remainder of two for Mary.

3. (plus (minusp -6) 7) Value = 1   [LVM]
   (times (add1 6) (sub1 5)) Value = 28
   (greaterp (intp 7) (minusp -8)) Value = TRUE
   (atom (divide 6 2)) Value = NIL [Recall that **divide**
           returns a <u>list</u> of the quotient and remainder]
   (atom (divide 7 2)) Value = NIL
   (atom (/ 6 2)) Value = TRUE
   (divide (oddp 5) 2) Value = (2 1)
   (quotient (* 3 2) (+ 2 1)) Value = 2

4. Both CL and LVM have the predicate function **minusp**, but they don't behave the same way (*see* Tables 1.1 and 1.2).
   (* (1+ 6) (1- 5)) ==> 28

The functions **intp** in Lispvm and **integerp** in Common Lisp do not behave in the same way. You cannot, therefore, replace one with the other. You will see later in the text, however, that **intp** can be defined as a function for Common Lisp.

$$
\begin{aligned}
&(\text{atom (truncate 6 2)}) ==) \text{ T} \\
&(\text{atom (truncate 7 2)}) ==) \text{ T} \\
&(\text{atom (/ 6 2)}) ==) \text{ T}
\end{aligned}
$$

The function **oddp** in Common Lisp does not behave the same way as in Lispvm (see Tables 1.1 and 1.2).

(/ (* 3 2) (+ 2 1)) ==) 2.0   [Note the difference in decimal point, however.]

5. (+ 1.5 (/ 425. 55.))   Value = 9.22727272727
6. (equal (+ 5 5) (* 2 5))   Value = TRUE
7. (* 3.14 (* 5.75 5.75))   Value = 103.8162
8. (equal (/ 5 2) (/ 5 2.0))   Value = NIL   (in LISPVM only)
    [Explanation: (/ 5 2) = 2; (/ 5 2.0) = 2.5]   [LVM]
9. (setq x 5) ==) 5   [CL]
         (= x) ==) T
         (/= 1 x 10) ==) T
         (<= 1 x 10) ==) T
         () 7 x 3) ==) T
         ((7 x 5) ==) NIL
         () -3 7 x 10) ==) NIL

10. In Common Lisp, **eql** is sensitive to number types, because numbers with decimal points and their equivalent integers are stored separately (see Section 4.3).

SECTION 1.8

1. (a) This function takes a numerical argument (which we can interpret as a temperature reading) and returns comments about it.
    (b) This function converts Fahrenheit temperature readings to Celsius.
    (c) In this recursive function, in each cycle 1 is subtracted from the second argument and 1 is added to the first argument. When the value of the first argument reaches 100, the value of the second argument is returned. Examples:

X1	X2	X1	X2
95	3	95	90
96	2	96	89
97	1	97	88
98	0	98	87
99	−1	99	86
100	−2	100	85
	⇒ −2		⇒ 85

What would be the result of the following function calls?

$$(\text{addition2 } 100 \ 0) ==\rangle \ ?$$
$$(\text{addition2 } 125 \ 10) ==\rangle \ ?$$

2. '(* 2 3) is treated as data (because of the quote) and is assigned as the value of x. Thus, if you type "x," the value (* 2 3) will be returned, and the **car** of this list is *. However, **eval** is a system function that evaluates its argument, so that (eval x) will return the result of $2 \times 3 = 6$. But (eval 'x) that is (eval (quote x)), will return the assigned value of "x." (eval "x), that is (eval (quote (quote x))), will return "x," which is the same as 'x if "x" was unbound.

3. ```
(defun howmany (L)   [LVM]
   (cond ((null L) 0)
         ('t (add1 (howmany (cdr L))))))   ;;use 1+ for CL
(howmany '(a b c d e))   Value = 5
```

4. ```
(defun power (m n)
   (cond ((equal n 1) m)
         ('t (* m (power m (- n 1))))))
```

5. ```
(defun count-arts (sent)   [CL]
   (cond ((null sent) 0)
         ((member (car sent) '(a an the))
          (1+ (count-arts (cdr sent)))) ;;use add1 for LVM
         (t (count-arts (cdr sent)))))
```

6. The following function written in Common Lisp will add any number "n" without overtly using a "+" operator:

```
(defun add-n (n)                                           [CL]
   (do ((sum 0) (n1 n (decf n1)))
       ((zerop n1) sum)
       (incf sum n1)))
(add-n 100) ==〉 5050
```

SECTION 1.10

1. ```
(defun product (m n)   [CL]
   (do ((p 0) (n1 n (1- n1)))   ;;use sub1 for LVM or
       ((zerop n1) p)   ;;(- n1 1) for both
       (setq p (+ p m))))
```

2. ```
(defun check (word sentence)
   (prog ()
      tag (cond ((null sentence) nil)
                ((equal word (car sentence))
                 (return 'found))
                (t (setq sentence (cdr sentence))
                   (go tag)))))
```
```

A much simpler noniterative solution to this is:

```
(defun check2 (word sentence)
   (cond ((null sentence) 'no)
         ((member word sentence) 'yes)
         (t 'no)))
```

We will see later in the text that there can be even a further, simpler version:

```
(defun check3 (word sentence)
   (if (member word sentence) 'yes 'no))
```

3. This is an iterative function that finds the value of a number "m" raised to the power "n." This is, of course, an inefficient and awkward way of writing this function—given here for demonstration only. See the discussion in the text.

4. (a) Defines *plus* as a word in the vocabulary of Common Lisp. But it can only add two numbers.
   (b) Defines *difference* for Common Lisp. But it can only subtract two numbers.
   (c) x ==> (+ 1 2 3)   y ==> ((+ 1 2 3))
       In "y," **cons**ing embeds (+ 1 2 3) in another list. See the Solution to Exercise 2, under Section 1.8 earlier.
   (d) x ==> (+ 1 (* 5 6))
   (e) name ==> FIDO   kind ==> DOG   sex ==> FEMALE
       age ==> 3

5. First we will define a dictionary as a simple list:

```
(setq dict '(dog cat mouse rabbit raccoon))
```

Now the function:

```
(defun add-dict (w dictionary)
   (setq x (check w dictionary))
   (cond ((equal x nil) (cons w dictionary))))
```

Note that, in the **add-dict** function, we used the **check** function, defined under the Solution to Exercise 2, earlier.

```
(add-dict 'bees dict) ==> (BEES DOG CAT RABBIT RACCOON)
(add-dict 'mouse dict) ==> (DOG CAT MOUSE RABBIT RACCOON)
```

In Common Lisp, there is a system function **adjoin** (**addtolist** in Lispvm) that does the same thing—adds an element to a list if it is not there.

```
(adjoin 'tiger dict) ==> (TIGER DOG CAT MOUSE RABBIT RACCOON)
(adjoin 'cat dict) ==> (DOG CAT MOUSE RABBIT RACCOON)
```

In the solution for Exercise 5, the **add-list** function was deliberately designed to call another function. The following solution is a simpler version:

```
(defun add-dict2 (w dictionary)
   (if (not (member w dictionary))
           (cons w dictionary)))
```

The special form **if** is similar to the function **cond**. It will be described in detail later in the text. Neither of the above versions will change the contents of DICT permanently. To make a global change in DICT, the function can be called in the following way:

```
(setq dict (add-dict2 'wolf dict))
   (WOLF DOG CAT MOUSE RABBIT RACCOON)
dict ==> (WOLF DOG CAT MOUSE RABBIT RACCOON)
```

6. `(multiply '(2 3 7)) ==> 0`
The way this function is written, when the list is exhausted, a zero value is returned, which is multiplied by the previous result, always returning zero as output. To correct this, you must change the zero in the second line of the function to 1:

```
(cond ((null nums) 1), then (multiply '(2 3 7)) => 42
```

SECTION 2.5

1. (a) This function takes an integer "n" and a list l as its argument, and deletes the nth element in the list.
   (b) This function takes an item and a list as arguments, and determines whether the item is equal to an element in the list at the top level. If equal, it returns T, otherwise it will return NIL. (Compare with the system function **member**.)
   (c) This function takes two items and a list as arguments and replaces every occurrence of the second item in the list by the first item.
   (d) `(kinship '(john mary nick sue) '(husband wife son daughter))`
   `==> ((JOHN HUSBAND) (MARY WIFE) (NICK SON) (SUE DAUGHTER))`
   In the following, slightly different version of the function, the output is the same:

```
(defun kinship2 (names relations)
   (cond ((or (null names) (null relations)) nil)
         (t (cons (list (car names) (car relations))
               (kinship (cdr names) (cdr relations))))))
```

2. `(defun gt (x y) (> x y))`   [CL]
   `(defun sub1 (x) (1- x))`

3. The following function can be written in a much simpler and more elegant way after you have studied more of the system functions in Common Lisp. We urge you to reconsider this exercise after you have read Chapter 5! In the following example, we assume that the text is a list of lists, where each sublist is a sentence.

```
(defun word-count (word text)
   (prog ((counter 0) (sent nil))
tag1   (cond ((null text) (return counter))
             (t (setq sent (car text)) (go tag2)))
      tag2   (cond ((null sent)
                    (setq text (cdr text))
                    (go tag1))
```

```
                        ((equal word (car sent))
                         (setq counter (+ counter 1))
                         (setq sent (cdr sent))
                         (go tag2))
                        (t (setq sent (cdr sent))
                           (go tag2)))))
```

4. `(defun divides-3 (num-list)`   [CL]
`   (cond ((null num-list) nil)`
`         ((zerop (rem (car num-list) 3))`
`          (cons (car num-list) (divides-3 (cdr num-list))))`
`         (t (divides-3 (cdr num-list)))))`

To run this function in Lispvm, the function **rem** in line 3 should be changed to
remainder.

SECTION 2.9

1. The order of elements in the output of the **union** and **intersection** functions is implementation-dependent. In this exercise, we use a special function, which we will call
order, to preserve the order set-1 set-2.

```
            (defun order (s1 s2)
               (cond ((null s1) s2)
                     ((null s2) nil)
                     ((member (car s2) s1)
                      (order s1 (cdr s2)))
                     (t (cons (car s2) (order s1 (cdr s2))))))
            (defun my-union (s1 s2)
               (cond ((null s2) s1)
                     (t (append s1 (order s1 s2)))))
```

Example: `(my-union '(1 2 3) '(a 1 b 3 c 5))`
`              ==) (1 2 3 A B C 5)`

```
            (defun my-intersection (s1 s2)
               (cond ((null s1) nil)
                     ((member (car s1) s2)
                      (cons (car s1) (my-intersection (cdr s1) s2)))
                     (t (my-intersection (cdr s1) s2))))
```

Example: `(my-intersection '(a b c d e f g) '(x a b y w c g))`
`              ==) (A B C G)`

2. Elements that are less than 3 are removed.

3. ```
   (Defun delete-last (L)
       (reverse (cdr (reverse L))))
   ```

   ```
   (defun put-dashes (L)
       (cond ((null L) nil)
             (t (append (delete-last L) '(---)))))
   (put dashes '(this is the man who came))
   ==> (THIS IS THE MAN WHO ---)
   ```

4. In the following example, we will assume that there are two registration lists, called CL4 and CL6, for the courses with the same names (CL4 and CL6). The arguments of the function **schedule** are the name of a student from a general list of names, and the two lists. The function returns the appropriate message or messages for each student.

   ```
   (defun schedule (name cl4 cl6)
       (cond ((and
                (member name cl4)
                (member name cl6))
                  (print '(Change time CL4 /
                    CL2 and CL5 are prerequisites
                         for CL4 and CL6 respectively)) nil)
             ((member name cl4)
                (print '(CL2 is prerequisite for CL4)) nil)
             ((member name cl6)
                (print '(CL5 is prerequisite for CL6)) nil)
             (t nil)))
   ```

   Examples:
   ```
   (setq cl4 '(mary sue john clide amanda))
   (setq cl6 '(jack lee mitsu clide mary jill))
   (schedule 'mary cl4 cl6) ==>
   ```

   ```
   (CHANGE TIME FOR CL4 / CL2 AND CL5 ARE PREREQUISITES FOR
   CL4 AND CL6 RESPECTIVELY)
           (schedule 'mitsu cl4 cl6) ==>
               (CL5 IS PREREQUISITE FOR CL6)
           (schedule 'renee cl4 cl6) ==> NIL
   ```

5. At this point, the following function requires that the lists NAMES and RELATIONS be selected judiciously with certain fixed orders and contents for the results to come out sensibly (e.g., (husband (john mary)) and not (husband (mary sue))). Later, in Subsections 4.5.2 and 4.5.3, we will discuss how to assign properties to names, so that John, for example, will have a feature *husband* as its property. We can then enter names and relations in any order in the lists and have the function pick up the right relationships.
   ```

```
(defun kinship3 (names relations)
    (cond ((or (null names)
               (null relations)) nil)
          (t (print (list (car relations)
                          (list (car names)(cadr names))))
             (kinship3 (cdr names)(cdr relations)))))

(kinship3 '(john mary andy sue)
          '(husband mother brother))

(HUSBAND (JOHN MARY))
(MOTHER (MARY ANDY))
(BROTHER (ANDY SUE))
```

6.  ```
    (defun my-reverse (L)
        (cond ((null L) nil)
              (t (append (my-reverse (cdr L))(list (car L))))))
    ```

7.  ```
    (defun book-sale (x)                                    [CL]
        (cond (((<= x 5) (* x 3))    ;;In Lispvm use le instead of <=
               (t (+ (* 5 3) (* (- x 5) 2))))))
    ```

    ```
    (book-sale 3)==> 9  (book-sale 5)==> 15  (book-sale 12)==> 29
    ```

    In anticipation of Section 2.11:

    ```
    (mapcar 'book-sale '(3 5 12) ==> (9 15 29)
    ```


SECTION 2.12

1. (a) Inserts a number into a sequence in the sequence order:

    ```
    (insert-number 5 '(1 2 3 4 6 7)) ==> (1 2 3 4 5 6 7)
    ```

    (b) Repeats the elements of a list:

    ```
    (repeat-list '(a b c)) ==> (A A A B B B C C C)
    ```

    (c) ==> (A B C D)

    (d) ==> (TOM)The value of the last expression; equivalent to non-nil (= T) for the function.

    (e) Returns true if all members of the list are numbers:

    ```
    (list-numbp '(2 3 4 5)) ==> T
    (list-numbp '(2 a 3 4)) ==> NIL
    ```

    (f) ==> (NIL T T NIL NIL T T)

    (g) (sum-list '(2 3 4 5)) ==> 14

2. The following two functions provide a solution to this exercise that is more general,

in that the arguments can be a phrase of any size and a text of multiple sentences. The sentences containing the phrase will be displayed.

```
(defun find-phrase (phrase text)
  (cond ((null text) nil)
        (t (setq sentence (car text))
           (cond ((null (match-list phrase sentence))
                   (find-phrase phrase (cdr text)))
                 (t (print sentence)
                    (find-phrase phrase (cdr text)))))))
  (defun match-list (p s)
    (prog ()
      tag1 (cond ((null p) (return t))
                 ((null s) (return nil))
                 ((equal (car p) (car s)
                   (go tag2))
                 (t (setq s (cdr s))
                    (go tag1)))
      tag2 (setq p (cdr p) s (cdr s))
           (cond ((null p) (return t))
                 ((equal (car p) (car s)) (go tag1))
                 (t return nil)))))

(setq text '((Mary said dont hammer away at john)
             (I thought about it for a while)
             (Then I said if I dont hammer away at him)
             (The work will never get done)
             (And the boss will hammer away at me)))

(find-phrase '(hammer away at) text) ==>
     (MARY SAID DONT HAMMER AWAY AT HIM)
     (THEN I SAID IF I DONT HAMMER AWY AT HIM)
     (AND THE BOSS WILL HAMMER AWAY AT ME)
     NIL
```

3.
```
(defun predq (verbs sentence)
  (append (intersection verbs sentence)
          (set-difference sentence verbs)
          '(?) ))

(setq verbs '(is was are were)) ==> (IS WAS ARE WERE)

(pred-q verbs '(john is my friend)) ==> (IS JOHN MY FRIEND)
(pred-q verbs '(John and Mary McCarthy were absent today))
     ==> (WERE JOHN AND MARY MCCARTHY ABSENT TODAY ?)
```

4. The general formula for computing the compound value of the principal and interest is $v = m(1+i)^n$ where $i = p/k$ and $n = ky$. "p" is the interest rate, "k" is the number of compounding periods in a year (in our example, "k" would be 4, since the problem says compounding is every three months), "y" is the number of years, and "m" is the amount of the principal. We will use the general formula in the following exercise to make it general. Since the problem asks for the accumulated interest, we will subtract "m" from "v" to get the result.

```
(defun interest (m p y k)
  (setq i (/ p k))
  (setq n (* k y))
  (setq v (* m (expt (+ 1 i) n)))
  (print (- v m)) nil)

(interest 1000 .06 5 4) ==) 346.853
```

SECTION 3.4

2.
```
(defun sum (nums)
  (cond ((null nums) 0)
        (t (+ (car nums) (sum (cdr nums))))))

(defun mean (nums) (/ (sum nums) (length nums)))

(defun factorial (n)
  (cond ((zerop n) 1)
        (t (* n (factorial (- n 1))))))
```

The following function computes the number of combinations of "n" objects taken "r" at a time:

```
(defun binomial-coefficient (n r)                    [CL]
  (cond (() r n) nil)          ;;Lispvm use GT for )
        (t (/ (factorial n)
              (* (factorial r)
                 (factorial (- n r)))))))
(defun sumsqdiv (L)
  (+ (expt (- (car L) (mean L)) 2)
     (sumsqdiv (cdr L))))

(defun variance (L) (/ (sumsqdiv L) (length L)))

(defun standard-diviation (L)
  (sqrt (/ (sumsqdiv L) (length L))))
```

In the above function, **sqrt** is the system function for square root. If your system does not have this function implemented, you can write the function as follows:

```
(defun s-d (L) (expt (/ (sumsqdiv L)(length)) .5))
(defun range (L) (- (max L) (min L)))
```

SECTION 3.9

1. ```
   (defun prettyprint (f)                                              [CL]
      (pprint (symbol-function 'f)))
   ```
2. `(setq pprint prettyprint)`   [LVM]
3. At this point, you can use the following simple approach. In the next chapter, you will learn better ways of doing this.

   ```
   (setq car-records '((ny-abc-567 john-adams 23-w-678-st-
           albany-ny-12457 phone-222-555-9878) (ma-kj-678
           amy-vanderland 234-bandy-st-arlington-ma-23453
           phone-201-555-9988) ...))

   (defun car-search (x r)
      (cond ((null r) nil)
            ((member x (car r)) (car r))
            (t (car-search x (cdr r)))))

   (car-search 'ma-kj-678 car-records) ==>
   (MA-KJ-678 AMY-VANDERLAND 234-BANDY-ST-ARLINGTON-MA-23453
    PHONE-201-555-9988)
   (car-search 'john-adams car-records) ==>
   (NY-ABC-567 JOHN-ADAMS 23-W-678-ST-ALBANY-NY-12457
    PHONE-222-555-9878)
   ```

   If you further separate some of the items in **car-records**, you can search on those. For example, if the zipcode were not connected to the address with a dash, you could search on the zipcode as well.
4. We can prove that by using the formula in a function that can generate all natural numbers.

   ```
   (defun formula (a b)
      (cond ((or (not (numberp a))
                 (not (numberp b))) nil)
            (t (* .5 (+ (expt (+ a b) 2) (* 3 a) b)))))

   (formula 0 0) ==> 0.0      (formula 0 1) ==> 1.0
   (formula 1 0) ==> 2.0      (formula 0 2) ==> 3.0
   (formula 1 1) ==> 4.0      (formula 2 0) ==> 5.0
   (formula 0 3) ==> 6.0      (formula 1 2) ==> 7.0
   (formula 2 1) ==> 8.0      (formula 3 0) ==> 9.0
   (formula 0 4) ==> 10.0

                          ⋮

   (formula 10 15) ==> 335.0  etc.
   ```
   ```

```
5. (defun sum-nums (L)
      (cond ((numberp (car L))
             (setq sum (+ sum (sum-nums (cdr L)))))
            (t (print (list (car L) 'is-not-a-number))
               (sum-nums (cdr L)))))
```

SECTION 3.11

1. See MY-MEMBERP in Section 2.3.
2. In the following solution, we will use the function **find-phrase** defined for the Solution to exercise 2, in Section 2.12, shown earlier.

```
(defun reader ( )
   (terpri)
   (princ "Type a phrase enclosed in parentheses")
   (terpri)
   (setq p (read))
   (terpri)
      (cond ((equal p nil) nil)
            (t (princ "Type a list of sentences
                          in parentheses")
               (terpri)
               (setq s (read))
               (find-phrase p s)
               (reader) )))
```

```
(reader)
Type a phrase enclosed in parentheses
(a b c)
Type a list of sentences in parentheses
((a b c d e)(j k a b c m)(t k l m n))
(A B C D E)
(J K A B C M)
Type a phrase enclosed in parentheses
(1 2 3)
Type a list of sentences in parentheses
((1 2 a b)(1 2 3 a b)(a 1 2 3 b c)(a 1 b 2 c 3))
(1 2 3 A B)
(A 1 2 3 B C)
Type a phrase enclosed in parentheses
( )
NIL
```

SECTION 4.4

1.  ```
    (setq numbers '(one two three))
    (setq colors '(red blue yellow green))
        (defun adj (x y)
            (cond ((or (null x)
                       (null y)) nil)
                  (t (setq adjectives
                       (append (list (car x) (car y))
                               (adj (cdr x) (cdr y)))))))
    ```

    (adj numbers colors) ==> (ONE RED TWO BLUE THREE YELLOW)

    Note also the following solution:

    ```
              (mapcar 'list numbers colors)
              ==> ((ONE RED) (TWO BLUE) (THREE YELLOW))
    ```

2. The answer depends on how you write the problem. Consider alternatives (a) and (b), below:

    (a) ```
        (setq n (/ (length (adj numbers colors)) 2)) ==> 3.0
        (setq m (min (length numbers) (length colors))) ==> 3
        (equal n m) ==> NIL
        (eql n m) ==> NIL
        (eq n m) ==> NIL
        (= n m) ==> T
        ```

    In this case in Common Lisp, only the symbol '=' shows that the results are equal, because the other equality forms are sensitive to type.

    (b) ```
        (setq n' (length (adj numbers colors))) ==> 6
        (setq m' (* 2 (min (length numbers) (length colors)))) ==> 6
        ```

    In this case, all of the four equality forms will return T.

3.

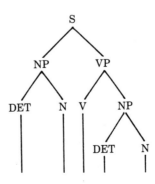

or the following:
        ```

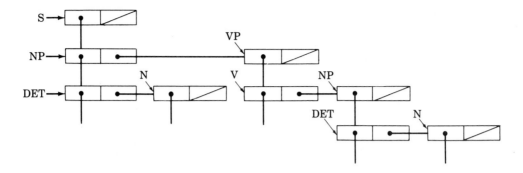

4. (a) ((J & M) and (B & L) are friends)

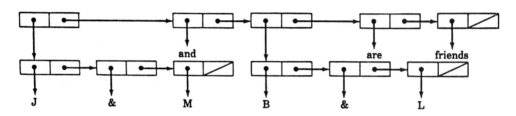

(b) ((father (Max Liza)))

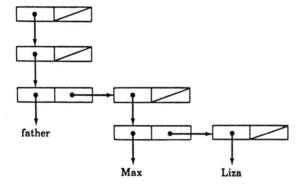

SECTION 4.5.5

1. In the solution for this Exercise, first a function, **invt-const**, is defined for constructing an inventory of a store. Then a second function, **order**, is provided for checking the inventory items and ordering those that fall below the *low* stock figure. The **invt-const** function prompts the user to give, first, a list of identifiers for the items in the inventory. Additional prompts are, then, given for inputting items to be associated with each identifier. Note that each entry consists of three pairs: name:value, quantity:value, and low:value. The last pair provides for initiating the order.

```
(defun invt-const ( )
   (print "Type a list of item identifiers")
   (print "Each identifier must begin with a letter")
   (setq ident (read))
     (do ((invent nil) (n ident (cdr n)))

         ((null n) (reverse invent))
          (print "Type inventory list for each identifier")
          (setq pl (read))
          (setf (symbol-plist (car n)) pl)
          (setq invent (cons (car n) invent))))

(defun order (ivt)
   (cond ((null ivt) nil)
         ((< (get (car ivt) 'quantity)
             (get (car ivt) 'low))
          (print
            (list 'order (get (car ivt) 'name)))
               (order (cdr ivt)))
         (t (order (cdr ivt)))))

(setq inventory (invt-constant))
   ==> "Type a list of identifiers"
       "Each identifier must begin with a letter"
         (a2345  a6543 a7896 a4356 a9548)
       "Type inventory list for each identifier"
         (name shirts quantity 500 low 700)
       "Type inventory list for each identifier"
         (name coats quantity 300 low 200)
       "Type inventory list for each identifier"
         (name pants quantity 400 low 500)
       "Type inventory list for each identifier"
         (name socks quantity 700 low 800)
       "Type inventory list for each identifier"
         (name ties quantity 200 low 100)
       "Type inventory list for each identifier"
         (name jackets quantity 300 low 400)
       (A2345 A6543 A7896 A4356 A9548)

(order inventory
   ==> (ORDER SHIRTS)
       (ORDER PANTS)
       (ORDER SOCKS)
       (ORDER JACKETS)
       NIL
```

2. The functions given here for Exercise 2 in this section can be used to start a new phone book or to update an existing one by adding names in the proper order. In the function **phones** we have used the macro *dotimes,* which is described in Section 5.6. It is a variant of the **do** macro. You can use **do** or **prog** here for iteration, but then the function would be perhaps less efficient.

```
(defun phones (n)                                          [CL]
  (let ((phone nil))
    (do times (i n)
      (print "Type name and number in string form")
      (setq name (read))
      (setq number (read))
      (cond ((null phone) (setq phone (acons name
                                               number nil)))
            ((and (setq x (assoc name phone :test 'string-equal))
                  (setq x (rassoc number phone :test
                   'string-equal)))
             (format t "~&The entry ~a is already
              there" x))
            (t (setq phone (aux-phones phone name number))
               (dolist (x phone) (print x)))))))

(defun aux-phones (tlist n1 n2)
  (cond ((null tlist) (acons n1 n2 nil))
        ((string-lessp n1 (caar tlist)) (acons n1 n2 tlist))
        (t (cons (car tlist) (aux phones
                                (cdr tlist) (n1 n2))))))

(phones 7) ==>
```

```
"Type name and number in string form" "Gasman, Judith" "656-3232"
"Type name and number in string form" "Gartner, Elias" "444-5656"
("Gartner, Elias" . "444-5656")  ;;order changed
("Gasman, Judith" . "656-3232")
"Type name and number in string form" "Gatkann, Peter" "777-8787"
("Gartner, Elias" . "444-5656")
("Gasman, Judith" . "656-3232")
("Gatkann, Peter" . "777-8787")  ;;Gatkann inserted properly
"Type name and number in string form" "Gassmann, Fred" "888-7766"
("Gartner, Elias" . "444-5656")
("Gasman, Judith" . "656-3232")
("Gassmann, Fred" . "888-7766")  ;;Gassmann inserted
("Gatkann, Peter" . "777-8787")
"Type name and number in string form" "Gasman, Judith" "656-3232"
The entry (Gasman, Judith . 656-3232) is already there
"Type name and number in string form" "Gasman, Judith" "656-4545"
("Gartner, Elias" . "444-5656")
```

```
("Gasman, Judith" . "656-3232")  ;;duplicate names with different
("Gasman, Judith" . "656-4545")  ;;phone numbers accepted
("Gassmann, Fred" . "888-7766")
("Gatkann, Peter" . "777-8787")
"Type name and number in string form" "Gasman, Alex" "656-3232"
("Gartner, Elias" . "444-5656")
("Gasman, Alex" . "656-3232")  ;;Gasman with different first name
("Gasman, Judith" . "656-3232")
("Gasman, Judith" . "656-4545")
("Gassmann, Fred" . "888-7766")
("Gatkann, Peter" . "777-8787")
NIL
*
```

The final phone list is:

```
"Gartner, Elias" . "444-5656"
"Gasman, Alex"   . "656-3232"
"Gasman, Judith" . "656-3232"
"Gasman, Judith" . "656-4545"
"Gassmann, Fred" . "888-7766"
"Gatkann, Peter" . "777-8787"
```

3.
```
(setf (get 'the 'pos) 'det)                                    [CL]
(setf (get 'man 'pos) 'n)
(setq dict '(the man))

            (defun look-up (s d)
               (cond ((null s) nil)
                     ((member (car s) d)
               (list (list (car s) (get (car s) 'pos))
                     (look-up (cadr s) d)))
               (t (print (format nil
                    "~s is not in the dictionary" (car s)))
                  (look-up (cdr s) d))))

        (look-up '(the tall man came home) dict)
        ==>  "TALL is not in the dictionary"
             "CAME is not in the dictionary"
             "HOME is not in the dictionary"
             ((THE DET) ((MAN N) NIL))
```

4.
```
(defun common-list-items (x y)
   (do ((sum 0) (x1 x (cdr x1)))
       ((null x1) sum)
       (if (member (car x1) y) (incf sum))))
```

```
(common-list-items '(a b c d e) '(f g a k b e)) ==) 3
;; a, b, and e occur in both lists.
```

However, a much simpler solution to this exercise is this:

```
(length (intersection list1 list2))
```

Both these versions will count duplicates in the first list. The following form will not count the duplicates: (length (intersection (delete-duplicates list1) list2))
Compare:

```
(setq x '(a b c a a d)) ==) (A B C A A D)
(delete 'a x) ==) (B C D)
(delete-duplicates x) ==) (A B C D)
```

5. First, we will write a small dictionary for adjectives only, since those are what we are concerned with in this exercise.

```
(setf (get 'hungry 'pos) 'adj)
(setf (get 'fat 'pos) 'adj)                          [CL]
(setf (get 'sweet 'pos) 'adj)
(setq dict '(hungry fat sweet))
```

Now the function:

```
(defun emphasize (s d)
   (cond ((null s) nil)
         ((and (member (car s) d)
               (equal (get (car s) 'pos) 'adj))
          (append (cons 'very (cons (car s)
                                    (emphasize (cdr s) d)))))
         (t (cons (car s) (emphasize (cdr s) d)))))
(emphasize '(the fat hungry bear ate the sweet honey) dict)
==) (THE VERY FAT VERY HUNGRY BEAR ATE THE VERY SWEET HONEY)
```

6. In the solution for this problem we will first construct a COURSE-LIST. Then the function **course-update** will take a course identifier and COURSE-LIST as its arguments and return the course description, if it is in the list. If the course is not in the list, it will be added to the list and, then, the updated list is printed. The function **print-list** prints the course list.

```
(setq course-list
   '((phil-1 729 room 1231 prof jones)
     (phil-2 750 room 1524 prof chamka)
     (phil-25 832 room 1219 prof peters) ))

(defun course-update (c cl)
   (cond ((equal (assoc c cl) nil)
          (print "Course not listed, enter description")
```

```
            (terpri)
            (setq course (read)) (terpri)(terpri)
            (print-list c1))
      (t (assoc c c1)))))

(defun print-list (x)
   (cond ((null x) nil)
         (t (print (car x)) (print-list (cdr x))))))
           (course-update 'bio-17 course-list)
           "Course not listed, enter description"
           (bio-17 695 room 1734 prof gonzalis)
           (BIO-17 695 ROOM 1734 PROF GONZALIS)
           (PHIL-1 729 ROOM 123 PROF JONES)
           (PHIL-2 750 ROOM 1524 PROF CHAMKA)
           (PHIL-25 832 ROOM 1219 PROF PETERS)
           NIL

(course-update 'phil-2 course-list)
(PHIL-2 750 ROOM 1524 PROF CHAMKA)
```

7. The Solution to Exercise 7 is due to Elenor Batchelder. The function **trimming** removes the excess blanks around entries and calls the **sort** function, which uses the **strlessp** function to determine the order of strings. Note that the **sort** function has also been written. The *&rest* keyword in the lambda list of the function **strlessp** provides an 'extension' to the lambda list, which is discussed in Section 5.4. The **dolist** macro in this function is an iterative function and is discussed in Subsection 5.7.1. The **strupcase** function converts the entries in the phone book to upper case, as required by the Exercise. The **dotimes** macro has already been mentioned in Exercise 2 in this section. The **phone-update** function simply prints the phone list after it undergoes the changes. We begin now by constructing the "phone book." Notice the order of entries, excess blanks, and upper/lower cases.

```
(setq phone-book '(("   Gastronomy assoc.  " . "222-1234")
                   ("gassman, fred  " . "999-8976")
                   ("gatkan, Peter" . "777-5463")
                   ("Gartener, Elias  " . "444-5656")
                   ("barkov, alex" . "333-4433")))
```

The functions are now listed in the order of their use:

```
(defun trimming (phone-book)
   (sort 'strlessp (mapcar '(lambda (x)
         (setq x (cons (strupcase (string-trim " " (car x)))
                       (strupcase (string-trim " " (cdr x)))))))
            phone-book)))

(defun sort (fun list)
   (cond ((> 2 (length list)) list)
```

```
                ((and (listp (car list))
                        (apply fun (list (caar list)(caadr list))))
                    (if (apply fun (mapcar 'car list)) list (sort
                            fun (cons (car list)
                        (sort fun (cdr list))))))
                (t (sort fun (cons (cadr list)
                                    (sort fun (cons (car list)
                                            (cddr list)))))))))))

        (defun strlessp (a &rest more)
          (cond ((atom a) (strlessp (cons a more)))
                ((null a) t)
                (t (setq d (car a))
                    (dolist (c (cdr a) t)
                        (if (string-lessp d c)
                            (setq d c)
                            (return nil))))))

        (defun strupcase (str)
          (dotimes (n (length str) str)
            (setf (char str n) (char-upcase (char str n)))))

        (defun phone-update (x)
          (dolist (a X) (print a)))
```

The **phone-update** function can now be called with **trimming**, and its argument phone-book, as its argument:

```
        (phone-update (trimming phone-book))
          ("BARKOV, ALEX"  .  "333-4433")
          ("GARTENER, ELIAS"  .  "444-5656")
          ("GASSMAN, FRED"  .  "999-8976")
          ("GASTRONOMY ASSOC."  .  "222-1234")
          ("GATKAN, PETER"  .  "777-5463")
          NIL
```

8. `(defun count-char (a s n)`   [CL]
      `(do ((sum 0) (n 0 (1+ n)))`
          `((equal n (length s)) sum)`
          `(if (equal (char s n) a) (incf sum))))`

```
(count-char #\a "abcaadae") ==> 4
(count-char #\a "alabama") ==> 4
(count-char #\x "xxxyxxx") ==> 6
```

A slightly more compact variant of the above function (after you have studied Sections 5.3 and 5.6) is the following:

```
(defun count-char2 (a s)                                          [CL]
  (let ((sum 0))
    (dotimes (i (length s) sum)
      (if (equal (char s i) a) (incf sum)))))
```

9.  ```
    (defun strg (n a)                                             [CL]
      (make-string n :initial-element a))
    ```

    ```
    (strg 10 #\x) ==) "xxxxxxxxxx"
    ```

SECTION 4.5.8

1. The function **take-a-walk-in** lists all of the nodes (including leaves) of its argument tree in a depth-first search procedure. Applied to MAGNOLIA, the following output will be given: (A B D E H M N C F I J O P G K L Q).

3. The function **take-a-walk-in** can do the task required in this exercise. Note that the tree structure of the arithmetic expression given in the exercise can be represented by the following form:

    ```
    (setq arith '(+ (* (x) (y)) (+ (* (w) (v)) (Z) )))
    (take-a-walk-in arith) ==) (+ * X Y + * W V Z)
    ```

4. Use the function given in the text to output the leaves of a tree.

SECTION 5.5

1.  ```
    (defun complex-num (x)                                        [CL]
      (format t "~& The real part of ~s is ~s " x (car x))

      (format t "~& The imaginary part of ~s is ~s" x (cadr x)))
    ```

    ```
    (complex-num '(5 3)) ==) The real part of (5 3) is 5
                             The imaginary part of (5 3) is 3
    ```

2. There are several ways of doing this, none of which are particularly interesting unless your dialect has implemented ratio as a data type. The system function **explode** in Lispvm or **string** in Common Lisp can be used to expand x/y to (x / y) or x/y to "X/Y" and then extract the first and the last elements of the list for answers. In Common Lisp, this can be obtained with the **char** function.

3. Use the function **type-of** to verify the types of the elements. For example, (type-of 55) ⇒ FIXNUM.

4.  ```
    (defun my-typep (x y)                                         [CL]
      (if (typep x y) t nil))
    MY-TYPEP
      (my-typep 5 'number) ==) T
      (my-typep 'a 'symbol) ==) T
      (my-typep 'a 'number) ==) NIL
    ```

5.  ```
    x ==) (A B C D)  ;;The global value of x does not change.
    ```

6. There will be an error message, because **let** tries to bind the values of "X" and "Y" simultaneously, and at the time of binding "Y," "X" has not been bound. If you change **let** to **let***, the function will work.

7. There is an error message because **psetq** tries to assign values to "X" and "Y" simultaneously.

8. The values are the following, in the order of the forms in the exercise.

$$(1\ 2\ 2\ \text{NIL}\ \text{NIL})$$
$$(1\ 2\ T\ (3\ 4\ 5\ 6))$$
$$(2\ 3\ T\ 4)$$

The outputs from the function **new-exam** are the following, in the order given in the exercise.

```
ERROR: Not enough arguments for NEW-EXAM
(5 6 NIL 11 NIL NIL NIL)
(5 6 3 11 NIL NIL NIL)
(5 6 3 7 T NIL NIL)
(5 6 3 7 T 8 (9 10 12 A B))
1
((1 2 3 4 T 5 (6 7 8)))
((1 2 3 4 T 5 (6 7 8)))
```

SECTION 5.8

1.
```
(defun vec-sum (v1 v2)                              [CL]
  (setq n (length v1))
  (setq v3 (make-array n))
    (dotimes (i n)
      (setf (aref v3 i) (+ (aref v1 i) (aref v2 1))))))
VEC-SUM
(vec-sum #(2 3 4) #(1 1 1)) ==> #(3 4 5)
```

2.
```
(defun inner-product (v1 v2)                        [CL]
   (setq n (length v1))
    (let ((sum 0))
      (dotimes (i n sum)
        (setq sum (+ (* (aref v1 i) (aref v2 i)) sum)))))
INNER-PRODUCT
(inner-product #(2 3 4) #(1 2 3)) ==> 20
```

3.
```
(defun odd-even-vec (vec)                           [CL]
   (setq n (length vec))
    (let ((L1 nil) (L2 nil))
      (dotimes (i n)
        (setq x (aref vec i))
        (if (oddp x) (setq L1 (cons x L1))
                     (setq L2 (cons x L2)))))
```

```
(setq v-odd (make-array (length L1) :initial-contents L1))
(setq v-even (make-array(length L2) :initial-contents L2))))
ODD-EVEN-VEC
(odd-even-vec #(1 3 5 4 6 8 12 10 2 7)) ==>
                #<VECTOR T 6 904F:B410>
```

We will use the function **show-vector**, defined under Example (5.41) in Section 5.6,
to observe the contents of the two arrays produced by the above function call.

```
(show-vector v-odd) ==> (1 3 5 7)
(show-vector v-even) ==> (4 6 8 12 10 2)
```

4. ```
   (defun string-concat (s1 s2)                          [CL]
       (string-append s1 s2))
   STRING-CONCAT
   (string-concat "abc" "def") ==> "abcdef"
   ```

5. [2 25]
   [2 4]

6. ```
   (defun power (m n) (expt m n))  !
   ```

7. ```
   (defun class-a (L y)
       (setq a (/ (+ L (* y (* L .10))) (* y 12))))
   (defun class-b (L y)
       (setq b (/ (+ L (* y (* L .12))) (* y 12))))
   (defun class-c (L y)
       (setq c (/ (+ L (* y (* L .18))) (* y 12))))

   (defun bank (x L y)
       (cond ((equal x 'a) (funcall 'class-a L y))
             ((equal x 'b) (funcall 'class-b L y))
             ((equal x 'c) (funcall 'class-c L y))
             (t nil)))
   BANK
   (bank 'a 100000 5) ==> 2500.0
   (bank 'b 100000 5) ==> 2666.67
   (bank 'c 100000 5) ==> 3166.67
   ```

SECTION 5.10

1. ```
   (defun sum-list (list)                               [CL]
       (let ((sum 0))
         (loop
           (setq sum (+ (car list) sum))
           (setq list (cdr list))
           (if (endp list) (return sum)))))
   SUM-LIST
   (sum-list '(2 3 4 5)) ==> 14
   ```

2. (defun compute ( )   [CL]
    (dotimes (i 10)
    (terpri)
    (princ "Please type four numbers")
    (terpri)
       (setq a (read))
       (setq b (read))
       (setq c (read))
       (setq d (read))
       (print (sqrt (/ (+ a b) (- c d))))))))

```
COMPUTE
(compute) ==> Please type four numbers
1 0 2 1
1.00000000001399D0
Please type four numbers
8 7 6 2
1.9364916731521800
:    :    :
Please type four numbers
5 6 7 2
1.4832396331224200
NIL
```

3. (progn (setq a 5) (setq b (1+ a)) (setq c (1+ b))
     (setq d (1+ c)) (setq e (1+ d)) (list a b c d e))
    ==> (5 6 7 8 9)

4. If we compute the expressions by hand, we get

$$(a + b)^0 = 1$$
$$(a + b)^1 = 1a + 1b$$
$$(a + b)^2 = 1a^2 + 2ab + 1b^2$$
$$(a + b)^3 = 1a^3 + 3a^2b + 3ab^2 + 1b^3$$

If we take the coefficients of each expression and order them in sequence, we get the Pascal triangle:

$$1$$
$$1\ 1$$
$$1\ 2\ 1$$
$$1\ 3\ 3\ 1$$
$$\text{etc.}$$

The general formula for solving for any power of n, also known as the *Binomial Theorem* is this:

$$(a + b)^n + \binom{n}{0} a^n + \binom{n}{1} a^{n-1} b + \binom{n}{2} a^{n-2}b^2 + \ldots + \binom{n}{n-1}ab^{n-1} + \binom{n}{n}b^n$$

which can also be abbreviated in the following summation notation:

$$(a + b)^n = \sum_{r=0}^{n} \binom{n}{r} a^{n-r} b^r$$

You can write Lisp expressions to solve these equations. You can find the formulas explained in any elementary book on mathematics.

In the following Lisp function, we can use the predictable facts about each row of the triangle. Given any row, the function produces the next row. Note that the input and output are in the form of vectors, and we use the function **show-vector** developed under Example (5.41) in Section 5.6 to display the contents of each row.

```
(defun pascal (vec1)                                         [CL]
 (setq m (length vec1))
 (setq n (+ m 1))
 (setq vec2 (make-array n))
 (setf (aref vec2 0) 1)
   (dotimes (i (- m 1))
     (setf (aref vec2 (+ i 1))
             (+ (aref vec1 i) (aref vec1 (+ i 1))))))
   (setf (aref vec2 (- n 1)) 1)
   (show-vector vec2))
PASCAL
(pascal #(1)) ==>              (1 1)
(pascal #(1 1) ==>             (1 2 1)
(pascal #(1 2 1) ==>           (1 3 3 1)
   :        :                     :
(pascal #(1 4 6 4 1) ==>       (1 5 10 10 5 1)
   :        :                     :
(pascal #(1 6 15 20 15 6 1)    (1 7 21 35 35 21 7 1)
```

The problem with the **pascal** function is that it produces one row of the triangle in each run. We can modify the function in the following way to produce a triangle of *n* rows in one application of the function.

```
(defun pascal2 (vec1 k)                                      [CL]
   (print '(1))
   (dotimes (i k)
     (setq m (length vec1))
     (setq n (+ m 1))
     (setq vec2 (make-array n))
     (setf (aref vec2 0) 1)
       (dotimes (j (- m 1))
         (setf (aref vec2 (+ j 1))
                 (+ (aref vec1 j)(aref vec1 (+ j 1))))))
       (setf (aref vec2 (- n 1)) 1)
       (setq v (show-vector vec2)))
   (print v)
```

```
          (setq vec1 (make-array (length v) :initial-contents v))))
     PASCAL2
     (pascal2 #(0) 7)
     (1)
     (1 1)
     (1 2 1)
     (1 3 3 1)
     (1 4 6 4 1)
     (1 5 10 10 5 1)
     (1 6 15 20 15 6 1)
     (1 7 21 35 35 21 7 1)
     NIL
```

5. ```
   (defun count (n)                                                    [CL]
      (let ((l nil))
        (dotimes (i n l)
          (setq l (cons i l)))))
   COUNT
   (count 10) ==> (9 8 7 6 5 4 3 2 1 0)
   (reverse (count 10)) ==> (0 1 2 3 4 5 6 7 8 9)
   ```

6. Put objects in a package named by you. Make the objects that you want to share publicly *external*. *Import* the objects that you want to share with specific packages into them.

7. There are several ways that you can construct a block world. For example, in a simple approach, you can use **defstruct**.

   ```
   (defstruct block-world cube pyramid sphere)                         [CL]
   ==> BLOCK-WORLD
   (setq my-blocks (make-block-world
     :cube 'red :pyramid 'blue :sphere 'yellow))
   ==> #s(BLOCK-WORLD :CUBE RED :PYRAMID BLUE :SPHERE YELLOW)
   (block-world-cube my-blocks) ==> RED
   ```

8. ```
   (defstruct s art n verb art1 n1)                                    [CL]
   (defun sentence (a nn vv a1 nn1)
       (setq ss (make-s :art a :n nn :verb vv :art1 a1 :n1 nn1))
       (list (s-art ss)(s-n ss)(s-verb ss)(s-art1 ss)(s-n1 ss)))

   (defun print-sentences (k)
      (dotimes (i k)
         (print (sentence (nth i dets)(nth i nouns)(nth i verbs)
                 (nth (+ i 1) dets) (nth (+ i 1) nouns)))))

   (setq dets '(the many some several all few most))
   (setq nouns '(boys girls women men cats dogs people poets))
   (setq verbs '(left missed saw kicked greeted smelled found))
   ```

```
(print-sentences 7) ==>
(THE BOYS LEFT MANY GIRLS)
(MANY GIRLS MISSED SOME WOMEN)
(SOME WOMEN SAW SEVERAL MEN)
(SEVERAL MEN KICKED ALL CATS)
(ALL CATS GREETED FEW DOGS)
(FEW DOGS SMELLED MOST PEOPLE)
(MOST PEOPLE FOUND NIL POETS)
NIL
```

There are several modifications and enhancements that one can make in the above program. In selecting elements from the lists DETS, NOUNS, and VERBS, instead of selecting the *i*th element, you can use the **random** function to make it more unpredictable. Recall that the **random** function takes an argument "n" and returns a number between zero and "n," inclusive. For example, several applications of **random** with argument 3 may return the following values: (random 3)⇒ 0, (random 3)⇒ 2, (random 3)⇒ 3, etc. In the **print-sentences** function, then, you can write such expressions as

$$\text{(nth (random (length dets)) dets)}$$

You can also write separate **defstruct** structures for noun-phrase (NP), verb-phrase (VP), and S to reflect the rules in the little grammar given in the exercise. In a larger dictionary with less judiciously selected words than the above lists, you might get such anomalous and ungrammatical sentences as *the trees slept a house, many house walked an cat* and so forth. To avoid this, your dictionary must have parts-of-speech feature for selection. In addition, each entry must have properties such as animate/inanimate, transitive/intransitive, human/nonhuman, and others, and these properties must be checked in making selections for constructing sentences.

SECTION 5.14

1. For example,

```
(setq broadcast (make-broadcast-stream outs1 os))        [CL]
    (print "abcdef" broadcast)
    (get-output-stream-string outs1)
        ==> " THIS-IS-STRING-ONE
              THIS-IS-STRING-TWO
              ABCDEF "
    (get-output-stream-string os)
        ==> AB
            " ABCDEF "
```

(outs1 and os are on pages 213 and 215, respectively) In some implementations, **make-broadcast-stream** returns the value of operation on the last stream in its arguments and discards the results from other streams.

3. (defun convert (n)   [CL]
        (format nil "Decimal number ~s is binary ~b, octal ~0,
        and hexadecimal ~x" n n n n))
    CONVERT
    (convert 20) ==> "Decimal number 20 is binary 10100,
                    octal 24, and hexadecimal 14"

4. We assume that a dictionary DICT has been defined, and the function **neg**, defined
    in Subsection 4.5.3.1, is available.

    (defun neg-? (dict)   [CL]
        (print '(type a progressive sentence in parentheses))
        (terpri)
        (setq sent (read))
        (y-or-n-p "Do you want a negation of the sentence?")
        (setq w (read))
        (if (equal w 'y) (neg dict sent)))
    NEG-?
        (neg-? dict)
        (TYPE A PROGRESSIVE SENTENCE IN PARENTHESES)
        (last night i was reading a book)
        Do you want a negation of the sence? (Y or N) y
        y
        (LAST NIGHT I WAS NOT READING A BOOK)

5. (setq out (open "newf.lsp" :direction :output))   [CL]
    (print '(setq dic '((book . books) (tree . trees)
                    (glass . glasses)) out))

    (print '(defun find-pl (w d)
                (cond ((null d) nil)
                        ((equal w (caar d)) (cdar d))
                        (t (find-pl w (cdr d))))) out)
    (close out)
    (load "newf.lsp")
    (find-pl 'book dict) ==> BOOKS
    (find-pl 'glass dict) ==> GLASSES
    'find-pl 'mirror dict) ==> NIL

6. We will use the NEWF.LSP file, created in the Solution to Exercise 5, above, to make
    a copy and change its type specification.

    (setq in (open "newf.lsp" :direction :input))   [CL]
    (setq out (open "newf.bak" :direction :output))
    (setq x (read in)) ==> (SETQ DICT (QUOTE ((BOOK . BOOKS)
                (TREE . TREES) (GLASS . GLASSES))))
    (print x out)

```
(setq x (read in)) ==> (DEFUN FIND-P (W D) (COND ((NULL D)
        NIL) ((EQUAL W (CAAR D)) (CDAR D)) (T (FIND-PL
    W (CDR D)))))  ;; Recall that every application
                        ;; of READ to a stream, reads the
                        ;; next record.
(print x out)
(close-all-files) ==>
  (#.(PATHNAME "NEWF.BAK") #.(PATHNAME "NEWF.LSP"))
```

7. We will assume that * is the end marker for a stream.

```
(setq instr (make-string-input-stream                    [CL]
            "this is a string of words *"))
```

```
(defun count (st)
   (do ((m 0 (1+ m)))
       ((equal (read st) '*) m)))
COUNT
(count instr) ==> 6
```

References

Aho, Alfred V. and Ullman, Jeffrey D., 1972. *The Theory of Parsing, Translation, and Computing*. Vol. I: Parsing. Englewood Cliffs, NJ: Prentice-Hall.

Bundy, A. (ed.), 1978. *Artificial Intelligence*. New York: North-Holland.

Charniak, Eugene and McDermott, Drew, 1984. *Introduction to Artificial Intelligence*. Reading, MA: Addison-Wesley.

Milner, Wendy L., 1988. *Common Lisp:* A Tutorial. Englewood Cliffs, NJ: Prentice-Hall.

Moyne, John A., 1985. *Understanding Language: Man or Machine*. New York: Plenum.

Penrose, Roger, 1989. *The Emperor's New Mind*. New York: Oxford University Press.

Steele, Guy L., 1984. *Common Lisp: The Language*. Billerica, MA: Digital Press.

Winograd, Terry, 1972. *Understanding Natural Language*. New York: Academic Press.

Winston, Patrick H., 1984. *Artificial Intelligence*. (Second Edition). Reading, MA: Addison-Wesley.

Winston, Patrick H. and Horn, B.K.P., 1984. *Lisp*. (Second Edition). Reading, MA: Addison-Wesley.

Yuasa, Taiichi and Hagiya, Masami, 1987. *Introduction to Common Lisp*. New York: Academic Press.

Yuasa, Taiichi, 1988. *Common Lisp Drill*. New York: Academic Press.

Index of Lisp Symbols and Terms Used in This Text

Boldface numbers denote definitions or more in-depth discussion of the entry material.

General Index

Entries in capitals in this index are names of user-defined functions. In the text, user-defined functions are given in bold characters, along with the system functions. The latter are listed in the Index of Lisp Symbols and Terms.